Teaching Wallace Stevens

TENNESSEE STUDIES IN LITERATURE VOLUME 35

Teaching Wallace Stevens
Practical Essays

Edited by

John N. Serio and B. J. Leggett

The University of Tennessee Press / Knoxville

TENNESSEE STUDIES IN LITERATURE

Editorial Board: D. Allen Carroll, Don Richard Cox, Allison Ensor, Richard Finneran, Nancy Moore Goslee, Marilyn Kallett, Norman Sanders.

"Tennessee Studies in Literature," a distinguished series sponsored by the Department of English at The University of Tennessee, Knoxville, began publication in 1956. Beginning in 1984, with Volume 27, TSL evolved from a series of annual volumes of miscellaneous essays to a series of occasional volumes, each one dealing with a specific theme, period, or genre, for which the editor of that volume has invited contributions from leading scholars in the field.

Inquiries concerning this series should be addressed to the Editorial Board, Tennessee Studies in Literature, Department of English, The University of Tennessee, Knoxville, Tennessee 37996-0430. Those desiring to purchase additional copies of this issue or copies of back issues should address The University of Tennessee Press, 293 Communications Building, Knoxville, Tennessee 37996-0325.

Library of Congress Cataloging in Publication Data

Teaching Wallace Stevens: practical essays / edited by John N. Serio and B. J. Leggett.

       p.   cm. — (Tennessee studies in literature; v. 35)

    Includes bibliographical references (p.) and index.

    ISBN 0–87049–817–7 (cl.: alk. pa.)

    1. Stevens, Wallace, 1879–1955—Study and teaching. 2. American poetry—20th century—Study and teaching. I. Serio, John N., 1943– . II. Leggett, B. J. (Bobby Joe), 1938– . III. Series.

PS3537.T4753Z769   1994

811'.52—dc20   93-8866

                                                           CIP

Contents

Abbreviations

The following abbreviations of titles of works are used throughout this volume.

CP   *The Collected Poems of Wallace Stevens.* New York: Alfred A. Knopf, 1954.

CPWCW   *The Collected Poems of William Carlos Williams, Volume 1, 1909–1939.* Ed. A. Walton Litz and Christopher MacGowan. New York: New Directions, 1986; *Volume 2, 1939–1962,* ed. Christopher MacGowan. New York: New Directions, 1988.

L   *Letters of Wallace Stevens.* Ed. Holly Stevens. New York: Alfred A. Knopf, 1966.

NA   *The Necessary Angel: Essays on Reality and the Imagination.* New York: Alfred A. Knopf, 1951.

OP   *Opus Posthumous.* Revised, enlarged, and corrected edition, ed. Milton J. Bates. New York: Alfred A. Knopf, 1989.

SP   *Souvenirs and Prophecies: The Young Wallace Stevens.* Holly Bright Stevens. New York: Alfred A. Knopf, 1977.

Introduction

B. J. LEGGETT AND JOHN N. SERIO

I

To point to the "fabled difficulty" of Wallace Stevens's poetry, in Joseph Carroll's apt phrase, is to explain a great deal about the equally legendary difficulty of teaching Stevens. Jacqueline Brogan goes so far as to suggest that teaching Stevens in the way that we teach Yeats or other modern poets is simply impossible, and she locates Stevens's resistance to conventional teaching in the sheer play of his poetry and its shifting theoretical perspectives, both of which forestall interpretation and undermine our approaches to the poems. Seeking an analogy for an activity that is resistant to certainty or precision, Joan Richardson compares teaching Stevens to teaching the weather. In both cases, she finds, we must be open to variables that arrange themselves unexpectedly to produce major effects; the more exposure to the subtle changes of pattern and shade, the greater the possibilities for interpretation. Richardson does not pursue a further analogy with the weather—that although everybody talks about the difficulty of teaching Stevens, nobody, to this point, has done anything about it.

The various obstacles imposed by Stevens's poems constitute one of the major themes of these essays, but the essays also demonstrate at least implicitly that the solutions to Stevens's difficulty proposed by the criticism—the commentary and readings that have accumulated for more than fifty years—are not always enough in the classroom. Presumably, the problems presented by Stevens's work to the critic and the teacher overlap at numerous points; yet a group of essays on teaching Stevens will necessarily display a different character from a collection of scholarly or critical essays.

The critic may well be content to account for the eccentricities of Stevens's verse, but the instructor must find a way to get past them. This gathering of essays thus diverges from the usual collection principally in its practical intent. Although no single method of teaching Stevens will be of value to all readers—given the notoriously idiosyncratic nature of the activity—the book as a whole should be of some real help to the classroom teacher. The essays of both Eleanor Cook and Lauren Rusk, in fact, pursue the argument that Stevens's poems may have something useful to *teach us* about the kind of reading that goes on in the classroom.

To separate the classroom teacher and the scholar/critic is misleading in this instance, however, since the volume contains many of the critics who have established the direction of contemporary Stevens scholarship (and who have produced more than a score of books on Stevens's poetry). In this connection, one of the unintended interests of these essays is to observe someone we have known in a more formal setting—Helen Vendler, say, or Milton Bates—at work in the classroom. The experience, repeated often in the volume, may on occasion be as startling as when we observe at rare moments the teaching of our own colleagues (a situation that appears to have given rise to Helen Vendler's criticism here of one prevalent method of teaching poetry). A second unintended result of the essays then is the opportunity for readers to debate and even to correct (at least silently) their peers' methods of teaching Stevens and modern poetry.

The scholars represented here are accustomed to writing about Stevens and to teaching Stevens; they are not accustomed to writing about teaching Stevens. This in itself occasions a number of pieces that felicitously depart from the conventions of the scholarly essay—as in Janet McCann's imaginative computer exercises and Marie Borroff's demonstration of the adversarial character of Stevens's poetry. The testimony of some contributors is that one of the few tasks more difficult than teaching Stevens is composing an essay about it, and that is partly because of the uneasy position between two extremes that we have attempted to occupy. On the one hand, we did not wish these to be traditional scholarly or critical articles merely masquerading as teaching essays, pieces more at home in *PMLA* or the *Wallace Stevens Journal*. On the other, we wanted essays of substance—something more than the personal testimony of the successful teacher of Stevens. It is perhaps inevitable that each of the essays—"merely a state, / One of many, between two poles" (*CP* 197)—tends toward one or the other of these poles. George Lensing's account of Stevens's prosody, Lisa Steinman's discussion of Stevens and Williams, and Joseph Carroll's portrait of Stevens as a late romantic, for example, are closer to the scholarly end of the spectrum, while Elton Glaser's description of a Stevens seminar, James Ransom's instruction on teaching the long poem, David Dougherty's method of introducing Stevens's epistemology, and A. Walton Litz's situating of Stevens in the course on modern American poetry—by the very nature of their pragmatic aims—are closer to the pedagogical.

But, to move beyond the classroom, what of the many readers of Stevens who have no occasion to teach him and the many teachers of Stevens who are perfectly happy with their present instruction? Although the book was not designed primarily for these readers, its practical format does not prohibit its being read against the grain (in the way that movie reviews are enjoyed by readers who have no interest in going to movies). Among the issues pursued here that may engage such readers are Margaret Dickie's assessment of the direction of recent Stevens criticism; Lisa Steinman's and Robin Gail Schulze's discussions of the links between Stevens, William Carlos Williams, and Marianne Moore; and Joseph Carroll's and Charles Doyle's interpretations of the relation of Stevens's poetry to romanticism and to modern movements in painting. Readers uninterested in the practical issues of the classroom will also find an explication by J. M. Furniss of the early play *Three Travelers Watch a Sunrise,* George Lensing's account of the development of Stevens's prosody, Michael Campbell and John Dolan's description of the rhetorical structures to which Stevens was drawn, Dean Bethea's argument for "Peter Quince at the Clavier" and "Sunday Morning" as versions of the same poem, and Alison Rieke's analysis of Stevens's verbal eccentricities. And even beyond the issues of Stevens's poetry, here are directions by Janet McCann for the use of computers in teaching creative writing, an account by Michael Beehler of the ethical philosophy of Emmanuel Levinas, an analysis by Janet Ellerby of postmodernist suspicions of representation, and the case by Helen Vendler for a holistic approach to teaching lyric poetry.

The ordering of the essays, although it follows a certain logic, is not intended as a constraint; readers of anthologies are, at any rate, accustomed to imposing their own sequences. We have grouped similar essays and moved from the specific to the more general. The first group is devoted to classroom practices and demonstrations. This gathering of exemplary approaches contains, among other things, exercises to help students understand the architecture of a stanza or the choice of a word or image, a way of organizing a Stevens seminar, and an entry into difficult long poems like "Notes toward a Supreme Fiction." This group also contains instruction on such strategies as using a single poem, such as "The Emperor of Ice-Cream" or "Thirteen Ways of Looking at a Blackbird," to introduce undergraduates to Stevens's distinctive qualities or to help them read other modern poems, and teaching a familiar Stevens poem such as "Anecdote of the Jar" from several different critical perspectives. The second group of essays focuses on teaching prosody, rhetorical structure, diction, and theme, and the third consists of comparative approaches—teaching Stevens with Williams, Moore, or twentieth-century painting; using an early play as an introduction to the poetry; using what at first appears the more difficult poem, "Peter Quince at the Clavier," to teach its companion piece, "Sunday Morning"; combining creative writing, group computer use, and Stevens's poetry. In the final group are essays that teach Stevens in a larger context—that, say, of romanticism or Victorianism or World Wars I and II or modernism or postmodernism or a contemporary theory of ethics. Our classification is, finally, arbitrary to a degree since an essay in one category may just as aptly illustrate the topic of another. Stevens once observed in trying to explain apparent inconsistencies in the three parts of "Notes toward a Supreme Fiction" that "[e]ven in a text expounding *it must change,* it is permissible to illustrate *it must give pleasure* without any law whatever" (*L* 445).

II

As James Ransom acknowledges in his teaching essay, a distinguished tradition of criticism has emerged on Stevens that invariably, if even at times intangibly, contributes to what goes on in the classroom. Although it is beyond the scope of this introduction to be comprehensive (at last count there were nearly two thousand books and articles on Stevens), we would nevertheless like to provide here for the nonspecialist teacher or student some suggestions for further reading.

The "fabled complaint" among Stevens specialists, to vary Joseph Carroll's phrase, is one pointed out by Alison Rieke in her essay: anthologies rely mostly on lyrics and do not adequately represent Stevens. Though one occasionally sees selections from the longer poems, anthologies can little afford the space to reproduce poetic sequences like "Notes toward a Supreme Fiction" or "An Ordinary Evening in New Haven." Fortunately, for those desiring comprehensiveness in advanced undergraduate courses or seminars, inexpensive paperback editions of the *Collected Poems of Wallace Stevens* and *The Palm at the End of the Mind*, edited by Holly Stevens, are available. Both have advantages—*Collected Poems* lets students appreciate how Stevens shaped his individual volumes, while *The Palm at the End of the Mind*, which contains the early play *Bowl, Cat and Broomstick*, the politically motivated "Owl's Clover," and a handful of late lyrics, conveys in its chronological arrangement a sense of Stevens's poetic development.

The solution we have chosen for references in this book, and one adopted for teaching Stevens by more than half of the specialists responding to our survey on this topic, is to combine the *Collected Poems* with *Opus Posthumous* (1989), edited by Milton Bates. Bates's edition is more accurate and richer than Samuel French Morse's earlier one, offering nearly two dozen more poems (from poetic cycles "Carnet de Voyage," "Phases," and "Primordia" to "From the Journal of Crispin," an early version of "The Comedian as the Letter C" salvaged from a trash can by Stevens's landlord and made public in 1974), as well as nearly two dozen more prose pieces (from "Poetry and War" to "Insurance and Social Change"). Most important, it corrects Morse's mistake of attributing H. D. Lewis's essay "On Poetic Truth" to Stevens.

Other important primary works include *Letters of Wallace Stevens* (1966), selected and edited by Holly Stevens, for it offers a cache of biographical information and contains Stevens's own explanations of many poems. Holly Stevens's *Souvenirs and Prophecies: The Young Wallace Stevens* (1977) sheds light on Stevens's transformation into a major poet by interweaving Holly

Stevens's personal recollections of her father and his times with the publication of his early journals, while Beverly Coyle and Alan Filreis's *Secretaries of the Moon: The Letters of Wallace Stevens and José Rodríguez Feo* (1986) reveals the later Stevens displaying a wide range of interests, from poetic theory and art to news of Rodríguez Feo's chickens raised on red peppers. And we have no better demonstration of Stevens's maxim that "Poetry is the scholar's art" (*OP* 193) than in the recently published notebooks *Sur Plusieurs Beaux Sujects: Wallace Stevens' Commonplace Book* (1989), edited by Bates, in which Stevens recorded and commented on passages from his sundry reading for over twenty years and in which one often discovers a Jamesian *ficelle*. The remainder of Stevens's essays, collected in *The Necessary Angel: Essays on Reality and the Imagination,* discuss in highly poetical terms Stevens's reflections on the sanctifying function of art and his conviction that "the structure of poetry and the structure of reality are one" (*NA* 81).

Secondary works detailing Stevens's biography are Morse's *Wallace Stevens: Poetry as Life* (1970)—useful on the formative years and influences but anchored to the poetry and letters; Peter Brazeau's *Parts of a World: Wallace Stevens Remembered* (1983)—an oral biography packed with intriguing details of the poet as businessman, husband, and "one of the boys"; and Bates's *Wallace Stevens: A Mythology of Self* (1985)—a literary and intellectual history doubling as a superb biography and revealing, among other things, the disturbing effects of a fractured home life. Joan Richardson's encyclopedic two-volume study *Wallace Stevens: The Early Years, 1879–1923* (1986) and *Wallace Stevens: The Later Years, 1923–1955* (1988) parallels Stevens's life and values with the transition of the United States into the twentieth century. It examines the impact of Stevens's reading and mixes biography with psychological speculation in an attempt to get at the man behind the poems.

A number of scholars have provided lucid overviews of Stevens's principal ideas and themes, and though some of these may seem dated, they continue to be useful at the introductory level. R. P. Blackmur's groundbreaking essay "Examples of Wallace Stevens" (1932)—really the first critical article—establishes the precision of Stevens's diction in the early poetry, while Louis Martz's "Wallace Stevens: The World as Meditation" (1958; rpt. 1966) elucidates the meditative quality in the later poetry by comparing it to that of the seventeenth-century Jesuit tradition. J. Hillis Miller's

"Wallace Stevens' Poetry of Being" (1964; rpt. 1965 as "Wallace Stevens") gives a sound overview of Stevens's philosophical ideas, while his more recent entry on William Carlos Williams and Stevens in the *Columbia Literary History of the United States* (1988) clarifies Stevens's difficulty and even irrationality by demonstrating their necessity to Stevens's expression of a complex perception of reality. Helen Vendler's introduction to Stevens in *Voices & Visions: The Poet in America* (1987) is crystalline in its delineation of the various phases of Stevens's poetic development from its beginning in the vacuum created by religious loss and its early experimental phases, to its concern in the middle period with social issues, to its expression in the later poetry of the poet's role in reshaping culture. Teachers will also find handy a number of collections, both of original material—as in Frank Doggett and Robert Buttel's *Wallace Stevens: A Celebration* (1980) and Albert Gelpi's *Wallace Stevens: The Poetics of Modernism* (1985)—and of previously published essays—as in Ashley Brown and Robert S. Haller's *The Achievement of Wallace Stevens* (1962; rpt. 1973), Marie Borroff's *Wallace Stevens: A Collection of Critical Essays* (1963), Harold Bloom's *Wallace Stevens* (1985), and Steven Gould Axelrod and Helen Deese's *Critical Essays on Wallace Stevens* (1988).

A handful of books also offer useful introductions, though some tend to favor the early poetry or to stress the ordering principle of the imagination. These include William Van O'Connor's *The Shaping Spirit: A Study of Wallace Stevens* (1950; rpt. 1964), Robert Pack's *Wallace Stevens: An Approach to His Poetry and Thought* (1958), Frank Kermode's *Wallace Stevens* (1964, rpt. 1989), and William Burney's *Wallace Stevens* (1968). More recent generalist studies include Susan Weston's refreshing *Wallace Stevens: An Introduction to the Poetry* (1977). Focusing on the underlying theme of the search for a new knowledge of reality, it is wittily written: "Creating fictions is the essential gift of the human mind; believing them is its curse." Robert Rehder's *The Poetry of Wallace Stevens* (1988) utilizes previously published primary material to present an astute sketch of both the life and the poetry but unfortunately contains typographical errors that, in the case of dates, mislead the unwary. Although only one book explicitly devotes itself to explicating poems—Ronald Sukenick's *Wallace Stevens: Musing the Obscure* (1967)—Joseph Riddel's *The Clairvoyant Eye: The Poetry and Poetics of*

Wallace Stevens (1966; rpt. 1990) remains indispensable: organized around the various stages of Stevens's evolving poetics, it discusses in detail virtually every major poem.

Studies in the last twenty-five years have begun to narrow their focus, isolating periods, influences, themes, or approaches. Since there are far too many to enumerate, we can suggest only a few of the more basic ones. Robert Buttel's *Wallace Stevens: The Making of Harmonium* (1967) initiated a series of books devoted to Stevens's poetic development; it has been followed by A. Walton Litz's *Introspective Voyager: The Poetic Development of Wallace Stevens* (1972), George S. Lensing's *Wallace Stevens: A Poet's Growth* (1986), and B. J. Leggett's *Early Stevens: The Nietzschean Intertext* (1992). Works emphasizing Stevens's later development include Thomas Hines's *The Later Poetry of Wallace Stevens* (1976) and Charles Berger's *Forms of Farewell: The Late Poetry of Wallace Stevens* (1985). Students or teachers interested in pursuing Stevens's philosophical affinities should consult Frank Doggett's *Stevens' Poetry of Thought* (1966) and James Leonard and Christine E. Wharton's *The Fluent Mundo: Wallace Stevens and the Structure of Reality* (1988), while those interested in literary and philosophical influences should read B. J. Leggett's *Wallace Stevens and Poetic Theory: Conceiving the Supreme Fiction* (1987). Helen Vendler's emphasis on rhetorical strategies, *On Extended Wings: Wallace Stevens' Longer Poems* (1969), has been extended by others, including Marie Borroff ("Wallace Stevens's World of Words" [1976]), Jacqueline Vaught Brogan (*Stevens and Simile* [1986]), and Eleanor Cook (*Poetry, Word-Play, and Word-War in Wallace Stevens* [1988]). For those wishing to discover the deeply personal elements embedded in Stevens's poetry, Vendler's *Words Chosen Out of Desire* (1985) is the most revealing. Although numerous works explore romantic links, Harold Bloom's *Wallace Stevens: The Poems of Our Climate* (1977) and Joseph Carroll's *Wallace Stevens' Supreme Fiction: A New Romanticism* (1987) are the most comprehensive. The newest turn in Stevens criticism aims at recapturing connections with the real world; two works along these lines are Alan Filreis's *Wallace Stevens and the Actual World* (1991) and James Longenbach's *Wallace Stevens: The Plain Sense of Things* (1991).

Bibliographical studies, of course, provide an excellent starting point for research in any number of directions. J. M. Edelstein's *Wallace Stevens: A Descriptive Bibliography* (1973) remains the standard guide to Stevens's publication history and includes a secondary bibliography of books, articles, reviews, and dissertations. Joseph Riddel's survey essays in the *Sixteen Modern American Authors* series (1973, 1990) give brief though evaluative descriptions of what has been published, while books by Abbie Willard and Melita Schaum supply much more detail. Willard organizes her *Wallace Stevens: The Poet and His Critics* (1978) around thematic issues (poetic growth, literary heritage, poetic theory) and reviews various scholars' contributions to each, while Schaum, in *Wallace Stevens and the Critical Schools* (1988), examines prominent theoretical movements that have emerged in the twentieth century (new criticism, phenomenology, poststructuralism) and shows how they have each emphasized, in turn, different facets of Stevens (order, experience, language). Another useful resource is Thomas F. Walsh's *Concordance to the Poetry of Wallace Stevens* (1963), for it enables one not only to examine Stevens's word usage, but also to locate particular passages in poems from both the *Collected Poems* and Morse's edition of *Opus Posthumous*. Finally, John N. Serio's *Wallace Stevens: An Annotated Secondary Bibliography* (1994) annotates criticism on Stevens from 1916 to 1993. In supplying informative summaries of nearly two thousand books and articles and in indexing poems, themes, approaches, and influences, it serves as a valuable reference guide.

Part I. Classroom Strategies

Wallace Stevens:
Teaching the Anthology Pieces

HELEN VENDLER

I want to say a few general things about teaching poems before I come to the case of Wallace Stevens. As Wordsworth pointed out long ago, poems propose for their immediate object pleasure, not truth. It follows that a student who has not had aesthetic pleasure from a poem has missed what it has to offer. We are responsible for making aesthetic pleasure available to students who often derive it easily from music or landscape, but who find words, and especially words composing poems, a difficult source of enjoyment. The several aesthetic pleasures available from poetry include one that poetry shares with other representational arts (film, photography, narration)—that is, the recognizable representation of physical, perceptual, psychological, moral, and topographical reality. But this is not a pleasure peculiar to poetry; and we would all like, I think, to bring our students to some of the particular things that poetry, and poetry alone, has to give.

This attention to what is special to poetry is what has been missing in most classes on poetry that I have attended. Class discussion has rarely gotten beyond a description of the speaker, of the concerns voiced by the speaker, and of the narrative or plot of the poem. To extract this information from the students (by, for example, having a student tell what each stanza adds to the one before, or by posing questions such as "Who is the speaker?" and "What is the event out of which the utterance comes?") takes up all the class time. Or, if a little time is left, it is given over to asking students their response to the position of the lyric speaker: "Do you feel this way about *your* childhood?" "How would *you* feel if a man said this to *you?*" These questions refer the plot of the poem to the actual life situations of the students.

These information-retrieval and opinion-giving responses are not specific to poetry; they could equally well be solicited from the students with respect to a newspaper editorial or a political speech that they had read. It is understandable that teachers would like students to respond to a poem as a "human document," but too often that purpose is achieved at the expense of students' responding to it as a work of art. And response on the documentary level is indifferent to the poet's genre-mastery; incompetent poems, as much as good ones, have speakers, announce a situation, and pursue a plot complete with imagery, climax, and conclusion. It is no service to students to train them to identify and discuss things that are irrelevant to the competence of a piece of art. It is much more useful to train them to see how good poems produce aesthetic surprise, imaginative pleasure, and moral ratification. To do that, it is indispensable to lead students to aesthetic response—something very different from the ability to paraphrase, or to give their opinion of the opinions of the lyric speaker, or to identify blank verse when they see it. Though none of these is irrelevant, none of them is primary.

It is common in the classes I have seen to take the students through a poem part by part, even line by line, inquiring of students the "meaning" of the first stanza, then the second stanza, and so on. But in any well-constructed poem stanza one—even line one—has "meaning" only in the light of the whole. To proceed line by line is like asking a student to comment on the upper left quadrant of a painting, then on the lower left quadrant, and so on, before it has been perceived that the painting represents, as a whole, a man on horseback. In aesthetic construction, the whole is that which confers meaning on the parts; and though the notion of the hermeneutic circle (testing the part by the whole and the whole by the part) has some theoretical truth to it as a model for the approach to more and more refined understanding (especially of extended objects like novels or operas) it has no validity for the first grasp of a small aesthetic object, which is always, because of the nature of perception, a holistic grasp. Since I'm here addressing lyric, I take it that we generally see the whole before we see its parts, and that students, too, should be taught to grasp wholes first.

How, then, can we bring students more directly into the precincts of the art of poetry itself, while not shortchanging those considerable moral and documentary powers it shares with other representative genres, and the general human interest that it shares with all position-taking verbal objects, from oratory to advertisements? And how can we bring them to see the whole poem before they inquire into its means and its manner?

It seems to me that we dishearten students by making them puzzle out the "meaning" of poems that are often written in archaic or learned language, and that use (often allusively) complicated theological, philosophical, and literary concepts. Stevens is in many ways a "difficult" poet in these respects. I find that I get to "real questions" (i.e., aesthetic ones) sooner if I "give" the whole poem to my students first, sketching it quickly in paraphrase and removing thereby most obstacles to understanding. Of "The Snow Man" (*CP* 9), for instance, I might say,

> Keats, when he heard the diminished music of autumn—crickets' songs and the twitter of swallows—remembered how much more opulent the spring songs of the nightingales had been and said in protest, "Where are the songs of spring? Aye, where are they?" Someone else might say, seeing bare trees in winter, "Where are the leaves of summer?" These are moments of nostalgia, and in the life of the emotions, vanished songs or fallen leaves stand for the loss of life, or energy, or happiness—so that in misery one says, "Where is the happiness I used to have?" or in old age, "Where has my youth gone?" Keats sympathized with that pained response, but decided that it was the wrong attitude to take, because it poisoned life. He proposed that one should stop looking for the past joy, and try to find, *in* the present, an attitude that springs *from* the present and not from some nostalgic comparison of the present with the past. So, after asking "Where are the songs of spring?" he counters by saying to Autumn, "Think not of them, thou hast thy music too"—and then he describes that music in ways that reveal its natural beauty as well as its pain, stoicism, and even joy. But Stevens, in "The Snow Man," pushes on beyond autumn—which after all does have some musical sounds left—to ask about winter. "Can one be in winter without misery? Can one turn oneself into a snow man? Can one live in winter with a mind of winter? Is there anything left to listen to once the birds and the crickets are gone? Is there anything to see once the leaves have fallen?"

Then I would read the poem aloud, since intonation conveys so much of the import of any verbal object.

Once "meaning"—the meat thrown to the dog by the burglar, as Eliot said—is cleared up (and "meaning" in lyric poetry is usually simple and rapidly paraphrasable, even in Stevens) the real investigation—why, in order to give aesthetic pleasure, the meaning is conveyed to us *in this manner*—can begin. Arrangement as the determiner of import is the source of all aesthetic pleasure, and if students are to have that pleasure—as is their right—we have to teach them what import-by-arrangement amounts to, how to recognize it, and what sorts of things can be said about it. "Arrangement" applies, of course, to a single case—a single painting, a single sonata, a single poem; once several cases are assembled, many different taxonomies of their mutual relations can be attempted (by genre, by school, by period, by a developmental hypothesis), but that is not likely to occur unless one is spending a whole course on, say, Stevens.

In a really accomplished poem, arrangement occurs on every possible level, from the phonetic to the philosophical (in fact, it is the density of multilevel arrangement that usually distinguishes the good poem from the incompetent one). A teacher can begin anywhere in pointing out signs of arrangement, of course, but I believe the cause of poetry has been ill served by emphasizing such minor patternings as alliteration, assonance, and rhyme over such gross patterns as "plot" (by contrast to "story"), lyric subgenre, conceptual architecture, speech acts, and tonal dynamics. In the case of "The Snow Man" the major aesthetic move is looking/listening/looking. Other moves include the preeminent negativity ("not to think . . . nothing himself . . . Nothing . . . not") turning suddenly to quasi-positivity ("the nothing that is"), the replacement of bare deciduous trees in the winter topos by shagged and crusted evergreens, the increasing enjambment as a sign of the wind, the infinitives as a sign of purpose yielding to the active present tense of "listens" and "beholds," etc. I'd probably hand out Stevens's precursor poem, Keats's "In drear-nighted December," to establish the subgenre of seasonal nostalgia.

It remains to be said that the best way into a poem is to learn it by heart, so that it becomes indistinguishable from a potential (I had first typed "poetential" and perhaps that is what I mean) utterance of one's own. If the class is small enough to have student reports, anyone reporting on a poem should have learned it by heart, and should have written it out at least once in longhand. Students learn aurally and kinesthetically as well as visually, and multiple possession of a poem (which has been learned by heart, written out, and recited) brings the student halfway home to mastery of the poem, to a knowledge of its secret arrangements.

Stevens's poems fall into two large kinds, and most anthologies have some of each. The first kind is meditative, relatively "classical," and rhapsodic: "Sunday Morning," "The Idea of Order at Key West," "To the One of Fictive Music," and "To an Old Philosopher in Rome" can stand for this kind. These are, in effect, "easier" poems than Stevens's cryptic riddles, but because of their long sentences, lofty diction, rhetorical address, and allusive texture, they can initially appear more forbidding. The second kind of poem, the short conceptual lyric, can be represented by "Ploughing on Sunday," "Disillusionment of Ten O'Clock," "Thirteen Ways of Looking at a Blackbird," "The Snow Man," "The Paltry Nude Starts on a Spring Voyage," "Bantams in Pine-Woods," etc. A good way to draw the students' attention to this large division in Stevens is to teach a long poem together with a short poem that shares its subject matter, e.g., "Sunday Morning" with its later version, "Ploughing on Sunday," both of them "blasphemous" poems taking off from Emily Dickinson's lyric (which I would quote) "Some keep the Sabbath going to Church — / I keep it, staying at Home — / With a Bobolink for a Chorister — / And an Orchard, for a Dome." Brief explanations of the seriousness of Sabbath-blasphemy (the refusal to attend divine service, the "servile work" of ploughing), and of the importance in Christian belief of the Resurrection—Jesus leaving his grave, his absence announced by angels lingering at the tomb—need to be offered to students, as does a sketch of the three-stage cultural progress described in the poem, from an all-divine Zeus to a half-divine, half-human Jesus to an (envisaged) totally human god; the attractions and repellencies of the various classical and Judeo-Christian ideas of the afterlife and paradise need to be mentioned, too.

This is the point at which reading aloud needs to take over, preferably of one or two of the most accessible sections of "Sunday Morning" (*CP* 66), such as "Why should she give her bounty to the dead?" (so that students can see the polemic force—anti-Christian, pro-pagan—of the poem) or "Is there no change of death in paradise?" (so that students can see Stevens's inquiry into the psychological need for a terminus in order to provoke erotic ecstasy and aesthetic pleasure). There is no point in having students read aloud unless they have had prior warning and a chance to reflect and practice; even with reflection, they have so little experience with reading verse aloud that their rhythmic scansion tends to be wrong and their emphases consequently misplaced; one has to know a poem very well to read it aloud competently. I prefer to do the reading myself, since so much of the import of a poem can be conveyed by hearing it accurately expressed aloud.

After my sketch of its themes, and my reading of part of it aloud, students will have seen the general argument of "Sunday Morning" and will consequently have more confidence in their perception of details. For the next class, two students might be asked to prepare a report on individual cantos. I might give one student a "scrambled" canto with its sentences rearranged, and ask for comments on the architectural difference between it and the original, especially the difference in tonal dynamics and in closure:

> Is there no change of death in paradise?
> Why set the pear upon those river-banks
> Or spice the shores with odors of the plum?
> Does ripe fruit never fall? Or do the boughs
> Hang always heavy in that perfect sky,
> Unchanging, yet so like our perishing earth,
> With rivers like our own that seek for seas
> They never find, the same receding shores
> That never touch with inarticulate pang?
> Death is the mother of beauty, mystical,
> Within whose burning bosom we devise
> Our earthly mothers waiting, sleeplessly.
> Alas, that they should wear our colors there,
> The silken weavings of our afternoons,
> And pick the strings of our insipid lutes!

Or I might do a handout of a canto with different words (more literal or more abstract ones) in some of the "slots," and ask about the difference made by these substitutions:

Is there no change of *time* in paradise?
Do young men never die? Or *does maturity*
Live ever perfect in that perfect sky,
Unchanging, yet so like our *mortal* earth,
With rivers like our own that *flow toward* seas
They never *reach,* the same *far-distant* shores
That never touch with *silent space between?*
Why set the *apple on* those river-banks
Or *decorate* the shores with *bough* of plum?
Alas, that they should wear our *textures* there,
The silken weavings of our *morning work,*
And pick the strings of our insipid *harps!*
Time is the *giver* of beauty, mystical,
Within whose *deep abyss* we *may surmise*
Our earthly *parents preceding us in death.*

This is close enough in paraphrasable "meaning" to press students away from paraphrase and toward the more precise import of particular words and metaphors. I encourage my students always to try to substitute words for important "slots"; I've also given out "skeletons" of poems they do not know with blanks for crucial adjectives or adverbs, asking them to fill in the blanks:

> . . . It is like the strain
Waked in the elders by Susanna.

Of a _____ evening, clear and warm,
She bathed in her _____ garden, while
The _____ elders watching, felt

The basses of their beings throb
In _____ chords, and their thin blood
Pulse _____ of Hosanna. (*CP* 90)

Given their own (usually more literal) choices, students can then be asked to speculate why an evening should be seen as "green," how a garden can be "still," why elders should be "red-eyed," what sorts of chords "witch-ing" ones are, and what "pizzicati" adds to the imagery of musical chords.

"Sunday Morning," its argument sketched in the first class, can be completed in the next class when students report on individual cantos. In the first class, after sketching the main lines of "Sunday Morning," I can go on to "Ploughing on Sunday," and ask why someone who had written "Sunday Morning" might rewrite it a few years later in this nonclassical, nonfemale, nativist, non–upper-class (and apparently nonwhite) way. Having seen the gorgeousness and opulence that is the central aesthetic value of the writing in "Sunday Morning," students now see the polar opposite of such diction, both in "Ploughing on Sunday" and in "Thirteen Ways of Looking at a Blackbird" (*CP* 92) with its dismissive reference to "the bawds of euphony." Stevens's suspicion, in this phrase, of high rhetoric and the limitation it imposes, in the service of euphony, on feeling-tones, will convey to students why Stevens had to write, in self-defense, his "angular" conceptual poems. At the same time, "Disillusionment of Ten O'Clock" (*CP* 66) will warn them that he also fears the minimalist style, which can entail wearing only "white night-gowns." Mediating between the opulent and the minimalist, "Thirteen Ways of Looking at a Blackbird" will show students how "the essential gaudiness of poetry" (*L* 263)—multiple ways of looking, odd diction—can coexist with stanzaic and syntactic minimalism.

It is only after students understand that maximalist euphony and minimalist colorlessness, Euro-culture and American bareness, are aesthetically troubling and divisive issues for Stevens that the teacher can begin to show them why accuracy of representation must be the artist's standard of moral responsibility. "The accuracy of accurate letters is an accuracy with respect to the structure of reality" (*NA* 71). What is the structure of reality; how could one go about ascertaining it in any given case; and, if it were ascertained, how could one accurately represent it in letters? These questions drive Stevens to his aspectual treatment of reality, evident in "Thirteen Ways," which intimates that there are an infinite number of ways of looking at and symbolizing any piece of reality (the blackbird is equated with the Heraclitean river of change, the erotic bond between the sexes, death, eccentricity, ambivalence, causation, and so on).

The difference between philosophy and poetry (too often blurred in discussion of Stevens's work) can be perfectly exemplified by "Thirteen Ways of Looking at a Blackbird," which raises philosophical issues in fabular, enigmatic, and aphoristic form. It is essential, of course, to raise with students the life-issues scrutinized in this, as in any other, poem, before seeing how they are aesthetically reframed, and so for purposes of illustration I list the chief life-issues implicit in each stanza of "Thirteen Ways":

I

Among twenty snowy mountains,
The only moving thing
Was the eye of the blackbird.

[The emotional and transcriptive significance of consciousness, the blackbird's eye as a "moving" (in the emotional sense) thing, a variant of the *Rubáiyát*'s "moving finger" that transcribes an otherwise lifeless universe.]

II

I was of three minds,
Like a tree
In which there are three blackbirds.

[Ambivalence to the point of eccentricity (being of three minds instead of two)—the intellectual's fate.]

III

The blackbird whirled in the autumn winds.
It was a small part of the pantomime.

[The insignificance of individual fate in the huge theater of nature.]

IV

A man and a woman
Are one.
A man and a woman and a blackbird
Are one.

[The inevitable intrusion of consciousness into erotic physical union.]

V

I do not know which to prefer,
The beauty of inflections
Or the beauty of innuendoes,
The blackbird whistling
Or just after.

[Ambivalence between experience (including song) and its reverberations. (This is a place where the legal meaning of *innuendo*—a comment following a principle—and the Latin roots of both *inflection* and *innuendo* can be usefully brought up.)]

VI

Icicles filled the long window
With barbaric glass.
The shadow of the blackbird
Crossed it, to and fro.
The mood
Traced in the shadow
An indecipherable cause.

[Experience as necessarily mediated, never unmediated. The poet's mood is caused not by the blackbird, but by its shadow, itself transmitted through two panes of glass—the "civilized" architectural window and the natural "barbaric glass" of the icicles outside it. The blackbird's contrary movement "to and fro" and the haunting of the window by the blackbird's shadow convey the interior distress of the speaker, who sees experience through so many mediations that it becomes "indecipherable."]

VII

O thin men of Haddam,
Why do you imagine golden birds?
Do you not see how the blackbird
Walks around the feet
Of the women about you?

[Idealization and its erotic motivation; the local (Haddam, Connecticut) as the site of reproach.]

VIII

I know noble accents
And lucid, inescapable rhythms;
But I know, too,
That the blackbird is involved
In what I know.

[Nobility and euphony, as cognitive objects, fatally contaminated by the temporality and alienation of consciousness.]

IX

When the blackbird flew out of sight,
It marked the edge
Of one of many circles.

[The dizzying infinite extension possible to consciousness, a series of circles distanced from the perceiver-center by a radial length determined by the locus of attention.]

X

At the sight of blackbirds
Flying in a green light,
Even the bawds of euphony
Would cry out sharply.

["Even the ranks of Tuscany / Could scarce forbear to cheer" (Macaulay, "Horatius" 359) probably lies behind "Even the bawds of euphony / Would cry out sharply": aesthetic effect as commanding even its opponents.]

XI

He rode over Connecticut
In a glass coach.
Once, a fear pierced him,
In that he mistook
The shadow of his equipage
For blackbirds.

[On perceptual and cognitive error; the fear of the invasion of one's own self-extensions (carriage, livery) by "blackbirds" even if one protects oneself inside a glass coach. The de-enchanting of Cinderella lurks in this schema of appearance/reality/error/fear.]

XII

The river is moving.

The blackbird must be flying.

[The correspondence theory of truth (Baudelaire as precursor in "Correspondances").]

XIII

It was evening all afternoon.

It was snowing

And it was going to snow.

The blackbird sat

In the cedar-limbs.

[Apprehension; menace; the eccentric (thirteen) as the base of design.]

These are the life-issues of the poem, but they are not the poem. "Thirteen Ways of Looking at a Blackbird" is a good poem by which to teach students the foreign language I call "poetic"—which is not the same language as "English," but rather a sociolect spoken by poets, which (as the students see by working through how each life-issue has been given a poetic shape) accomplishes its ends by indirection, concision, symbol, suggestion, riddle, and, especially, a never-suspended ironic inquiry—brought into being by the very act of art-writing itself—into its own procedures and products. The symbolic indefiniteness of reference of the blackbird—and of its two poles, immobility and mobility, which organize the poem—is frustrating to some students, attractive to others.

When students wonder why anyone would want to write in this sociolect, they raise the whole question of verbal stimuli to aesthetic pleasure—that is, the question of verbal stylization. Stylization (by contrast to mimetic documentary reproduction) is best explained to them, as the shorthand it is, in visual terms; one can present the notion of cartoons, caricature, advertisements, traffic signs, and so on, as representing, for an artist, the challenge of conveying a certain quantum of information by the least possible means. Students may recognize instances like the single-line trademark sketch of Hitchcock, or the logo of a company, or the single exaggerated trait of caricature, or the animal symbol of a political party. The appeal of visual stylization is that it involves the viewer in cooperative recognition; similarly, poems of maximum stylization (like "Thirteen Ways") make the reader the co-creator of import, a role students can learn to value.

Once they understand the constructivist aesthetic of "Thirteen Ways," students can inquire into its variety of productive means. They can look at its choices—of stasis versus flight, of exterior versus interior landscapes; of varying tenses (present, imperfect, preterit, future) and moods (indicative, interrogative, conjectural, conditional, definitional); of changing forms of self-reference ("I," "he," "man," "thin men of Haddam," "the bawds of euphony")—some of them lyric, some impersonal, some self-satirizing. They can discuss its opening and its closure (both "impersonal"), and see the role in poetry of "impersonal" proposition and description as a marker for "universally accepted fact," enabling the poem to distinguish between personal experience (marked by "I" or "he") and, respectively, generally acknowledged law ("A man and a woman and a blackbird / Are one"), inference ("The blackbird must be flying"), and prediction ("it was going to snow"). These and other speech-acts in the poem can be shown to be among the poem's resources for variety, just as certain standard volumes (the cylinder, the sphere, the cone) are among the sculptor's standard resources in assembling his figures.

The literal unpredictability of "Thirteen Ways"—who can say, having read the first four stanzas, what the fifth stanza might be?—can be usefully contrasted with the thematic rationality and continuity of argument in "Sunday Morning"—and a perception of this contrast will help students understand the difference between a linear and a radial (aspectual) architecture. The fact that human beings are able to enjoy both structures—the linear and the radial—suggests that both are structures we often perceive (as by X-ray vision) in "reality," or, to put this another way, are lenses through which we shape reality—the linear structure a directed motion in the narrative realm, the radial structure one that is implicitly faceted and multiple. Other comparable structures—the "framed narrative" of "Peter Quince at the Clavier" with its lyric brackets around the plot of Susanna, the apostrophe and prayer of "To the One of Fictive Music," the spiral "turnings" of "Domination of Black," the concentric circles of "Frogs Eat Butterflies . . . ," the confrontational structure of "Bantams in Pine-Woods"—these are all arrangements that mimic, in poetic structures, rec-

ognizable social structures. It is chiefly at the level of structural arrangement, and not at the level of documentation, that the poetry of Stevens is
mimetic of social reality.

In teaching Stevens, one should probably vary epistemological and self-
reflexive poems with poems more narratively accessible to the students,
such as those on social problems ("Mozart, 1935"), or death ("The Emperor of Ice-Cream"), or love ("Le Monocle de Mon Oncle"), or old age
("The Planet on the Table," "The River of Rivers in Connecticut," "To
an Old Philosopher in Rome"). Of course we need to show students that
a poet writes about economic depression, or concupiscence and a corpse,
or marital failure, or the distress of old age (as well as about the fresh beginnings possible at each stage of loss). But that is not enough. It is useless
to draw to students' attention the human relevance and moving power of
Stevens's work without introducing them to the specific stylizing means of
art—the only means, after all, through which, in art, relevance and power
are attained with any longevity.

"The Emperor" and Its Clothes

MILTON J. BATES

Teach Wallace Stevens? The prospect still strikes terror into my heart, though for eighteen years I have been trying to teach his poetry to students from the freshman through graduate levels. It is futile to pretend that Stevens is transparently accessible to most students, so I have shamelessly exploited every resource known to pedagogy to maximize the pleasure of reading his poems and minimize the pain. I have distributed handouts with *Norton Anthology*-style notes, played tapes of Stevens reading his poems, placed helpful books and articles on reserve in the library. I have mentioned contemporary films, popular songs, and other media that illustrate the continuing relevance of his main theme, the mind's negotiations with physical reality. (Not all of these analogues are very sophisticated or even very serious. Among the items in my Stevens file is a "Mother Goose & Grimm" cartoon by Mike Peters. It shows a familiar-looking locomotive with headphones, obviously listening to a self-help tape as it repeats, "I'm visualizing that I can . . . I'm visualizing that I can. . . .") Most recently, I have taken to showing selected portions of the *Voices & Visions* videotape program on Stevens.

Each of these sheds a ray of light into the palpable obscure between the covers of the *Collected Poems*. However, I have found that our consideration of Stevens's work often lives or dies depending on which poem we take up first. The ideal "first poem" should do at least five things: (1) introduce the themes and vocabulary necessary for discussion of subsequent poems; (2) identify the distinctive qualities of Stevens's poetic style; (3) deliver intellectual and emotional rewards that repay the effort of understanding; (4) confront head-on the issue of his obscurity, which is so unlike that of Pound, Eliot, or Yeats; and (5) suggest the role played by historical and cultural context in the creation of meaning. This may be asking too much of a single poem, which would explain why I have tried and rejected so many "first poems" over the years. These have included "Anecdote of the Jar," "The Snow Man," "Cy Est Pourtraicte, Madame Ste Ursule, et Les Unze Mille Vierges," "Of Modern Poetry," and the fable Stevens himself chose as the entrée to his *Collected Poems,* "Earthy Anecdote."

The poem I have recently found most satisfactory is that old anthology chestnut, "The Emperor of Ice-Cream" (*CP* 64). Rather than offer another explication of the poem here, I will indicate step-by-step how it might be presented to an undergraduate class so as to achieve the objectives just mentioned.

It is essential, first, that the student spend some time grappling with the poem before class and have a personal stake in its interpretation. At our previous meeting I therefore distribute the following handout, assigning a paraphrase of the poem and glossing several words likely to perplex even those who take the trouble to consult a dictionary:

Stevens's "The Emperor of Ice-Cream": Paraphrase Assignment

A poem is not a straightforward prose statement that the poet has "dressed up" in such devices as imagery, allusion, sound effects, and so forth. It embodies a complex intellectual and emotional experience that is communicated fully *only* in the form and language the poet has chosen. Consequently, critics of literature regard paraphrase as a form of "heresy," a violation of the poem's meaning as poem.

It is nevertheless useful to attempt a prose paraphrase as a first step toward understanding the full meaning of a poem. Prior to our discussion of Stevens's "The Emperor of Ice-Cream" on [date], please write a paraphrase of the poem on the back of this page. Don't forget to sign your name to your work.

The paraphrase should take the form of a series of directives and observations addressed to an implied audience. When referring to people and objects mentioned in the poem, you should also indicate your *attitude* toward them—e.g., "Do *x* because I feel this or that way about *y*." Wherever possible, use words other than those chosen by Stevens. When you encounter a poetic image ("concupiscent curds," for example) you will need to "translate" it into language that conveys both the literal reality and its emotional overtones.

Notes to Poem:

line 9: *deal*—pine or other cheap wood

    11: *fantails*—fantail pigeons

    13: *horny*—calloused

As the wording of the assignment suggests, I was too thoroughly schooled in the New Criticism to feel entirely comfortable with this exercise. Thus I characterize the paraphrase somewhat defensively as a form of heresy. Having shared this scruple with my students, I nevertheless urge them to follow Martin Luther's advice and sin courageously.

I initiate the class on "The Emperor" by reading the poem in a deliberately flat, noncommittal voice, since I want to postpone consideration of its tone until later. I then ask if any of the students wants to read his or her paraphrase, an invitation almost certain to go begging. I waste little time before calling on a student, whose effort generally provokes some blend of shock and amusement in the rest of the class. Stevens's poems give pleasure even when misconstrued. I then invite the other students to question the writer of the paraphrase about details they find confusing or without basis in the poem. Those who jump into the fray—remember, they have a stake in the "correct" reading—are then impressed into reading their paraphrases. By the time three or four of these have been aired, it is clear that there are as many interpretations of the poem as there are people in the room.

Once, I discovered that every student had somehow overlooked the dead woman whose wake is the occasion of "The Emperor." Since then I have come prepared with copies of Helen Vendler's prose rendition of the poem from *Words Chosen Out of Desire*. Her narrative is not so much a paraphrase as it is a first-person account of the kind of experience that might have prompted the poem. Consequently, it is addressed to no one in particular, and its verbs are all in the indicative mood. These differences aside, Vendler's pre-"Emperor" can serve the same purpose as a paraphrase in the classroom. It reads,

> I went, as a neighbor, to a house to help to lay out the corpse of an old woman
> who had died alone; I was helping to prepare for the home wake. I entered,
> familiarly, not by the front door but by the kitchen door. I was shocked and repelled

as I went into the kitchen by the disorderly festival going on inside: a big muscular neighbor who worked at the cigar-factory had been called in to crank the ice-cream machine, various neighbors had sent over their scullery-girls to help out and their yard-boys bearing newspaper-wrapped flowers from their yards to decorate the house and the bier: the scullery-girls were taking advantage of the occasion to dawdle around the kitchen and flirt with the yard-boys, and they were all waiting around to have a taste of the ice-cream when it was finished. It all seemed to me crude and boisterous and squalid and unfeeling in the house of the dead—all that appetite, all that concupiscence.

Then I left the sexuality and gluttony of the kitchen and went in to the death in the bedroom. The corpse of the old woman was lying exposed on the bed. My first impulse was to find a sheet to cover the corpse; I went to the cheap old pine dresser, but it was hard to get the sheet out of it because each of the three drawers was lacking a drawer-pull; she must have been too infirm to get to the store to get new glass knobs. But I got a sheet out, noticing that she had hand-embroidered a fantail border on it; she wanted to make it beautiful, even though she was so poor that she made her own sheets, and cut them as minimally as she could so as to get as many as possible out of a length of cloth. She cut them so short, in fact, that when I pulled the sheet up far enough to cover her face, it was too short to cover her feet. It was almost worse to have to look at her old calloused feet than to look at her face; somehow her feet were more dead, more mute, than her face had been.

She is dead, and the fact cannot be hidden by any sheet. What remains after death, in the cold light of reality, is life—all of that life, with its coarse muscularity and crude hunger and greedy concupiscence, that is going on in the kitchen. The only god of this world is the cold god of persistent life and appetite; and I must look steadily at this repellent but true tableau—the animal life in the kitchen, the corpse in the back bedroom. Life offers no other tableau of reality, once we pierce beneath appearances. (50–51)

If Vendler's *ur*-narrative is introduced at all, it should not be played as a trump card. Rather, it should be offered as another text to be challenged and criticized, like the student paraphrases. Since it is over four times as long as the poem, it also serves to illustrate the remarkable compression of poetry.

We then proceed more systematically through the poem, specifying the dramatic situation and the *dramatis personae* if these are not already clear from the paraphrases. Discussion of how the wake prescribed in the poem differs from those the students have attended leads to consideration of the diction. Why "wenches" rather than "girls" or (to be hopelessly old-fashioned) "young ladies"? Why "concupiscent curds" rather than "ice cream"? Why "Let the lamp *affix its beam*" rather than, say, "Let the lamp *shine on her*"?

We are at last ready for the poem's thematic line, "Let be be finale of seem." Having paraphrased this to our satisfaction, we sort the various elements in the poem into the categories of *be* and *seem*, listing them on the chalkboard as we go. Those in the *seem* column are almost wholly implicit in the poem, but would include such things as belief in a divine "emperor" and an afterlife, the ceremony with which we surround and to some extent disguise the reality of death, the manners and clothing that would transform wenches and boys into proper young ladies and gentlemen, even such embellishments as a tastefully furnished parlor, a catered luncheon, an elegant shroud, and indirect lighting. We will return to the contrast between *be* and *seem* in our discussion of such poems as "Sunday Morning," "The Snow Man," "Tea at the Palaz of Hoon," and "The Idea of Order at Key West." Thus "The Emperor" has already supplied us with a central Stevens theme and a way to talk about it.

Of course, the students are not privy to this scheme. They are of two minds at the moment, like a tree in which there are two blackbirds. On the one hand, they are dismayed that no single paraphrase has accounted for the poem as neatly as the diagram on the board. On the other hand, they feel a sense of relief; the rage for order has been assuaged, not to mention the rage for a formula that can be repeated on the final exam. The poem's meaning has been determined, indeed overdetermined. As the students dot the last *i* and cross the last *t* in their notebooks, I tell an amusing story about another group of college students, living on the opposite side of the world, who had to struggle through "The Emperor of Ice-Cream" half a century ago.

In 1945 a professor at the University of Ceylon asked his students to explicate the poem. Professor E. F. C. Ludowyk described his procedure—inspired, Alan Filreis has shown (174–77), by I. A. Richards's *Practical Criticism*—and his results in a letter to a friend, who passed the letter on to Stevens. Trying to account for his students' misreadings, Professor Ludowyk wrote,

> There was one source of error which might interest Stevens—as you know ice cream still is for a large number of people a Sybaritic treat. That coupled with emperor gave them the impression that the poet was inviting them to a Bacchanalian orgy with ice cream instead of wine. The occasion was completely left out in these accounts. Those who noticed the business of flowers, dress, and the second stanza thought that the lines referred to the ice cream machine—you know our churns. I don't know how they worked in the 'horny feet', they must have left it alone as a canny piece of poetic licence. I felt the difficulty was the too powerful draw of ice cream as a luxury here.[1]

Where did the experiment go wrong, I ask my students. Having heard of cultural relativism, they are shrewd enough to see that the Ceylonese students brought to Stevens's poem a set of cultural values—notably the "luxurious" aspect of ice cream—that were not shared, or were shared only in part, by the American poet and their Cambridge-educated professor. Ceylon was still Ceylon, though it was also a British colony. One might well argue that luxury *is* germane to the poem's meaning, especially as Professor Ludowyk himself went on to paraphrase it in the next sentence of his letter: "'Because you had better accept things as they are ("be"), it wouldn't be out of place to celebrate the "being" with a fanfare' (all that wonderful opeining [*sic*] of the poem)." The point remains that meaning, in poetry as in other human endeavors, is constructed by individuals and social groups. It does not inhere in the event, the action, the natural object, the artifact, or the ice cream.

Stevens's response to Professor Ludowyk's paraphrase is revealing, for it betrays his sense of the inadequacy of the New Criticism as a way of understanding poetry. Writing to his Ceylon connection he remarked,

Dr. Ludowyk seems to have the right understanding of it. But, after all, the point of that poem is not its meaning. When people think of poems as integrations, they are thinking usually of integration of ideas: that is to say, of what they mean. However, a poem must have a peculiarity, as if it was the momentarily complete idiom of that which prompts it, even if that which prompts it is the vaguest emotion. (L 500)

Conceding the validity of Professor Ludowyk's interpretation at the level of meaning, and apparently overlooking his sensitivity to the poem's "wonderful opening," Stevens objects that "The Emperor" cannot be reduced to its argument. Its "point" includes another dimension, what Stevens calls the "peculiarity" of its "momentarily complete idiom."

There is a stir of consternation in the classroom. Brows furrow and pens are again poised over notebooks. After all, if the professor was as wide of the mark as his students, then we too have missed the point of the poem in our search for determinate, paraphrasable meaning. Perhaps we had better read it again, aloud. This time I ask for coaching on my delivery. Shall I read it in a funereal tone? Angry? Solemn? Flippant? Someone says it reminds him of a carnival spiel, so I make that my dominant note, infusing it with overtones of regret and worldly-wise cynicism. No one ever said this would be easy.

Read in a monotone, "The Emperor of Ice-Cream" remains more or less an *argument.* It tries to persuade us that reality, however abhorrent, must replace illusions, however seductive. Read with attention to its peculiar rhetoric, however, the poem is also a *performance,* and its panache—what Professor Ludowyk called its "fanfare"—is part of its point. In fact, the word that marks the boundary between seeming and being is lifted from the lexicon of theatrical or musical performance: *finale.* The more sophisticated New Critics never reduced poetic meaning to argument. Where the less adroit affixed their beams and saw only a lifeless cadaver, these critics were careful to treat the poem as a vital organism in which idea is inseparable from mode of expression. Stevens's interest in the relation between sound and meaning, a relation he explores most thoroughly in his essay "The Noble Rider and the Sound of Words," is a distinctive feature of his poetry and a major source of its emotional and intellectual rewards. Our discussion has therefore accomplished the second and third objectives specified above.

What Stevens meant by the "point" of "The Emperor" is spelled out more fully in a paragraph he wrote in 1933. William Rose Benét had asked Stevens and forty-nine other poets to submit their favorite poems for inclusion in an anthology, together with notes explaining their choices. Stevens sent "The Emperor of Ice-Cream," saying,

> I think I should select from my poems as my favorite "The Emperor of Ice-Cream." This wears a deliberately commonplace costume, and yet seems to me to contain something of the essential gaudiness of poetry; that is the reason why I like it. I do not remember the circumstances under which this poem was written, unless this means the state of mind from which it came. (*OP* 212)

Stevens's note indicates, first, that the poem expresses a state of mind rather than a response to a specific physical event. Furthermore, it reverses the analogy we typically use (the first sentence of my paraphrase assignment is a case in point) to describe the relation between a poem's argument and its style. According to his note, the essence or "body" of "The Emperor" is its gaudy rhetoric, while the commonplace subject matter—dawdling wenches, shabby furniture, horny feet, the woefully inadequate bedsheet—is mere costume.

To understand why Stevens exalted style over argument, the "momentarily complete idiom" over the "integration of ideas," we must turn again to historical and cultural context to understand how these shape the meaning of the poem. In the process, we learn something about the nature of Stevens's obscurity and so achieve our last two objectives. As A. Walton Litz has reminded us, Stevens published "The Emperor" at a time (1922) when many poets sought to write a "pure" poetry that subordinated idea and subject matter to the pure sensation of sound and image ("Wallace Stevens' Defense of Poetry"). His first community of readers understood this convention and construed the poem accordingly. They saw (or heard) both the emperor and the clothes. But poetic meaning was one thing in the 1920s and another in the 1940s, just as ice cream was one thing in Hartford and another in Ceylon. For later generations of readers, "The Emperor" became obscure in a way that stems neither from esoteric allusion, as in Pound and Eliot, nor from reference to a private mythology, as in Yeats, but from revisions of the implied reader-writer contract.

No, I have not forgotten the forty or fifty restive students who want all this confusion cleared up in the last minute before class ends. Turning back to the chalkboard, I add the word *poetry* to the list of words and phrases in the *seem* column. That, too, is what "The Emperor of Ice-Cream" is about, I tell them—and not only "The Emperor" but also several of the other Stevens poems we will be reading. At the level of argument, it exhorts us to confront the squalor of life without any illusions. At the level of style, however, it virtually turns that argument on its head: some kinds of *seem* can sustain and even delight us in the daily struggle with *be*. Poetry is one of these, which is why Stevens liked to say that it helps us to live our lives. That is the point of "The Emperor," and a good point of departure for our next class.

Note

1. Unpublished letter to Leonard C. van Geyzel of 13 March 1945, used with the permission of Carmen Ludowyk Holt and the Huntington Library. Stevens quoted from this letter when writing to Alfred A. Knopf on 17 May 1945, transcribing "the business of flowers, dress, and the second stanza" as "the business of flowers, trees in the second stanza" (*L* 502). This passage, together with the other quotations included here, can be reproduced on a class handout or displayed by overhead projector.

How Stevens Teaches Us to Read:
"Thirteen Ways of Looking at a Blackbird"

LAUREN RUSK

"Thirteen Ways of Looking at a Blackbird" (*CP* 92) is a poem that works by teaching us what questions to ask of it. It does so by demonstrating the inadequacy of the questions novice readers tend to ask: What is the poem about? What does *X*—in this case, the blackbird—symbolize? Finding these queries unanswerable, one is forced to consider the poem as an event that creates meaning rather than as a nugget that contains it, to ask what the poem *does,* how its images speak to each other, and to observe the process it takes one through. Coming to terms with Stevens's strategies makes it easier, I believe, to read other modern poems—that is, to approach them with fruitful questions. This particular work is a good one to use in an undergraduate course on poetry and poetics because its sensuous simplicity and mystery engage the students' interest, making them want to figure it out. I teach it in the latter part of the course, as a primary instance of poetry that foregrounds process.

When teaching a difficult poem like "Thirteen Ways," it is especially important to empower the students, so that they can look forward to approaching such works on their own. A class reading must, I believe, be based on the students' impressions; otherwise they'll think they need a teacher to decipher the poem. On the other hand, there are particular things I hope they'll see about the meaning manifest in the poem's structure and diction, and I want specifically to offer ideas that come from my experience of Stevens's other work. The problem is how to find a way to balance these needs.

An approach to demonstrating what "Thirteen Ways" can teach us about reading poetry that I've found rewarding is to design one session in which students work with the poem in small groups, followed by two meetings in which I lead a discussion that builds on what the groups have found. The last session ends with our making a list of questions that students can use to inquire into other poems as well.

"Thirteen Ways of Looking at a Blackbird" is conducive to group investigation because it is not highly allusive and repays time spent; the more avenues of interconnection that are explored, the more meaningful the poem becomes. Moreover, working in groups telescopes the exploration time and allows students to compensate for each other's deficits of experience. Working together both makes it clear that multiple readings are possible and tends to knock out the most idiosyncratic notions (such as that of the student who fixated on the nursery-rhyme phrase "four and twenty blackbirds baked in a pie"—having himself missed lunch). And, most importantly, students enjoy the group work. They give up breaks to keep on talking. It's the kind of experience that gets people to start reading groups after college.

When the class reconvenes at the next meeting, the structure is that of a dialogue between groups who have already formulated their thoughts and me. This configuration, in contrast to the Socratic one, increases both the students' authority and the number of viewpoints voiced. Yet it allows me to add what seems to be missing and, with luck, to integrate the various views into a coherent whole. I find it important to punctuate the discussion with mini-lecture summations, since revelations about Stevens are as elusive as "a pheasant disappearing in the brush." (*OP* 198).

The first class begins with my proposition that "Thirteen Ways of Looking at a Blackbird" is a poem that can teach us how to read it—and much other modern poetry. The poem prompts us to ask a series of questions about it and thus to discover what kinds of queries are the most productive. We can then use such questions to illuminate other poems that may at first seem opaque. On the board is one of Stevens's own propositions to keep in mind: "To read a poem should be an experience, like experiencing an act" (*OP* 191). After sketching out the plan for the three classes, I read "Thirteen Ways" aloud.

Then the class divides into groups of four or so (a two-hour session is ideal), and I give the following printed instructions.

> Each group has two tasks: to work with the poem to reach an understanding of what's happening in it and to observe the process you go through. At the next class a spokesperson is to report briefly what the group has discovered, and then we'll see how we can put our various ways of looking at the poem together. As you investigate the poem, don't be constrained by its linear order. Work back and forth through it, looking for patterns of imagery, subject matter, and tone. In doing so, consider the effect of Stevens's choices of particular words; dictionaries are available.
>
> Each group is to appoint a scribe (who need not be the spokesperson) to take notes on your process and what you discover. The notes should include
>
> - what questions you pursue and where they lead,
> - what you find out about the poem,
> - what points you disagree on,
> - what questions are left unanswered for you.
>
> In the last ten or fifteen minutes the scribe should read the notes aloud so the rest of the group can help make them into a five-minute report for the next meeting.

During this session my role is that of a wandering scribe, jotting down observations and questions I hear that get at the essentials of the poem. Since I tell the students I'll be writing down helpful remarks, my note-taking may at times encourage them to continue along a certain line, as when one says, "I don't think the blackbird means anything by itself. Maybe we should ask what its *function* is in each part."

Using these notes to frame the issues of the next two sessions is crucial to maintaining the students' sense of empowerment. Although I design the agenda, the students can see that it is built from their own concerns and insights. As much as possible, when posing questions for discussion, I refer to those I've heard students raise in their groups. Conversely, when one person raises an issue and no one jumps in, I may remind other students of remarks they made that speak to the issue. Citing such comments allows me to reinforce perceptions that the thinkers themselves may not have valued; the groups' summaries often omit glancing insights that they did not pursue. By repeating the best of what I've heard, I hope to help the students discriminate among their own ideas.

The rest of this essay describes how such a discussion might proceed, citing remarks and questions students have contributed in class. I begin the second session by saying that I have two aims for the next couple of days. The first is to raise issues I think we should investigate further, using what the students have discovered so far, and see if we can come up with a collective reading of the poem. The second aim, for the end of the last day, is to derive from this experience a list of questions that will help in the reading of other poems. The spokespersons then give their reports, after which I summarize and compare their processes and interpretations, noting questions to which we'll return.

The most striking similarity of process among the groups is that they have all started by attempting to determine what the blackbird "means." They have tried out various ways of translating the word *blackbird,* only to find that no single translation fits all the sections. I open the discussion by inquiring further into how this process takes place. The groups have reported, in essence, that the poem makes them want to pin down the figure of the blackbird and assign a single meaning to it. I ask how it does this. The title directs our attention to the blackbird, they say; it is a dark, mysterious silhouette; it appears in every section, and in surprising contexts. For one student, reading the poem is like watching the blackbird "migrate" through it, always changing. Another says the blackbird seems like the key to the poem because it is the constant term that unifies very different sections. Someone else points out, however, that the blackbird is not really a constant—it changes according to its context. Thus the class gathers a sense of how Stevens sets us up to look for a fixed symbolism, and to fail.

Though the poem foils our attempts to make the blackbird *stand for* a *single* thing, the reports indicate that it *suggests various* things in different sections. I observe that these suggestions fall into two categories. In certain parts, students have said, the blackbird suggests such things as vision, self-knowledge, the use of language—"black marks on a white page," the muse, the poetic imagination, and "not just the poet's imagination but everyone's." In other sections, they've said, it has to do with ordinary reality, the commonplace, and nature. I propose that we call these two categories *mind* and *world,* or *imagination* and *physical reality.* I see relief in some faces, renewed effort in others; clarity seems possible. And the clarification stems from their own perceptions, which, though incomplete, are proving to be valid and useful.

Is there some way, I ask, that we can put these two categories together to formulate a statement about what the poem concerns? One or two students oblige by saying, essentially, that it concerns the mind's apprehension of, or attempts to understand, the natural world. I paraphrase these statements, combining and fine-tuning them, and invoke the concepts of subject and object that we've used before. (The term *subject* is especially useful when one wants to talk about the imaginative responses of the man in the coach, the men of Haddam, and the bawds of euphony, together with those of the speaker.) Next I ask whether students find sections that suggest the merging of nature and the imagination or, in other words, that describe the interrelation of the blackbird as a physical object and the subject's imagination. They propose VI and XI, in which the blackbirds seem associated with nature though they are not actually present but only projected by the subject, and VII, in which a real blackbird, overlooked by the thin men, stimulates the speaker's imagination.

After helping to hone these points, since no one has brought up section IX, I say that I find it a particularly eloquent image of the imagination making something of reality. (The students are familiar with my Poundian use of the term *image* to mean "that which presents an intellectual and emotional complex in an instant of time" [Pound, *Literary Essays* 4].) Stimulated by the motion of a real bird, the speaker's imagination creates out of the randomness of nature an abstract order, the geometric perfection of a circle. And, seeing it as "one of many circles," the speaker also envisions the possibility of other such orderings. (A reference to "The Idea of Order at Key West" fits nicely here.) I then propose that section IX also describes the activity the poem aims to engage us in. We too are pursuing an elusive object: the meaning expressed through the images in which "the blackbird is involved." And in the process of trying to perceive it fully, we too, the group reports indicate, begin to seek order by constructing and reconstructing circles, or clusters, of associated images.

These associative groups, I continue, are the structures that express the meaning of the poem since, as students have observed, the poem's linear order doesn't tell us much. Thus, during the first session people soon begin grouping sections they find to be similar in mood, suggestiveness, or visual imagery. I ask the students what sections they think of as related, and then jot these groups of section numbers on the board, circle them, and label them with a key phrase to denote what they share, such as "snow imagery," "the sinister," "ideas of beauty," and "riddles." As the discussion goes on, I continue to add sections to these groups and to add new groups. Overlapping the circles when certain sections appear in more than one group gives an indication of the poem's complexity.

I then choose the order in which we will talk about the clusters, beginning with sections I and XIII, which the students see as paired because of their wintry landscapes. I ask what differences students find in the language, tone, and suggestiveness of the two images. One person notices that section XIII refers to the blackbird in terms of stasis, section I in terms of motion. Another finds XIII depressing because of the darkness and sameness it depicts. I refer to Stevens's letter stating that he meant XIII to "convey despair" (*L* 340) and suggest that, in contrast, the mood of the first section is one of expectancy. Birds watch to see if they can spot something moving. Thus the eye of the blackbird is not only a sign of motion but of the potential for further motion. It's on the lookout for change. As one student says, section I "initiates the motion of the poem." Someone else adds that reading section XIII makes her return to section I; others agree.

The invitation to circle back—from the austerity of XIII with its bare branches to the expectancy of section I with its proliferation of mountains, I say, is an example of a conceptual cycle in Stevens's poetry that J. Hillis Miller identifies in *Poets of Reality* (223–76). Miller views some of Stevens's poems as representing different parts of the cycle, others as enacting the entire process. The cyclic process is that of the mind trying to conceive of the physical world it faces. "The Rock" is a poem in which this cycle is particularly explicit. In one part of the cycle, the mind attempts to connect with the world imaginatively, by "seeing something in it" or "making something of it." However, the mind comes to realize that its conception of the world is false, either because it has gone too far and fancified reality, or because reality, which is always in flux, has already changed and has thus evaded capture. The thinker then resolves to look upon, and some-how realize, the bare bones of the world-in-itself, not fleshed out and deco-rated by the lushness of the imagination. Stevens's poem "The Snow Man" demonstrates this part of the cycle, the mind's trying to see the world clearly without adding anything to what it sees. Inevitably, though, this restraining of the imagination comes to feel like alienation from, instead of connection with, the world. Consequently, the mind turns again to finding meaning by investing the world with personal, imaginative associations. This cycle ultimately leads to the sense that the mind and the world, or imagination and reality, are not finally separate but, rather, interrelated parts of a universe that is continually in motion. Stevens has to resolve this dual-ity of mind and world in his poems over and over again. When he does so, Miller says, he "finds that there is after all only one realm, always and ev-erywhere the realm of some new conjunction of imagination and reality" (274).

Next, since we've been focusing on the beginning and end of the poem, I ask how section I relates to the title. Someone remarks that in the first section the bird is doing the looking; another, that we're looking at the blackbird looking. Then in that image, I suggest, the blackbird embodies both the thing looked at and the act of perception. And what about the title itself, I ask. What is it concerned with? A blackbird? I quote a student I heard saying crossly that the poem "doesn't tell us anything about the blackbird. It might as well be a red bird or a squirrel or a camel." Yes, but it has to be a living creature, something that moves and changes, another adds. Someone else disagrees that the word *blackbird* is expendable, on the grounds that the color black, like the number thirteen, is associated with death. A couple of people say that that idea only works in a few of the sections; their group tried and rejected the interpretation. Another student says she thinks the number *thirteen* is arbitrary, like the *twenty* in "twenty snowy mountains." They could just as well be any number, except that they sound right. We take a moment to examine the stress patterns, conso-nance, and assonance of the two phrases. But the *thirteen* couldn't be *one,* someone amends. Another student agrees: what's important is that there are a lot of different ways of looking. I ask whether they are saying that the crucial part of the title is "Ways of Looking." There is general agreement.

We often use the expression *ways of looking at* something to refer to the ways we conceive of it, I continue. Similarly, the words *perception* and *vision* can refer both to physical sight and to one's understanding of what one's nervous system has recorded. Clearly, Stevens is interested in how one makes an object of perception meaningful, how one can imaginatively recreate it for oneself, without distorting it. And he gets his readers involved in this problem by giving us the task of "making something of" the object of the poem.

Interpreting the color black and the number thirteen as ominous is one of the possible ways of looking at them, I say, turning to the cluster of sections labeled "the sinister," which contains sections VI and XI. We've already begun to talk about these sections in terms of the interaction of imagination and reality, and students have grouped them because of a similarity in tone. I ask them to say more about the mood the sections evoke. They say that both sections convey a sense of fear, vulnerability, and mystery; that they have a Gothic or Poe-like feeling; but that XI is more spooky, VI more contemplative. I ask what the subject in these sections seems to fear; the students say that it's death, injury, the natural or primitive world, the unknown—all of these things, which are all related. We examine the words and images that give rise to these associations. People observe that images of breakable and splintered glass and the word *pierced* suggest injury; the word *shadow,* death and the unknown. I then inquire what in these sections makes the students associate the blackbird with nature. The subject is inside and the blackbirds outside, they respond, and in XI the blackbirds are contrasted with the artificiality of the coach (see Sukenick 76), which is emphasized by the word *equipage.* I then ask in what way the subject's imagination responds to the natural world in these two sections. The class concludes that the sections demonstrate the imagination investing nature, or in XI the *idea* of nature, with a sense of mystery and foreboding.

Death is often associated with the transience of natural phenomena— seasons, flowers, or effects of light and shadow as in VI—but such effects can evoke a variety of moods other than the sinister. What sections other than VI, I ask, convey feelings that are stirred by transitory effects of nature? The students suggest III, V, IX, and X; I jot the sections on the board and label the cluster "transience." Although I've talked about IX, we haven't considered its tone. When I ask how students would describe the tone, they use words like *cerebral, meditative,* and *contemplative.* Earlier someone also referred to VI as contemplative; we decide that most of the sections in this group have that quality, among others. The transitory effects of nature evoke contemplation, and sometimes fear. I inquire what other emotions are suggested, in section III, for instance. One student finds its mood one of celebration. When I ask what words contribute to that mood, students point to *whirled* and *pantomime.* I then ask what they visualize when they read the section. "A bird that flutters like a falling leaf" and "bright-colored leaves," two of them answer. Summing up and extending these remarks, I observe that the section depicts a season defined as transitory by its falling, dying leaves, and by analogy it shows the life of the blackbird to be brief. Yet the scene is celebratory, carnivalesque—because of the way the speaker imagines its motion and because of the way readers participate, for example, by adding colors that the speaker doesn't name.

The other two sections in the "transience" cluster, V and X, are also part of the group we have labeled "ideas of beauty," students note. I add that in V, by analogizing the moment after the whistling with innuendo, Stevens again stresses the audience's activity: innuendo only exists if the audience construes meaning "between the lines," or in the silence after the sound. The image of transience I've saved for last is "the sight of blackbirds / Flying in a green light." When I inquire about the emotional tone of section X, the class agrees that it mainly expresses unexpected, intense pleasure, but that the phrase "cry out sharply" also has connotations of fear and pain, reinforced by the section that follows. Perhaps, I suggest, the tone is complicated because the beauty of the sight depends on its evanescence. In other words, as Stevens writes in "Sunday Morning" (*CP* 66), "Death is the mother of beauty."

There is also, of course, an argument in section X that we need to clarify. Having worked with the dictionary during the first class, students know the meaning of *bawds* and *euphony.* People from the different groups tell what interpretation of the section they arrived at; most gave it quite a bit of attention. Combining their readings, the students arrive at the understanding that the section critiques those who waste themselves producing poetic utterances that are merely lovely, and those who are taken in by them. What such poetry lacks, the class decides, is a connection with the real—I offer the word *authenticity*—that the sight of the blackbirds recalls (see Sukenick 75–76). In support of their view, I mention that in Stevens's poems the color green generally has to do with earthliness, blue with abstraction. One student points out how easy it is to misread the word *bawds* as *bards*, saying that this play on words shows the danger of mistaking inauthentic poetry for the real thing. Moreover, when asked, some students admit to associating "cry out sharply" with sexual ecstasy; all are delighted when I observe that the bawds are, for a change, not faking it.

I then inquire what other sections make a similar argument, and students point to the remaining members of the cluster that concerns beauty, sections VII and VIII. At first they tend to see VIII as disparaging pleasurable sound in poetry to the extent that X does. However, after I encourage them to consider the difference in tone, as well as the denotations of the adjectives in section VIII, most decide that "noble accents" and "lucid, inescapable rhythms" are positive poetic qualities but insufficient in themselves. How does the way the figure of the blackbird is used in VIII compare to its significance in X, I ask. In both cases, the students feel, the blackbird provides the connection to reality that was lacking. As one student puts it, "Unless you're talking about something real, you're not saying anything." Another makes a connection to Keats's "Beauty is truth, truth beauty." And similarly, the students find, section VII argues that the most profound beauty resides in ordinary reality, if only we will attend to it. Again, in VII students connect the blackbirds with ordinary, physical reality, because they are not golden, and because they walk around women's feet. Yet the blackbirds are also mysterious, others point out, because the thin men don't see them, and because the women they are associated with seem mysterious too. I agree, pointing out that the phrase *about you* makes the women seem, like the blackbirds, invisible; and that the women are represented as "others," whose thoughts are not given.

When I inquire about the tone of VII, one student says it sounds biblical. Like a prophet's exhortation, I suggest. Yes, but the tone leads the student to expect something exalted, and then the ending lets him down, he complains. "Stevens keeps pulling the rug out from under us—building us up and then giving us only blackbirds." The student's frustration is useful; he is cooperating with the poem more than he knows. I agree that that is just what Stevens does, and then ask the class what he is trying to get across with this maneuver. He's saying the ordinary is exalted, one answers, and others approve. I note that, perhaps because of the biblical tone as well as the spelling, students are pronouncing *Haddam* as "Hah-dáhm"; they are taken aback to hear that it is not the name of a Middle Eastern town but of one in Connecticut. Stevens has tricked them, pulling the rug out again. I ask whether the speaker's point of view seems religious. Most think not, and this is a good moment to introduce the following brief background and references in regard to Stevens's attitude toward religion.

Overall, Stevens's works give ample evidence that his perspective is one of humanistic atheism. Miller's essay offers an especially thorough and insightful analysis of the relation of Stevens's ideas about religion to his poetry (217–25). The most helpful of Stevens's own works to read are the poem "Sunday Morning" and the essay entitled "Two or Three Ideas." In the latter he writes, "in an age of disbelief, when the gods have come to an end, when we think of them as the aesthetic projections of a time that has passed, men turn to a fundamental glory of their own" (*OP* 262). Thus, while Stevens was not religious in the conventional sense, he was interested in the desire that turns people toward religion, the urge to find meaning and value in life. He was concerned with the transformation of the human spirit that must accompany the movement toward a secular culture, such as that which was occurring in the United States and Europe during World War I, when he wrote "Thirteen Ways."

At present my students who are not seasoned literature majors tend either to overlook religious allusions or to take religious tenets as fixed ideas rather than as ideas that writers work with and transform. Thus I go on to offer a suggestion that is otherwise unlikely to come up. Though Stevens's "Two or Three Ideas" includes other religions in its references to "the gods," his own source of religious symbolism is Judeo-Christian. I propose that sections II and IV, in similar ways, draw upon this symbolism and work changes on it. After I've given the students a nudge in this direction, they are ready to see that both sections represent threesomes, or trinities. Various students also link the man and woman to Adam and Eve, and the tree of minds to the tree of knowledge and also to the cross, noting the emphatic rhyming of *tree* and *three*. What is missing in these images of three-in-oneness, the class determines, is any suggestion of divinity. Instead, as the student said of section VII, they give us only blackbirds—which, I recall, we have viewed as having to do with physical reality, the human imagination, and the conjunction of the two. I make a new cluster on the board, of II, IV, and VII, and dub it "humanistic atheism." In contrast to the implied white dove of the holy spirit or mind of God, I continue, the blackbird is of this earth and of the human mind. It is interesting in reference to section IV, I add, that Stevens wrote of the imagination, "Like light, it adds nothing, except itself" (*NA* 61; Sukenick 75).

Then, noting that the students have grouped sections IV and XII together as "riddles," I mention having heard one group talk about XII as an assertion of causality. However, they found that no form of "this causes that" makes sense of it, especially since, as one said, rivers always move. When I ask for further thoughts on the kind of universe this image depicts, someone calls it a universe of "perpetual motion" (see Sukenick 74). Another student says it seems to be one that has no first cause—or, I offer, no prime mover, adding XII to our "atheism" cluster.

At this point I refer back to Stevens's assertion of secular humanism from *Opus Posthumous* and ask: What replaces religion for him, what is the "fundamental glory of [our] own"? The students respond with "the imagination," "the way the mind works," "how it sees the world." Why, I ask, does the way we see the blackbird keep changing? And why does the poem get us to keep rearranging it? Because reality and the way we see it are always changing, and the poem demonstrates this process, they answer in various ways. For emphasis, I restate their conclusions. I now feel satisfied that they understand the poem—except perhaps for how much it concerns their own process of confronting it.

After a pause, I ask a more open-ended question: Is Stevens an elitist poet? This gives the students a chance to air their feelings about the poem's constraints: the lack of cultural specificity, the level of abstraction, the difficulty—"It's like a puzzle." On the other hand, someone mentions that although the poem is hard, it's not necessary to look up allusions—"Everything's pretty much in there; you only need a dictionary." I contrast this aspect of

Stevens's work with that of Eliot and Pound, his expatriate contemporaries. Is there a way in which, despite his difficulty, one might consider Stevens a democratic poet, I ask. There is a startled, thoughtful silence. I quote the student who found that the poem concerns "not just the poet's imagination, but everyone's" and then the critic Roy Harvey Pearce, who says that Stevens aimed throughout much of his work to write a poem "of a creative process . . . that all men could share in" and "come to behold . . . that which made them human" (*The Continuity of American Poetry* 378). Is Pearce's observation relevant to the students' reading of "Thirteen Ways," I ask. What is the poem doing or trying to do to the reader? "It's trying to get us to see our own imagination working," a student ventures. Or at any rate to feel it, I say, referring to Stevens's proposition on the board that "To read a poem should be an experience, like experiencing an act."

In summation and by way of introducing our final task, I explain that the reason I believe "Thirteen Ways" teaches us how to read is that it focuses our attention on two poetic strategies that can be harder to perceive than others. One is common to all poetry—the construction of an underlying network of associations, which is, at first, less apparent than the linear chronology of the poem. Generally, meaning is created through the interplay of the associative patterns and the poem's linear structure. "Thirteen Ways," however, deemphasizes chronology by avoiding logical discourse, thereby forcing us to look for associative clusters as the major source of meaning. We have to examine how the images we group together illuminate each other and how the various groups work together. Thus "Thirteen Ways" exercises our ability to analyze patterns of association, a skill important for reading all poetry. The second strategy that "Thirteen Ways" calls to our attention is its focus on process rather than statement—a strategy that is characteristic of much modern poetry. All poems manifest a mind making something of the world, but Stevens's poems, as we've seen, are also, indeed primarily, about the process of understanding itself. "Thirteen Ways," we have said, concerns such things as change and death and being human in the natural world, but it is even more concerned with how the imagination conceives of these things. Moreover, it prompts us to experience this process of imaginative apprehension in our effort to come to terms with the world of the poem. The nature of poetry is that of action rather than statement, and the action takes place in the reader. Modern poems that at first seem impenetrable are often ones that foreground the process the poem takes us through, making it part of the subject matter. Having worked with Stevens makes it easier, I believe, to find a way into such poems, by identifying this strategy and talking about how the poem works.

Thus, by recalling our process of investigation we should be able to compile a list of general questions that will help in reading other poems. I begin by putting on the board some queries that seem useful to me. (This works much better than trying to get the students to say specifically what I have in mind.) As I do so, I frequently remind the class of what has occurred in the small and large discussions. For example, I observe that everyone's first question, what the blackbird stands for, was unanswerable, but considering what *various things* the figure *suggests* proved fruitful; then I write: What various things does X suggest? In regard to associative structure, I also put the following questions on the board: How do the images group themselves in your mind? What patterns emerge? How do the images and parts of the poem shed light on each other? Do parts of the poem seem to contradict each other? What do the contradictions indicate? Next I offer some questions that concern process. I introduce them with the observation that asking, early on, what the poem is *about* usually yields either a baffled or a superficial response. If poetry is action, then we might ask instead what the poem *does*. What does it get you to think? To feel? To wonder? Where do the specific questions it raises lead you? What assumptions does this process challenge? I then proceed to ask for and write up further questions that the students have found helpful and would use to explore other poems. The following are some of their contributions: What is the function of X? What do various parts of the poem make you see? What feelings do they convey? What particular words evoke these visual images and feelings? How does the title relate to the poem? What is the significance of how the poem begins and ends? What is the effect of its progression from one part to the next? Does the midpoint of the poem have special significance? (The student who offers this question points out that section VII of "Thirteen Ways" is the only one in which the word *imagine* appears.) Does the poem have a climactic point? What is the reader's role in the poem? And, interestingly put: What are the rules of the game? As a footnote, I add that near the end of such an inquiry it finally becomes appropriate to ask what the poem is about, because by then one is able to characterize it as a process rather than as a static, monolithic statement.

The next meeting should allow the students to use the questions we've arrived at to illuminate other poems. And since they are usually eager to practice working in small groups again, at this new level of inquiry, that is probably the best format to choose. Over the term I like to vary the way we proceed, to fulfill the needs of the students and the subject matter, and to "make it new." For the next readings, one might immediately follow "Thirteen Ways of Looking at a Blackbird" with more poems by Stevens. Otherwise, especially appropriate selections are works, like those of Eliot, Rich, and Ashbery, that foreground the dynamics of the speaker's thought process. After that, of course, the students should each write about what they discover when they inquire into such a poem on their own.

Accurate Songs or Thinking-in-Poetry

ELEANOR COOK

The logical faculty has infinitely more to do with Poetry than the
Young and the inexperienced, whether writer or critic, ever dreams of.
—William Wordsworth

What makes the new poetry so bad is its failure to realize that
there is no sound poetry without intelligence.
—James Wright

[T]he evil of thinking as poetry is not the same thing as the good
of thinking in poetry.
—Wallace Stevens

Suppose we reverse things. Instead of asking how we can teach the work
of Wallace Stevens, suppose we ask how he can teach us. What might we
learn from him about the art to which he was devoted—was "faithful," to
use his word? Some of Stevens's lessons are so advanced that only the best
poets and critics will recognize them. But he can also teach us something
obvious yet perhaps startling: that thinking matters crucially when we read
good poetry. Again and again, he emphasizes this, as do others, for example, Wordsworth and James Wright in my first two epigraphs. Here is
Stevens, offering advice to a young writer and friend:

> True, the desire to read is an insatiable desire and you must read. Nevertheless, you
> must also think. . . . [T]here is no passion like the passion of thinking which grows
> stronger as one grows older, even though one never thinks anything of any particular
> interest to anyone else. Spend an hour or two a day even if in the beginning you are
> staggered by the confusion and aimlessness of your thoughts. (L 513)

We need to remember this when we hear Stevens saying, "The poem must resist the intelligence / Almost successfully" (*CP* 350). *Resist,* not ignore or flee. *Almost* successfully, but not altogether successfully. How long was Stephen Hawking's *A Brief History of Time* on the best-seller list? And why was this, if not that people were hungry to know, to think about, what physicists make of our universe? At age twenty-six, Stevens noted "the capable, the marvellous [*sic*], poetic language; and the absence of poetic thought. . . . We get plenty of moods (and like them, wherever we get them). . . . But it's the mind we want to fill" (*L* 92). At age sixty-five, he wrote that "supreme poetry can be produced only on the highest possible level of the cognitive" (*L* 500).

As a long-term goal in teaching Stevens, or teaching any poetry, I like to show how all good poetry requires thinking. This means combating several stereotypes: first, the stereotype where thinking is what you do in mathematics or the physical and biological sciences or philosophy or psychology; second, the stereotype of an easy division between thinking and feeling, where poetry is assigned to feeling, and judgments about feeling go unexamined; third, the stereotype where poetry is divided between "content" (associated with thought, themes, arguments that are *already in existence*) and "form" (associated with ornament, purple passages, hyperbole, etc., that "express" what is already in existence); fourth, the stereotypes that prevent too many people from simply enjoying art, and this includes the enjoyment of thinking about it. I'll say a word or two about these long-term goals before some particular remarks about Stevens in the classroom.

1. Let's start with the atmosphere in which most teachers of literature work. Here's how Northrop Frye described it in 1975, and it doesn't seem to have changed much since. Teachers of literature are

> harassed and bedeviled by the dismal sexist symbology surrounding the humanities which [they meet] everywhere, even in the university itself, from freshman classes to the president's office. This symbology . . . says that the sciences, especially the physical sciences, are rugged, aggressive, out in the world doing things, and so symbolically male, whereas the literatures are narcissistic, intuitive, fanciful, staying at home and making the home more beautiful but not doing anything really serious, and are

therefore symbolically female. They are, however, leisure-class females, and have to be attended by a caste of ladies' maids who prepare them for public appearance, and who are the teachers and critics of literature in schools and universities. (102)

The tendency to assign thinking, serious thinking, to any subject but the arts or humanities is all part of this. So are fallacies of accuracy. I used to say, "Words are not as accurate as numbers," until it struck me that this was a meaningless statement. For what did I mean by "accurate"? I meant "accurate" as in $2 + 2 = 4$. So all I was really saying was that words are not accurate in the same way that numbers are accurate, which is not exactly news. It may sound odd to use the word "accurate" in connection with poetry, but it was Stevens's word: "My dame, sing for this person accurate songs" (*CP* 388). And Proust once observed: "In literature 'almost-parallel' lines are not worth drawing. Water (given certain conditions) boils at 100 degrees. At 98, at 99 the phenomenon does not occur. It is better, therefore, to abstain" (44)—if, that is, the author can't get it exactly right. Getting something just right in a poem: this can produce as much pleasure and knowledge as getting something just right in baseball. Getting just the right spin on a word or a group of words.

Baseball may help. Logically considered, it makes less sense than poetry. Grown men taking a stick of wood to a small object, and racing against a set of arbitrary rules? But it's intensely human, this exercise of physical and mental skill, and beautiful to watch when seemingly preternatural ability looks effortless. We know from our own softball games how gifted those major-league players are, and good commentators help us realize this. So with poetry. We all use words. Still, there's not much to encourage us to use them really well, let alone play games with them or write occasional poems. If we played softball games with words, and also regularly heard the major-league word-players, with good commentators. . . . It's a nice thought. And nobody supposes for a moment that baseball players don't think, even if they don't think in philosophical concepts or chemical numbers. They think in baseball: thinking-in-baseball, we might call it. Thinking-in-poetry is what poets do.

Movies may help too, except that there are so many third-rate ones around. We have higher standards in baseball by far. But movies have the advantage of being one art form that students are relaxed about and will reflect on. That includes questions of technique. Why this shot and not that one? What precisely makes Griffith or Chaplin or Renoir or Hitchcock or X, Y, Z so good? I've watched a number of student films from a very good film school. You can trace the progress in learning the mechanics of filmmaking. But the real challenge is different. It's *thinking,* imaginative thinking. It's avoiding the pitfalls of novelty or hyperbole or overambitious claptrap. It has to do with a sense of proportion, a sense of shaping. It has to do with attention, passionate attention, to details. It has to do with an active, examining, alive self, a thinking self, as against the passive self who just accepts without thinking whatever it's fed by the TV or movie screen.

2. As for thinking and feeling, there is one great hazard in separating them. We are accustomed to rigor and discipline in thinking. We prize it, we strive for it. But we usually do not think of rigor or discipline in connection with feeling. Our terminology for speaking of the emotions can be reduced to notions like "expression" and "suppression." As if these were the only alternatives or indeed were simple matters. Worse, "expression," any expression, becomes a good in itself, in the ignorant antipuritanism of pop psychology. What happens, T. S. Eliot asked, when our feelings are separated from our thinking, and both from our senses, so that the three function in different compartments? What happens to our capacity to feel? To use our senses? To think?

> [I]nstead of thinking with our feelings . . . we corrupt our feelings with ideas; we produce the public, the political, the emotional idea, evading sensation and thought. . . . Mr. Chesterton's brain swarms with ideas; I see no evidence that it thinks. ("In Memory" 46)

3. As for content and form, the first time that the content-form metaphor turns up in a class, I stop things. Time to examine this metaphor, which is nearly always based on a container-and-contained model. "Content" is the milk or beer or important substance, what sometimes gets wrongly called the "philosophy" of A or B. (Here insert growls from good philosophers and good poets alike.) "Content" can be poured into all kinds of containers. The container or form is just what's convenient or pretty. One way to shake up this stereotype is to remember an Aristotelian notion

of form, as in: the form of an oak tree is contained in an acorn. The form of an adult is contained in an infant. Or we might think of architecture. What's the "content" of a building and what's its "form"? Form suddenly becomes something vital in these examples of the oak tree or the human being or the building. Similarly with poems.

4. Enjoying, and this includes enjoying thinking. Here is where I usually start when teaching Stevens, in order to get students to relax with the work. Just listening to poems can help. I read myself or else play a record of Stevens reading. What poems? There are poems of immediate sense appeal, there are funny poems, there are quirky poems, there are protest poems. Try a few of the early Florida poems: "Nomad Exquisite," "Indian River," "Fabliau of Florida." You could include "Frogs Eat Butterflies . . ." or an early seashore poem, "Hibiscus on the Sleeping Shores." You could illustrate what Stevens is *not* doing by reading a bit of the hilarious mock-poem "Le Bouquet" from *Bowl, Cat and Broomstick* (*OP* 174). "Six Significant Landscapes," VI, is funny, centers on suggestive analogy, curves itself on the page like its theme, and uses the familiar hat metaphor. (Putting on your thinking cap. Putting on X hat for X job.) It can also start a class thinking about thinking. There are other possible groupings, a seasonal one, for example. A *New York Times* column once claimed that nobody wrote poems about February. Is that so? See Stevens's "Poésie Abrutie." Other possibilities would be river and seashore poems, starry-night poems, poems of ghosts and shades, love poems, and so on.

Any one of these groups will lead on to later work, and thereby show how Stevens enlarges his subjects as he goes on. Stevens's great river or seashore poems would include the challenging poem "The Idea of Order at Key West," as well as "Somnambulisma" and the intensely moving poem of Stevens's late years "The River of Rivers in Connecticut." But all this comes later.

Enjoying includes the pleasure we take in exactness. As for example, why this word and not that one? W. H. Auden is said to have given his students an exercise in which he blanked out several words in a poem they didn't know and asked them to fill in the blanks. I regularly use this exercise myself. (You have to play fair, keeping enough key words.) It's fun to look for poems that use different effects. For example, "Nomad Exquisite," with its utterly unexpected alligator. Or the third section of "Someone Puts a Pineapple Together," with its dozen one-line pineapple likenesses. Or "The Plain Sense of Things," especially the start of stanza 4. (Here the surprise is not in a single word or a fresh metaphor but in the force of logic.) This exercise helps to show readers their own presuppositions and sometimes their stock responses. (There's a handy essay by I. A. Richards on stock responses, and see also Christopher Ricks's opening chapter in his *T. S. Eliot and Prejudice*.)

All this can lead to the pleasure of dictionary exercises, the best dictionary by far being the generous multivolume *Oxford English Dictionary*. For any assigned poem, all students should know precise lexical meanings. For key words, they should pay attention to all the information in the *OED*: the word-root, cognates, and especially usage as in the illustrative quotations. These last help to give the connotations or associations of words, which are just as important as denotations. And we need to remember that poets help make dictionaries; they don't just follow them. On Stevens's unusual words, there's a useful essay by R. P. Blackmur. There's also Stevens's own wonderful remark: "Personally, I like words to sound wrong" (*L* 340). He did like throwing curveballs.

From enjoyment, to single words, to combinations of words. (And actually words in a poem never exist in isolation but always in relation.) Yeats once wrote that he only began to make a language to his liking when he sought a "powerful and passionate syntax" ("A General Introduction to My Work," *Essays and Introductions*). Watching sentence structure, our own and others, is always instructive. (Students may need a little teaching about basic grammar if their schools have deprived them of it—which is like depriving math students of the multiplication table.)

Here's one exercise that's fun. Consider James Merrill's observation about writing workshops:

Last winter I visited a workshop in which only one out of fifteen poets had noticed that he needn't invariably use the first-person present active indicative. Poem after poem began: "I empty my glass . . . I go out . . . I stop by woods . . ." For me a "hot" tense like that can't be handled for very long without cool pasts and futures to temper it. Or some complexity of syntax, or a modulation into the conditional— *something*. An imperative, even an auxiliary verb, can do wonders. Otherwise, you get this addictive self-centered immediacy, harder to break oneself of than cigarettes. That kind of talk (which, by the way, is purely literary; it's never heard in life unless from foreigners or four-year-olds) calls to mind a speaker suspicious of words. . . . He'll never notice "Whose woods these are I think I know" gliding backwards through the room, or "Longtemps je me suis couché de bonne heure" plumping a cushion invitingly at her side. (21)

Exercise: test this in Stevens. And yes, there are surprisingly few first-person present active indicatives, one being in the third of the "Six Significant Landscapes." But then, Stevens does seem to be saying something Merrill-like to the "I" who talks this way. (See the ants.) From here, students can go on to think about person in Stevens. Who *are* "we" and "he" and, and? (Students might think about the use of all those at-first-anonymous he's and she's in modern short stories in contrast to the properly introduced he's and she's in nineteenth-century fiction.) There are also matters of verb tense, active and passive voice, grammatical moods, and so on.

Of course, there's much more, and especially the large question of rhythm. Hearing poetry read aloud helps to develop the ear, and this should continue throughout a course. Students often don't hear the rhythms of poetry—of a phrase, a line, a stanza. (John Hollander's lively and instructive *Rhyme's Reason* is invaluable for this.) Try reading "The River of Rivers in Connecticut" or the first two stanzas of "Credences of Summer."

Sooner or later, the question of feeling will come up, often in the form of feeling versus thought or ideas. "Domination of Black," an extraordinary early poem, is a useful case in point. Here is what Stevens said about it, as he directed the readers away from "ideas": "I am sorry that a poem of this sort has to contain any ideas at all, because its sole purpose is to fill the mind with the images & sounds that it contains. . . . You are supposed to get heavens full of the colors and full of sounds, and *you are supposed to feel as you would feel if you actually got all this*" (L 251; emphasis added). Teachers could try blanking out the word *afraid* at the end of the poem, and asking students to surmise what feeling they are "supposed to feel." And then to work out just how we know that such a feeling has developed rather than, say, a "delightful evening" feeling. (And Stevens wrote a funny poem under that title.) Students might also be interested in thinking about different kinds of fear. See especially the six different sentences offered by Wittgenstein, all using the clause "I am afraid," together with his comment: "To each of these sentences a special tone of voice is appropriate, and a different context" (547).

Or take the feeling of rage, and the word *rage*. Take also the word *order*, and do a dictionary exercise with both these words. Consider likely rhythms for matters of rage and of order. Likely subjects, likely settings, other poetry on these two subjects. (Try Shakespeare, via a concordance.) Then turn to "The Idea of Order at Key West," beginning with the title.

Tracing the line of thought in a poem is always necessary, and should become a matter of course, just as hearing the rhythm, hearing the sentence structure, hearing the range of diction, hearing the exact form of verb and pronoun, and so on, should become matters of course. Even if a poem has a minimal line of thought, we should register this. (X is a minimal-thought poem, working with ABC.) Everyone is suspicious of paraphrases, but such suspicion should not banish the ever-useful précis, which should be tested, every word, against the actual words of the poem. Is it adequate? (Given that it's never meant to be a substitute for the poem.) Should it be modified? How? (Where I live, students used to be trained in the invaluable art of writing a précis. That has mostly gone, so that some students have trouble following an argument, and hence of recognizing what's at stake, if anything.)

See, for example, the implicit argument in "Tea at the Palaz of Hoon" (*CP* 65):

> Not less because in purple I descended
> The western day through what you called
> The loneliest air, not less was I myself.

"Not less was I myself"? Why say this? What's the logic? The day and the place ("The western day," "there") will turn out to be extraordinary, but why this opening response? Has someone said, "You were less yourself that day"? Do we ourselves say, "I was less myself that day"? No, the usual expression is simply, "I wasn't myself that day," period. That's how we often take care of extraordinary days and experiences, ones that don't fit into our regular routine, ones that are better (or worse) than usual. And so we guard ourselves against our other selves, the other better (or worse) selves. Not so Stevens. This means he can go on to say: "And there I found myself more truly and more strange."

Stevens talked about how we all carry within us a trunkful of characters (*L* 91). "Hoon" was his strange, true, sublime self (early style), and he was not about to say, "I wasn't myself the day I had tea at the palaz of Hoon—or maybe was Hoon himself, serving tea." (For poetry as tea, see his lovely little poem "Tea.") And so we learn to think a bit before we say, "I wasn't myself that day." Weren't we, now?

Thinking extends to the logic of figures. Take, for example, angels. "Am I not, / Myself, only half of a figure of a sort . . . ?" asks Stevens's late angel, in a wicked pun ("Angel Surrounded by Paysans" [*CP* 496]). There are angels galore in Stevens, a far better selection than the impoverished angels of modern movies, those broadly comic figures with standard properties attached—haloes and wings, "tepid aureoles," said Stevens of such haloes. "Tepid"? "I suppose that I shall feel sorry about paysans and tepid by the time this reaches you but they suit me very well today," Stevens wrote to a journal editor (*L* 650). "Tepid" is fine for a bath sometimes, but not for a cup of tea and not for most feelings and not for churches. (See Revelation, the last book of the Bible: "So then because thou art lukewarm, and neither cold nor hot, I will spue thee out of my mouth" [3.16].) An aureole or halo ought to be glowing, gold, or white-hot surely. A halo that is lukewarm to the touch is a property rejected by Stevens's necessary angel.

There are early angels in Stevens but he is mostly anxious to shed them. "Trees, like serafin" is a simile in "Sunday Morning" (*CP* 66), as if the highest order of angels, the seraphim, were being explained away in naturalistic terms. And sure enough, in "Evening without Angels" (*CP* 136), Stevens is explicit:

> Why seraphim like lutanists arranged
> Above the trees? And why the poet as
> Eternal *chef d'orchestre?*

It is "light / That fosters seraphim and is to them / Coiffeur of haloes, fecund jeweller." Stevens is still fighting the same battle. "Sad men made angels of the sun. . . ." For him, "Bare earth is best. Bare, bare, / Except for our own houses. . . ." The reasoning is clear, and the type of argument is common enough.

At some point, Stevens decided not to fight angels but to reimagine them. After all, they do seem to have appealed to the human imagination for a long time. Rather than lopping off angels and demons—which leaves their force in the hands of others—why not reinvent them? "Bare earth" is fine, but no angelic equivalents at all? This is poverty, Stevens came to think. And so they start to return, the angels, most remarkably in 1942 in "Notes toward a Supreme Fiction": the tired angels, the goatish angels, the angel on a pond in a park, the angel in the name of Nanzia Nunzio, the capital-A Angel who listens to Stevens, the Miltonic angel who leaps downward and never lands, the angels whose functions Stevens takes over in the end. "Notes toward a Supreme Fiction" is for advanced students, though teachers might like to try one or two cantos with junior students; Nanzia Nunzio is lots of fun.

Then there is the later "Angel Surrounded by Paysans" (1949), where Stevens invents "the angel of reality . . . the necessary angel of earth." He liked this angel well enough to use it as a title for his collected essays in 1951. Here is his comment on the creature:

> in Angel Surrounded by Paysans the angel is the angel of reality. This is clear only if the reader is of the idea that we live in a world of the imagination, in which reality and contact with it are the great blessings. For nine readers out of ten, the necessary angel will appear to be the angel of the imagination and for nine days out of ten that is true, although it is the tenth day that counts. (*L* 753)

Students often find it nearly impossible to read this angel without turning it into its contrary: an angel of imagination, after all, and an angel of heaven, after all. Our habits of thinking about all this are deeply ingrained. It takes discipline of thought to be able to imagine an angel of reality. Or discipline of imagination to be able to think of an angel of reality.

Either way, we hear Stevens writing accurate songs. We hear thinking-in-poetry. We understand more fully how Stevens can write that "the evil of thinking as poetry is not the same thing as the good of thinking in poetry" (*NA* 165).

Introducing Wallace Stevens:
Or, the Sheerly Playful and the Display of Theory in Stevens's Poetry

JACQUELINE VAUGHT BROGAN

When I made a campus visit a number of years ago, one of my interviewers asked me how I taught Wallace Stevens. My answer did not ease the inherent tension in these situations. It was, in fact, a conversation stopper, for I rather glibly announced, with no explanation, that you can't teach Wallace Stevens. I still believe that's true, but what I meant by that remark is complex enough to warrant writing the rest of this essay. In fact, I had just finished teaching Stevens in an introductory literature class only a few weeks earlier. It was not the first time I had attempted to introduce Stevens to undergraduates, but it was the first time I would have called that attempt in any way "successful." So I would like to describe the matrix I have developed for teaching Stevens, one that readily adapts itself to graduate courses as well. I have refined this matrix somewhat over the years, trying to make it "meet the men of the time" and "the women of the time," as it were. But in general what follows is the way I have been introducing Stevens to students for several years. "Introducing," I insist, is what we as professors must do with Stevens. We can teach Yeats—in fact, we almost have to teach Yeats (that is, by teaching his private system of symbolism)—and we can teach Stein, for that matter (by delineating her rhetorical and linguistic strategies). But I still believe it's impossible *to teach* Wallace Stevens.

The reason I find Stevens so resistant to being taught—and this is not, I believe, a personal failing on my part but something endemic to Stevens—

is twofold: first, the relentless sense of sheer play in his poetry that repeatedly forestalls any attempt to arrive at *any* interpretation and, second, a consistent display of theoretical perspectives that undermines even the attempt to describe *the range* of interpretations possible in a given poem. What are students to make of a poet who whips from himself that "damned hoobla-hoobla-hoobla-how" and "such tink and tank and tunk-a-tunk-tunk" and who, alternately, rejects totally the "rotted names" of poetry or embraces thoroughly the "theory / Of poetry" as the "theory of life"? It is, I would argue, ultimately the combination of these two qualities—the playful and the theoretical display—that makes Stevens's poetry so notoriously enigmatic (and, equally, so seductive). So my first objective is to have my students experience an *appreciation* of these qualities rather than to leave them feeling intimidated by Stevens's vocabulary, syntax, or philosophical speculations.

To achieve this objective, I do not assign any poems by Stevens ahead of time for the first day's discussion, but rather introduce my students to Stevens, collectively, in class, where our collective confusion and our collective brilliance have a chance for some hilarity—something like a support group for novice Stevens readers. With absolutely no introduction (other than the consolation that I have been working with Stevens for years and that there are entire lines—no, even entire poems—I still don't understand), I have the students break into three groups, and I assign each group one of the following poems: "Disillusionment of Ten O'Clock" (*CP* 66), "Domination of Black" (*CP* 8), or "Thirteen Ways of Looking at a Blackbird" (*CP* 92). At the same time, because I want to force the students into thinking critically and independently, I hand each group one or two quotations from a well-known Stevens critic and ask each group to complete three tasks: first, decide if they, as a group, agree with the critic's interpretation or not (and explain why); second, explain what the critic's interpretation failed to notice or account for; and, third, suggest any alternative readings or approaches for reading the poem that seem worthwhile after their group discussion. I have found that the following quotations from Joseph Riddel's *The Clairvoyant Eye* stimulate the most fruitful discussion of the poems being considered, not because Riddel's ideas are "wrong" (even if he would have it so later ["Postscript '90"]), but because Riddel's ideas are themselves complex enough to open up important aspects of Stevens's poetry, such as subjectivity or metaphysics, yet so artfully stated as to be accessible to the students.

Group A: "Disillusionment of Ten O'Clock":
The characteristic poem displays a very delicate balance, and occasionally a light ironic sweep, as in the mood piece, "Disillusionment of Ten O'Clock." This latter poem is a veritable spectrum of images, an exercise in color, beginning with the emptiness of houses "haunted / By white night-gowns" and modulating into the one authentic dream of an old sailor who "Drunk and asleep in his boots, / Catches tigers / In red weather." Concealed in the poem is Stevens' symbolic world of color in its earliest form: ranging from the blue of mind to the green of nature, from the purple-violet of total subjectivity to the violent reds of nature's rawness. The poem is a plea for the very real pleasures of merely thinking, of subjective escape, even if delight-fully oblivious to any conditions surrounding drunken sailors and their dreams. (64)

Group B: "Domination of Black":
For every poem of pure delight there is one, like "Domination of Black," equally absorbed by the perils of self-consciousness, the domination of time. (42)

"Domination of Black" is powerfully evocative. Enthralled by the dark mood of his isolation ("At night, by the fire . . ."), the poet finds that the ominous spirit of blackness without provokes a spirit of blackness within. The images of the poem are subjective images, but images in motion. "Turning" is the poem's dominant verb, and the direction of the turning is constantly downward toward darkness, as at the end of "Sunday Morning." (65)

Group C: "Thirteen Ways of Looking at a Blackbird":
[T]he refrain of the crying peacocks [in "Domination of Black"] echoes through the "color of heavy hemlocks" to catch a melancholic struggle of the self with its fate. Likewise, several of the "Thirteen Ways of Looking at a Blackbird," an epistemological tour de force, acquaint one with death's ever-presence in a mixture of wit and preciosity. Just as the blackbird is a part of man's reality (IV), it is also the symbol of his horizons (IX), of flux (XII), and in essence the piercing reminder of human mortality (XI):

He rode over Connecticut
In a glass coach.
Once, a fear pierced him,
In that he mistook
The shadow of his equipage
For blackbirds. (86–87)

In the classroom, I usually read these quotations aloud and then give the students around fifteen minutes to formulate their responses, which will then be shared with the class as a whole. Other than walking around the classroom and answering any particular questions (such as the meaning of "ceinture"), I stay out of the various discussions going on. What surprises me year after year is how readily and how energetically the students engage with the poems. (Usually, despite a few initial groans of despair, the room becomes punctuated with laughter, pleasant disagreements, even an occasional "I got it!") The surprise stems not from my feeling disparaging toward the students, but from the critical commonplace mentioned above—that Stevens is so enigmatic. It is refreshing to see people who haven't read Stevens before *enjoying* Stevens—as I'm sure all of us who teach Stevens did when we first encountered him. As should be obvious, this mood has something to do with that sense of play that I want my students to find and appreciate in his poetry.

When we reassemble as a class, most of the students usually look quite cheerful and confident. While conclusions vary from class to class, the students are normally quite insightful—so much so that it is usually true that they have "taught" their particular poem to themselves before I ever utter a word. A rather typical class comes back with something like the following account.

Usually, the students notice that the time of the "Disillusionment" is set at ten o'clock (and, most likely because of the "nightgowns," at 10 P.M.) and not at a more adventurous hour of night. People, they say, are "supposed" to be in bed at ten o'clock. And that's boring. Without my intervention, but with the help of Riddel, they usually conclude that this is a poem poised against the dual diseases of complacency and convention. Furthermore, as a group, they usually have worked toward the conclusion that the drunken sailor is a figure for the imagination, placed in contrast to those people who wear white nightgowns, who go to bed at ten o'clock, drive station wagons, and have 2.4 children. (I usually read the poem at this point, emphasizing, even exaggerating, the lure of "strange," "periwinkles," and certainly that "red weather.")

But then some members of the class usually admit to being somewhat puzzled, and they tentatively disagree with Riddel's neat configuration of color symbolism. Invariably, someone disagrees that the individual colors of this poem have assigned symbolic value. In fact, they usually conclude that all of the colors in this poem are collectively poised against the "white nightgowns"; and this realization typically leads to all sorts of critical extensions, such as the difference between taking a poem individually on its own terms and placing the poem in a larger context. Before leaving this poem, I ask them what Stevens has gained by using "ceinture," likely a word he borrowed from the French or that he knew from the very rare use of it by Thackeray noted in the *OED*. At this point I usually have to argue that it is all right for poets not only to *borrow* words but even to *coin* words—that language is really alive, creative, at play (all very much part of the poet's "point" or the experience of and in this poem).

When we turn to "Domination of Black," I find it typical that students agree with at least part of Riddel's comments and find this a very distressing, if not depressing, poem. Usually, someone has noted the date and wonders if this poem doesn't reflect Great War angst. Again we are forced to consider the difference between looking at a poem on its own merits and placing it in a "context." We discuss whether or not there are any particular "clues" in the poem that would specifically direct us to think of this poem in relation to the Great War or if we even need such internal directives to make that historical placement. I don't try to answer these questions here, but merely try to generate them and to expose just how difficult they really are.

Eventually, some students will disagree, however, with Riddel's assertion that "Domination of Black" is about the "perils of self-consciousness." On the other hand, they usually confess to not knowing what the poem *is* about. I suggest we read the poem at this point to see if there is anything in its actual sounds to help us, and invariably we end up laughing, for there is almost no way to read this poem aloud (with attention to the fact that Riddel rightly notes, that the dominant word is "turning") without experiencing the sheer metaphorical and metaphysical delights of the turns, the similes, the flux, and especially the repetitions *as sheer play*. As someone will always note, read aloud, the poem is exuberant, not downward toward darkness, almost celebratory (despite its counterpoint of pain). This insight allows us to discuss the importance of sound in poetry in general, as well as some of the particular sounds that variously modulate or stomp through this particular poem. (For example, the rather sharp "long i" sound of "cry" collides with the same sound in "striding," etc.)

If no one has noticed it, I direct the students to the structural arrangement of the "repetitions" from the internal vision to the planetary one—that, too, is part of the fun of this poem—and to the implied colors swirling almost everywhere (despite that domination of black). Depending upon the level of the class, I also introduce the philosophical difficulties of *repetition* itself, this last of which manages to validate Riddel's elliptical statement about "the perils of self-consciousness, the domination of time."

So far, at least with minimal help, the students have felt if not in control of the poetry at least not intimidated by it. But when we turn to the third group, we find confusion, near depression. That is an overstatement, of course, but the students assigned "Thirteen Ways of Looking at a Blackbird" have a decidedly different mood from the other groups. I reassure them that this poem is the most difficult of the three (for which I get a surly "Thanks") and ask for anything conclusive or inconclusive they've come up with. I find it curious that, invariably, at least one student will try to read Christian numerology onto this poem—that is, to replace the emphasis on "Thirteen" with TEN and then to extract the idea of a circle (from section IX, where it is actually "one of many circles") as an image for godly perfection. (This interpretive maneuver usually leads to a reading of sections II and IV as referring to the Trinity.) This proves to be a delicate moment in class, but ultimately a useful one for exposing how much more complicated the poem is than that reading would allow and, more important perhaps, for exposing our instinctive desire for some recognizable (though in this case, reductive) order. In the meantime, someone usually agrees with Riddel's interpretation of separate sections, including the "horizons" and "flux," but expresses irritation with still not understanding the poem as a whole. And it is this "irritation"—even more than the previously noted "rage to order"—that opens up a lot of discussion and, ultimately, the poem itself.

After some general murmuring and complaining, we begin to discuss our expectations about poetry and about interpreting poetry—I summarize essentially New Critical ideas about complexity and *unity*. We try to make that work. Without going line by line, or section by section here, I find that it becomes evident fairly quickly in class that some sections work well thematically with others, while other sections resist coherence altogether (except, of course, for the nominal recurrence of the blackbird). When I tell them, as I do at this point, that Stevens himself said that poetry should resist the intellect, "almost successfully," some are wryly amused and some disgusted. But over the course of the discussion, it gradually emerges that the predominant theme of the poem is precisely what is signaled by the title—i.e., perspective, particularly *multiple* perspectives. (It might seem that this fact would be self-evident, but I haven't found it to be so in the classroom.) I try to get them to see that the play with perspectives is itself pleasurable, even if such play is dependent upon a lack of "fixed accord," a lack that has metaphysical consequences (such as death, the possibility of meaninglessness, etc.). In other words, by the end of the class, I hope that the students will have experienced for themselves two of the three imperatives that dominate Stevens's poetry and that are articulated in "Notes toward a Supreme Fiction"—"It Must Give Pleasure" and "It Must Change."

If there is any time remaining, I sometimes introduce the particular historical context of the first publication of "Thirteen Ways of Looking at a Blackbird"—that it appeared initially in the 1917 issue of *Others* subtitled "A Number for the Mind's Eye, / Not to be read aloud." My objective here, in part, is to demonstrate how historical contexts can enhance interpretations discernible from the poem itself without overwhelming the poem. In addition, this historical fact leads not only to a discussion of visual poetry, but to a serious discussion of the importance of perspective, especially as it was being explored at that time in the visual arts in the form of cubism. I then hazard my own interpretation of this poem as a *cubist poem* in which multiplicity (rather than unity) becomes the interpretative and critical expectation (Brogan, *Part of the Climate* 12). I usually detect a sense of exhaustion at this point, so with a few handouts distributed for the next classes, we end the first day.

On Day Two of "Professor Tries to Introduce Wallace Stevens," I do something entirely different from Day One. Having assigned several poems ahead of time, I choose "Anecdote of the Jar" (*CP* 76) as the focus for one entire class period. The object of this day is again twofold: to have the students discover or experience the multiplicity of perspectives possible— or actually at play—in the interpretive choices we have in a given Stevens poem and to have students consider, at least in a minimal way, something of the ethical responsibilities involved in choosing (or projecting) a given perspective. To achieve these objectives, I break the class into small groups and assign each a particular critical perspective that it must bring to bear on the poem. I also give grossly reductive mini-lectures on what expectations each of the critical perspectives brings with it. (A New Critic is to find ambiguity resolved in unity and is, invariably, to conclude that the poem is "about poetry." A poststructuralist is to find a linguistic and/or temporal "gap" inscribed in the poem that forestalls closure or meaning. A Freudian is to look for sexual symbols and innuendoes, a feminist for phallocentric dominance.) I also have one group look at this poem as an allusion to Keats's "Ode on a Grecian Urn," much as Harold Bloom has done with another of Stevens's poems in *The Poems of Our Climate* (141), and I have another group approach the poem from the perspective of social or cultural criticism, as Frank Lentricchia has done in *Ariel and the Police* (3–27).

What is most remarkable about "Anecdote of the Jar" is that it is not only possible to interpret this poem from all these different perspectives, but that it is possible for students to do so and to do so persuasively and with great attention to detail. From a New Critical perspective, "Anecdote of the Jar" is clearly a poem about writing poetry—at the very least, a poem about art. The jar *is* art, a product of human creation, in opposition to natural fecundity. From a poststructuralist perspective, the poem proves convincingly to be one concerned with temporal and linguistic disjunction, exhibiting what Paul de Man might call "*dédoublement*" (de Man 213), especially in the convoluted syntax of the last two lines. With the double negative, past tense, and ambiguous comparison in the concluding lines

("It did not give of bird or bush, / Like nothing else in Tennessee"), the absolute meaning of this "anecdote" is convincingly and utterly forestalled. From a feminist perspective, the poem emerges, quite obviously, as a poem concerned with male (or phallocentric) dominance over a traditionally feminized landscape. With Keats's ode in mind, there is most definitely an all-American tone to that placement of a jar in Tennessee. Considered from the perspective of cultural criticism, the poem definitely evokes a sense of industrial imperialism. (I should note here that if I don't impose this reading, someone in the class will usually decide that the jar is a symbol for the glass housings associated with electricity and conclude that the poem is "about" the TVA in Tennessee.) Usually, it's the New Critics and the Freudians who get the most laughter. But this is characteristically a very animated class, which evolves into intense discussion and debate. By the end of the class, students *really want to know* which interpretation is *right*. Some will think the interpretation assigned to them *is* the better one. Some will have been persuaded that another group's interpretation is better. When the debate gets particularly intense, I introduce Roy Harvey Pearce's discovery of the Dominion canning jars (a picture of which I then pass around).

This historical "fact" is usually met with moans and some laughter. But it is not uncommon for several people to get angry. And this anger allows us to face again squarely our instinctive drive to try to determine *one* right answer, or one perspective—as if the existence of this historical information suddenly means the other interpretations are *therefore necessarily wrong*. But, as may be obvious to us, and as becomes obvious to students fairly quickly in the ensuing discussion, actual Dominion canning jars do not necessarily eradicate a feminist reading, a New Critical reading, etc. (They may even support some of the readings.) "Anecdote of the Jar," then, is an extremely useful poem not only for demonstrating *in praxis* the variety of theoretical perspectives that can be brought to bear on Stevens but also the way in which his poetry almost demands such conflicting theoretical approaches. Nonetheless, as I dismiss the class, someone still demands to know—"Which interpretation is right?" I have been known to say, "That depends upon which critical lens you put on for the rest of your life." I count it as a success if, at the end of Day Two, three or four members of the class get the joke.

Days Three, Four, and Five are organized quite differently, but ultimately toward a similar effect. It's something like Thirteen Ways of Looking at Wallace Stevens. Before these classes convene, I have had students choose from among a variety of topics (including particular poems and essays for each) to present to the rest of the class. If the class is large, I have them work again in groups. But if class size permits, each student chooses a different topic. Below are a few examples of the topics they choose among:

Stevens and Fictionalism

"A High-Toned Old Christian Woman"

"Asides on the Oboe"

"To an Old Philosopher in Rome"

"Notes toward a Supreme Fiction"

"The Noble Rider and the Sound of Words" (*NA*)

(See also, William James's "The Will to Believe")

Stevens in Relation to War

"The Death of a Soldier"

"Man and Bottle"

"Of Modern Poetry"

"Examination of the Hero in a Time of War"

"Effects of Analogy" (*NA*)

"Poetry and War" (*OP*)

Stevens and "the Thing Itself" (Kant and Nietzsche)

"Metaphors of a Magnifico"

"The Emperor of Ice-Cream"

"The Connoisseur of Chaos"

"Of Bright & Blue Birds & the Gala Sun"

"Not Ideas about the Thing but the Thing Itself"

"Description without Place"

"Imagination as Value" (*NA*)

Other optional topics I hand out include Stevens in relation to romantic writers, to other writers (notably Shakespeare), to imagism, to cubism, to other arts, to women, and to religion. For each topic, I supply a reading list that includes several short poems, one long (or "longer") poem, and one essay from *The Necessary Angel.*

The object of this particular assignment is to have the students discover again *in praxis* the richness, complexity, and depth of Stevens's poetry. This assignment also exposes, again, the consequences of determining a "fixed" perspective when approaching Stevens's poetry. We discover that certain insights are gained—that adopting a perspective has merits—and that other insights are excluded—each perspective is reductive. For example, the student working with Stevens and "the thing itself" is likely to discover the "Stevens" who has certain philosophical similarities with someone like Heidegger, which other students will have missed, but will not discover the "Stevens" who was responding to the actual world, which the person working with Stevens and war will find. Since the students usually choose a topic that really interests them already, they usually have enough background information on the subject to discover and to introduce very sophisticated ideas about Stevens's poetry. By the time we have finished this assignment, the students have really introduced Stevens to themselves—and to each other—and are far more ready to agree with Stevens that "it must not be fixed" (*NA* 34) than they were when we began studying his poetry.

For the conclusion (or last day), I focus upon the ethical component in Stevens's verse in the act of creating meaning—and of taking responsibility for that act. I have found that for this final phase in introducing Stevens two poems prove most successful. From a political perspective, particularly in relation to World War II and current affairs, "Description without Place" (*CP* 339) is the more powerful. From a more spiritual perspective, "Final Soliloquy of the Interior Paramour" (*CP* 524) is the more moving. I normally use them both. "Description without Place" has the particular advantage of encouraging students to realize that we still have responsibility for the future we describe for our world. For example, as we heard the news descriptions leading to the Gulf War—first, "Decision Day," then, "High Noon"—and, as we watched those descriptions assume a reality of global magnitude in the so-called Desert Storm, it became quite clear that

Stevens is completely right in "Description without Place" when he says that it is the "theory of description" that "matters most":

> It matters, because everything we say
> Of the past is description without place, a cast

> Of the imagination, made in sound;
> And because what we say of the future must portend. . . .

In addition, if this point has not been made previously by one of the students, I usually remind the class of what Stevens felt to be the concurrent need for "resistance," since, as we approach the turning of the millennium, we will certainly begin increasingly to hear descriptions of the coming apocalypse (descriptions that we could, if we believed them, then succeed in making a reality). I then turn to "Final Soliloquy of the Interior Paramour," a poem that readily opens that difficult question about Stevens— the question of belief. It is an important question that most students find very compelling. But I always end my introduction to Stevens by simply reading, again, "Final Soliloquy" aloud—without a final commentary—for it is, to my ear, so simply beautiful in its meaning, in its syntax, and especially in its sounds. I also like to think that the last three lines—"Out of this light, out of the central mind, / We make a dwelling in the evening air, / In which being there together is enough"—have come to describe what we, as a class, have accomplished together in reading Wallace Stevens, indeed, in reading any great poetry.

Stevens at the Seminar Table

ELTON GLASER

W. H. Auden once defined a professor as a person who talks in someone else's sleep. But this ruefully witty aphorism does not hold true for the teacher seated at a seminar table: the students are too few and too visible to risk dozing off during the class. The experience of teaching several graduate seminars on Wallace Stevens suggests that the seminar is the ideal pedagogic approach to his frequently difficult work. Having taught Stevens's poetry under other circumstances, I have come to realize that the best way to learn how to read Stevens is to read him in abundance; as he notes in "A Primitive like an Orb" (*CP* 440), "One poem proves another and the whole."

My approach to the Stevens seminar is the basis of this essay. If it is a personal account, it is also one refined in the fire of critical exchange and tempered in the cooler calm of reflection. I proceed by what might be called the Total Immersion Method, a saturated baptism in the works of Wallace Stevens. The intent is to enter Stevens in as many ways as possible, with the understanding that the more we read him, and the more of him we read, the better we learn to read him. In effect, he is both subject and teacher in the seminar, both source and resource. The class is asked to read most of Stevens's poetry, all of the essays collected in *The Necessary Angel,* selected pieces from *Opus Posthumous* (such as the aphorisms and short plays), and several of the critical studies proliferating on Stevens. In researching their seminar papers, the students also make use of Stevens's letters and journals, and I frequently refer to the letters in the seminar discussions.

By the end of the semester, the seminar has confronted Stevens from four different perspectives: (1) a full frontal look at the poems and plays;

(2) a side view through the poetics of his aphorisms and essays; (3) a rear view from remarks on his own poems in the journals and correspondence; and (4) an angled reflection from the standpoint of his critics. The experience is similar to walking around a large sculpture, taking in the figure from every prospect. The seminar, with its intense focus and its room for movement, makes possible an overlap of approaches that brings us to a multidimensional awareness of Stevens.

Because all this material has to be addressed in some organized way, structuring the seminar is the first responsibility the professor assumes. As we recognize that Stevens's poetry, despite its consistent attention to a few unresolvable questions, underwent changes during the more than forty years he was publishing (usually characterized as early, middle, and late Stevens), the most sensible approach to his work is chronological, beginning with those apprentice pieces either uncollected or jettisoned from the second edition of *Harmonium,* and ending with the post-*Collected* poems available in *Opus Posthumous.* Within each book, poems are best grouped by topic or stylistic strategy or shared imagery and theme, letting these poems talk to each other; if we are feeling particularly theoretical, we might even use the term "intertextuality" to designate this behavior of related texts.

An early session on *Harmonium* might be organized around the Paterian dictum "All Art Aspires to the Condition of Music." Several issues fall into a natural alliance in this discussion. We can turn to poems obviously concerned with music, such as "Peter Quince at the Clavier," to illustrate Lucy Beckett's contention that Stevens uses music as "a metaphor for the kind of significance which poetry also can create" (74). Many other poems offer passages in which Stevens employs musical figures to comment on poetry in general or on his own poems, from the epigrammatic pronouncement that "There is no pith in music / Except in something false" ("The Revolutionists Stop for Orangeade" [*CP* 102]), to the self-reflexive phrases about "idiosyncratic music" and "capricious fugues and chorals" in "Jasmine's Beautiful Thoughts Underneath the Willow" (*CP* 79), a poem that, like "Peter Quince at the Clavier," makes the Stevensian connection between music and eros. To establish a corollary point, "The Plot against the Giant" (*CP* 6), with its concluding lines about the power of "Heavenly labials in a world of gutturals," might be considered in support of Edward Kessler's observation that Stevens's poems refer more often to vocal than to instrumental music, because the voice has the *human* expressiveness and imperfections that we also encounter in poetry (114).

Two other aspects of the poetry are appropriate to this discussion of music. First is Stevens's use of the theme-and-variation form to develop poems throughout his career. It is instructive, for instance, to compare two improvisational poems like "Sea Surface Full of Clouds" and "Thirteen Ways of Looking at a Blackbird." As A. Walton Litz has noted, in the marine poem "the decorative imagination deals with a seascape of fluid colors and motion, almost without form, while in the other ["Thirteen Ways"] an austere imagination works constantly from the concrete details of a perceived landscape" (*Introspective Voyager* 151). The second approach considers the poem as a creative tension between two poles of energy, at one extreme music (the texture and movement of language), and at the other extreme philosophy (the overt or implicit ideational content of the poems). Especially relevant here is Ezra Pound's warning that poetry begins to atrophy when it gets too far from music. Almost any poem of Stevens will serve to register his attention to the musical properties of language, his concern with the *melos* and harmonics of the line. But a particularly good example is "Peter Quince," because in that poem Stevens varies his pitch and rhythm and dynamics from section to section, each change in prosodic attack appropriate to the material being developed.

Transitions from book to book can be effected in a way similar to the treatment of poems within a book; a class devoted to "The Tropics and True North" would move from the Florida and Caribbean poems of *Harmonium* to the poems of northern climes in *Ideas of Order,* with "Farewell to Florida" (*CP* 117) the pivot from book to book, from "the ever-freshened Keys" to the "wintry slime." We soon begin to notice the affinities that occur among Stevens's poems, within each book and from book to book. The theoretical formulation might be expressed in these terms: repetitions make connections, and connections make patterns, and patterns make meanings. The seminar, with its immersion in all of Stevens's writing, allows us to discover the larger patterns that develop within a book or among the books of poems, or between different literary forms, as when the postulates of the essays ring sympathetically with passages in the poems.

The nonpoetic materials—plays, aphorisms, essays—should serve as adjuncts to the poetry, and can be introduced either as a group or as separate items paired with a relevant assemblage of poems. The brief plays, for example, work best in tandem; they constitute a minor element in Stevens's oeuvre, and can be taken together without seriously disrupting the main attention to his poetry. The essays, however, if presented jointly, can act as a drag on the forward progress of the class; this mass of paragraphed print is less enticing than the shapely energy of the poems, and has the potential, when taken in bulk, of eliciting more tedium than insight. The prose pieces become most useful as supplements to the poetry, as theoretical reflections that support and explain what the poems practice. Attached to the appropriate set of related poems, an essay can clarify the ideas that the poems treat in an indirect fashion.

For example, we note an obvious connection between "The Irrational Element in Poetry" and *Owl's Clover,* both productions of the social upheavals of the 1930s. Not only is the first poem of the sequence, "The Old Woman and the Statue," specifically, if briefly, discussed in the prose, but Stevens also refers more broadly, in section VII of the essay, to the impulse behind such politically aware poetry. He recognizes that the "pressure of the contemporaneous" is an inescapable force acting on citizen and poet alike: "We are preoccupied with events, even when we do not observe them closely. . . . We feel threatened. We look from an uncertain present toward a more uncertain future. One feels the desire to collect oneself against all this in poetry as well as in politics" (*OP* 229). Such passages in the essay speak directly to analogous passages in the poetic sequence, like those lines in "Mr. Burnshaw and the Statue" that invoke the example of Shelley and consider the role of "the poets' politics . . . in a poets' world":

> . . . Yet that will be
> A world impossible for poets, who
> Complain and prophesy, in their complaints,
> And are never of the world in which they live. (*OP* 80)

The first essay to be discussed, no matter which one is chosen, ought to be given a thorough analysis on its own, since Stevens exhibits some habitual devices of thinking and composing of which students should be aware. For example, he frequently uses a quasi syllogism to develop his points: If A is true, and if B is true, then C must be true. Going slowly through the first assigned essay allows the class to pick up on such characteristic methods of developing his essays. That Stevens sometimes summarizes his argument in the latter part of an essay is also worth pointing out to students. It is helpful, for instance, to know that Stevens begins the final section of "The Figure of the Youth as Virile Poet" with a recapitulation of his earlier remarks, moving from the dense underbrush of his thought into the clearing of a single compendious statement about the poet: "He must create his unreal out of what is real" (NA 58).

Most of us, I suspect, are drawn less to the often ponderous elaboration of ideas in the essays than to the quick perceptions that glint in individual sentences, such as "It is one of the peculiarities of the imagination that it is always at the end of an era" (NA 22). In this sense, the best parts of the essays are associated with Stevens's aphorisms, most of them included in the "Adagia" section of Opus Posthumous. Important and delightful as these terse sayings are, though, they are very difficult to deal with in the classroom, except as obiter dicta to certain of the poems. An effective way of integrating the aphorisms into the seminar is to require their reading as part of a writing assignment.

This assignment is meant to engage the students with work by Stevens that is not scheduled for class discussion. I ask them to choose two aphorisms from Opus Posthumous, one on poetry (e.g., "The poet makes silk dresses out of worms" [OP 184]) and one on any other subject (e.g., "It is the belief and not the god that counts" [OP 188]), and to apply these aphorisms to any two poems not listed on the syllabus. This eight-page essay obligates the seminar members to familiarize themselves with much of Stevens that will not be covered in the classroom (the Total Immersion principle at work), and to test Stevens with Stevens: can his gnomic sayings on poetry and life provide a useful way of entering his practice as a poet? The work on this project also carries over into the seminar discussions; once the miniature mysteries of the "Adagia" get into the head, they are impossible to dislodge, and seem infinitely applicable, like verses from the Bible.

Stevens's dictum that "The theory of poetry is the theory of life" (*OP* 202) seems to be reversible; in other words, hypotheses about life can also be applied to poetry. In that sense, the two types of "Adagia" called for by the assignment actually come to the same thing, as the separate lenses in a pair of eyeglasses allow us to look out on one integrated world. To illustrate the relation between aphorism and poem that could serve as the basis for a paper, we can take this proposition from the "Adagia," one that is not often cited, probably because it lacks the hard finish or metaphoric force of his better-known statements: "Life cannot be based on a thesis, since, by nature, it is based on instinct. A thesis, however, is usually present and living is the struggle between thesis and instinct" (*OP* 187). For "life" and "living" read "poetry." These sentences, continuous with other remarks that he made about the nature of poems, might well become the point of departure for the student's commentary on Stevens's own practice as a poet, which could be usefully described as "the struggle between thesis and instinct." How many passages, after *Harmonium,* either begin with a thesis and end with an image, or open with a sudden flash of metaphor that settles into discursive lines? Nearly any page of the *Collected Poems* will yield an example, but the third section of "Things of August" (*CP* 489) can serve for innumerable others:

> The solemn sentences,
> Like interior intonations,
> The speech of truth in its true solitude,
> A nature that is created in what it says,
> The peace of the last intelligence;

> Or the same thing without desire,
> He that in this intelligence
> Mistakes it for a world of objects,
> Which, being green and blue, appease him,
> By chance, or happy chance, or happiness,
> According to his thought, in the Mediterranean
> Of the quiet of the middle of the night,
> With the broken statues standing on the shore.

The "thesis," the lines of philosophical musing, gives way to the earthier "instinct" of images that concludes the passage. These lines themselves illustrate the point of Stevens's aphorism, in that they oppose "intelligence" to "a world of objects"—terms for which we might substitute "thesis" and "instinct"—and then verbally demonstrate this struggle, moving from the abstract rhetoric of "The speech of truth in its true solitude" to the teasing glimpse of physical reality in "green and blue" to the mysterious solidity of those "broken statues standing on the shore." Any attention paid to the way the "Adagia" penetrate Stevens's poetry will earn dividends with compounded interest.

To supplement the limited scrutiny that can be given to poems at class meetings, each student also has to write two other types of papers. Unlike the aphorism paper, the second type of essay does require some burrowing in the library stacks. This twelve-page paper, on an open topic subject to my approval, can focus on anything relevant to the study of Stevens. By letting the students settle on their own subjects, I hope to avoid receiving pages that are little more than grudging exercises completed to fulfill the demands of the course. If the seminar members follow their own interests, getting deeply into topics that were only touched on in class discussions, or researching topics not covered at all by the course, the essays should be valuable to them and pleasurable to the professor. The last time I taught the seminar, one of the students, who was also taking a course in Milton, wanted to look at the links between "Sunday Morning" and *Paradise Lost,* with an emphasis on the lady in the peignoir as a version of Eve. Skeptical at first, I reluctantly agreed that he could pursue the connection; the premise sounded interesting but rather farfetched. Happily, the student turned in a paper impressive enough to be reworked later for submission to a critical journal.

The third type of required essay might be described as a glorified book report on a full-length study of Stevens's work. Each student must write two five-page papers summarizing a critical book's central argument and corollary theses, its scope, organization, and coverage of individual poems. After this objective account, the student has an opportunity to evaluate the book, considering such issues as the validity of the argument and the freshness of the interpretations. The intention is first to immerse the students more deeply in the study of Stevens by introducing them to the most prominent secondary sources on his poetry, and then to make sure they do not believe everything they read. At the first meeting of the semester, a bibliography of critical studies and essay collections is handed out, so that the class knows what material is currently available on Stevens. From this list, I assign certain indispensable books, such as Helen Vendler's *On Extended Wings* and Harold Bloom's *Wallace Stevens: The Poems of Our Climate,* with which any student of Stevens should be familiar, even if only for the fact that they are so often cited in other books and articles on Stevens. For the second set of book reports, I recommend other works of interest, like A. Walton Litz's *Introspective Voyager: The Poetic Development of Wallace Stevens,* but let the students pick their texts. These reports are then scheduled for class presentation at regular intervals during the semester, matching as much as possible a critical work to a seminar topic (Charles Berger's *Forms of Farewell: The Late Poetry of Wallace Stevens* and "The Auroras of Autumn," for example, are a natural fit). The discussion of poems becomes informed by the critical readings, without letting the secondary material intrude overbearingly on Stevens's work. And the students, each of whom has been given a photocopy of the reports, have models of literary analysis—both positive and negative models—against which they can gauge their own essays on Stevens.

Though I recognize the value of the seminar's intense and extensive classroom scrutiny of Stevens's poetry, I am also aware of the dangers in discussing Stevens—or any poet—in an academic setting. One danger is that discussions will focus too much on the intellectual affinities or sociological evidence of the poems. Harry Levin has acknowledged this problem of pedagogical practice: "Literature is in itself an enjoyment; consequently educators are always trying to make the sweet pill morally acceptable by coating it with the bitter taste of didacticism" (59). This sort of emphasis occurs all too often in scholarship on the poet; Thomas Hines's *The Later Poetry of Wallace Stevens: Phenomenological Parallels with Husserl and Heidegger* can stand for many other books that treat Stevens as a philosopher manqué. More recently, commentators have taken Stevens to task for not being, retroactively, as sociopolitically pure as the current intellectual climate—or at least its stormier element—demands. My own approach to poems is modeled not on some continental theory, but on the modest and sensible method espoused by the poet Richard Wilbur: I look at the poem, and see what it wants me to say about it.

Poems, as T. S. Eliot made clear decades ago, communicate before they are understood. It is necessary, then, to counteract early and often the classroom's tendency toward earnest pontification by treating the poems as poems, verbal constructs that (in Coleridge's terms) place "the right words in the right order." Poems, when read aloud, work first on the physical level—on the pulse, in the ear, on the tongue—linking us to primitive forces that bypass or predate the operations of the rational mind. This is another, and perhaps the most important, kind of immersion the seminar can promote: it steeps us in the *body* of Stevens's poetry. Unfortunately, very little work has been done on such topics as prosody in Stevens's poems. After bringing in Harvey Gross's chapter on Stevens in *Sound and Form in Modern Poetry,* Donald Justice's essay "The Free-Verse Line in Stevens" (and now, fortunately, the essay by George Lensing in this volume), or a handful of more theoretical papers published in a special issue on the structures of sound in the *Wallace Stevens Journal* (Fall 1991), where does one go for an informed and sensitive study of Stevens's versification? Uttering the poems aloud helps to keep the attention on the color and movement of the language, the breath and muscle of the lines; the greatest poverty, indeed, would be to remove Stevens's poems from the physical world where they make their first and lasting effect on us.

The second danger is to treat Stevens like one of the unassailable poets he has increasingly become, as he settles more comfortably every year into the pantheon of twentieth-century greats, one of the "strong" poets Bloom has canonized. No poet writes well all of the time, and it is a disservice to literature, and to Stevens, to limit discussions to explication and analysis: we also need to *evaluate* his work throughout the seminar. Beginning with some of his apprentice work is helpful; we can see the accomplished poet in his embryonic state, with many of the major themes already present, but handled in an uncertain, inept, or half-finished way. In section VI of "Architecture" (*OP* 37), for example, we witness the poet probing for his style, from the excessive alliteration of "guardians in the grounds, / Gray, gruesome grumblers," to a signature phrase like "sully the begonias."

And the lapses are not confined to these early pieces; they occur throughout his career. Even in a very late poem like "The Region November" (*OP* 140), which contains several impressive passages, we encounter a line like the penultimate one, "Deeplier, deeplier, loudlier, loudlier," which distorts the language to ill effect, an unsuccessful indulgence in one of Stevens's habitual stylistic tics, the unusual comparative or superlative form of an adjective. Set that line against the closing of "The Sense of the Sleight-of-Hand Man" (*CP* 222), where "the life / That is fluent in even the wintriest bronze" is miraculously right. To locate the missteps in Stevens's poetry is also to honor the many places where the verse strides ahead with vigor and confidence and absolute ease.

The final warning for the seminar is about the temptation to claim perfect knowledge. We must admit that much of Stevens's poetry is still mysterious and is likely to remain so. It is a mistake to force explanations of the unexplainable, to gussy up interpretations that paint smiles on a blank face. Many skillful critics have made previously obscure poems now seem relatively simple, and for that we should all be grateful. But it is no surprise that some poems seem altogether neglected, turn as we may to the library shelves for help in preparing our classes; even skillful critics know how to ignore a poem their acumen cannot penetrate.

It would also be a mistake, though, for the seminar to ignore such difficult poems or passages. Taking on long poems like "Notes toward a Supreme Fiction" is essential to any serious study of Stevens—and the seminar, with its single-minded devotion to the work of one author, is the ideal setting in which to air out those "endlessly elaborating" poems (*CP* 486). The challenge of explicating them brings the seminar members together in a shared effort to understand what Stevens is doing in these formidable sequences. If Stevens's meanings cannot always be brought to light, then we ought to recognize that these shadowy moments are also part of his work, perhaps even of his genius. If sometimes his poems resist the intelligence completely, then we can either blame him or blame ourselves, but we must not pretend that this obscurity does not exist, or that the knotty lines and seductive puzzles are not part of the charm and power and exasperation of Stevens's work.

The seminar format, with its small enrollment and intense concentration on a single writer, makes possible a closer, more extensive engagement with a unified body of work than does any other type of instruction. When we sit down with Wallace Stevens at the seminar table, master and ephebes, we greatly improve our chances of coming away with both the experience and the meaning, full partners immersed in the continuing construction of the "miraculous multiplex of lesser poems" and the central poem that is "the poem of the whole" (CP 442).

Teaching the Long Poem:
The Example of "Notes toward a Supreme Fiction"

JAMES C. RANSOM

To write about teaching is to be made immediately mindful of the degree to which teaching is a local event everywhere conditioned by the particulars of the scene in which it takes place, including the physical setting and institutional environment, of course, but most especially, the nature of the individuals involved, teacher and students. It is also to acknowledge how much good teaching depends upon what cannot be rehearsed, upon the spontaneous and even the accidental. Yet for such writing to be of more than anecdotal value, it must try to locate something of general use—a pedagogy that might be applicable in diverse scenes, a kind of "fake book," as it were, that might provide the painstakingly prepared ground from which the unrehearsed spontaneities of a good classroom could spring. This essay is such a try, spelling out the method and some of the materials that have worked for me in teaching "Notes toward a Supreme Fiction," and arriving at three general precepts that might guide the efforts of other teachers in different places.

I have taught "Notes" regularly in a course in American modernist poetry, where it is taken up late in the semester, when students are able to approach it with some background of preparation in reading Stevens's poetry and that of other American modernist poets. With respect to Stevens's work, the class will have already read and discussed a number of the shorter lyrics (e.g., "Sunday Morning," "Thirteen Ways of Looking at a Blackbird," "The Snow Man," "Tea at the Palaz of Hoon," "A High-Toned Old Christian Woman," "The Idea of Order at Key West," "Evening without Angels," "The Poems of Our Climate," "The Man on the Dump," "Of

Modern Poetry," and "Asides on the Oboe"). While the individual texts are certainly negotiable, and the specifically American context in which my students read "Notes" is more a function of our departmental curriculum than necessarily an optimal choice, the point here is that I have found it best to teach "Notes" to students who are prepared to read it in a context of modernist literary styles and concerns and where they have already become acquainted with examples of Stevens's own work.

Typically, we will spend two weeks, or six hours of class time, on "Notes"; and I like to initiate our reading of this poem with some remarks delivered prior to the first meeting for which it has been assigned, acknowledging its difficulty and indicating something of the overall character of the text. I tell my students that "Notes" was written at a time when Stevens was preoccupied with the theory of poetry, an interest sparked by his friendship with Henry Church (hence, the dedication) and fueled by his reading of two then-current works of aesthetic theory, I. A. Richards's *Coleridge on Imagination* (1934) and Charles Mauron's *Aesthetics and Psychology* (1935), both of which focus attention upon the psychological aspects of aesthetic experience and valorize the role of what Coleridge named imagination—and Stevens defines as "the sum of our faculties" (*NA* 61)— in providing human beings with the fundamental constructions of reality by which we come to know and even celebrate the actuality of our lives. I then quote Stevens: "the poet . . . gives to life the supreme fictions without which we are unable to conceive of it" and which "giv[e] life whatever savor it possesses" (*NA* 31, 30). I tell my students that Stevens, in letters written during the composition of the poem and in the year following its publication, says that by a supreme fiction he means poetry (*L* 407, 418, 430), which is what, they will remember, had been asserted by the speaker of "A High-Toned Old Christian Woman" (*CP* 59), where Stevens wrote, "Poetry is the supreme fiction." Stevens explains in another letter that, in the modern world, such poetry is "trying to create something as valid as the idea of God has been" (*L* 435).

I also tell my students that the composition of "Notes" was surrounded by the writing and public reading of two essays "intended to disclose definitions of poetry" (*NA* vii), from the first of which ("The Noble Rider and the Sound of Words") I have already quoted and in the second of which ("The Figure of the Youth as Virile Poet") Stevens explores the relationship of poetry to philosophy and to religious belief, suggesting that in his own day poetry "may be . . . superior" as a way of "find[ing] a sanction for life" (*NA* 43). Later in the essay he defines "poetic truth" as

> an agreement with reality, brought about by the imagination of a man disposed to be strongly influenced by his imagination, which he believes, for a time, to be true, expressed in terms of his emotions or, since it is less of a restriction to say so, in terms of his own personality. (*NA* 54)

This context from Stevens's letters and essays encourages students to be alert to the ways in which "Notes" advances ideas about the creative process and about poetry, with respect especially to those perennial concerns already familiar to them from our readings in Stevens's earlier lyrics: the negotiation of the intricate relations between human consciousness and its external environment, and the ways in which poetry might help people to live their lives under the conditions of modernity.

If we thus take Stevens's supreme fiction to be, generally speaking, poetry in its highest theoretical projection, the language of Stevens's title suggests that his "Notes" will be "about" poetry in the way of exploring necessary elements in an approach to what is not yet fully defined (*toward*: in the direction of; with a purpose to obtaining; in the vicinity of, near; just about arriving at; facing). "Notes" only very seemingly, I tell my students, "goes about" this project in any kind of systematic way. While its somewhat extraordinarily regular formal design—dividing the quest into an exploration of "three notes by way of defining the characteristics of supreme fiction" (*L* 407), each of which is given its own section consisting of ten poems (or, if one likes, "cantos") of twenty-one roughly iambic pentameter lines apiece, arranged in seven triplets, and with an introductory lyric of eight lines and a coda conforming to the twenty-one line pattern of the preceding thirty cantos—gives the reader a sense of being located quite securely within a firm architectonic structure, the actual development of each section, and indeed of any given canto, follows the kind of disjunctive and elliptical pattern to which we have become accustomed in our explorations of modernist poetry. Again, I read to my students from Stevens's letters:

the articulations between the poems are not the articulations that one would expect to find between paragraphs and chapters of a work of philosophy. . . . I very soon found that, if I stuck closely to a development, I should lose all of the qualities that I really wanted to get into the thing, and that I was likely to produce something that did not come off . . . as poetry. (*L* 431)

[W]e are dealing with poetry, not with philosophy. The last thing in the world that I should want to do would be to formulate a system. (*L* 864)

I have written a small series of poems dealing with the idea of a supreme fiction, or, rather, playing with that idea. (*L* 409)

I now ask my students to begin their own respective readings of "Notes" with the first of the three sections, watching for the ways in which Stevens's poetry (his "rhetoric" of sound and rhythm, diction, figuration, and trope) plays upon the thought that a supreme fiction must be abstract. I suggest that they look for evidences of continuity from canto to canto in the development of "It Must Be Abstract," but also to expect discontinuities and to allow for the rapid shifts and new beginnings of an improvisational structure as they move from canto to canto. I tell them to look for ideas of abstraction at work in individual cantos and to watch for how the actual rhetoric of these poems affects the articulation of such ideas. And I remind them of what they have already learned in earlier encounters with Stevens's poetry, that they will need to keep a good dictionary at hand.

Having thus set the students "to track the knaves of thought" (*CP* 42) through the rhetorical warp of Stevens's text, I conclude my introduction to "Notes" with reading the eight-line introductory lyric. And I offer the briefest possible explication, pointing out that the ambiguity of "except for you" (only for you *and* if not for you) allows one to read the addressee here not so much as the exclusive object of the poet's love as that which enables him to love at all. A supreme fiction, then, has everything to do with "the origin and course / Of love" (*CP* 18); the poetry of the act of the mind (thought) is also the poetry of the ebb and flow of emotion (desire); and I invite my students to enter Stevens's "Notes" along the twinned axis (twinned access?) of a pair of structuring tensions—one between ideology and rhetoric; the other between thought and desire.

Aiming to devote about two hours of class time to each of the three sections of the poem, we proceed by closely reading selected individual cantos against the backdrop of these provisional generalizations concerning what the poem is "about," in the sense both of "meanings" and of how it "goes about" doing what it does. We follow the general rubrics provided by Stevens's own headings, exploring how the individual cantos in each section develop the themes of, respectively, abstraction, change, and pleasure; and we remain always alert to the play of rhetoric upon and against ideology and to the ways in which the ebb and flow of desire subtend the act of the mind. The students will have already done quite a lot of close reading of modernist poems by this point in the semester, both working together in class sessions and individually on written exercises in explication. For "Notes," students are required to prepare written exercises involving close reading of assigned cantos in advance of class meetings where I anticipate taking up these poems. Each student is responsible for one such exercise during the two weeks, and I usually assign three or four cantos for each meeting. The number of students enrolled in the course is normally such that two or three students will be assigned to any given canto and I encourage them to work together outside of class in preparing this exercise.

I always begin the discussion of a given canto by reading the poem aloud; student exercises then serve as points of departure for our explorations of the poem. For any one student or group of students, the amount of guidance needed to steer away from "false engagements" (*CP* 317) and onto the genuine difficulties of a given canto may be varied by the extent of direction offered when the assignment is made. For example, in preparation for our first class, one student (or group) might be assigned the task of working out a brief paraphrase of the speaker's injunction to the ephebe in canto I of "It Must Be Abstract" and then commenting on the play of the central figuration of "the sun" upon this general sense; another student or group could then be shown where, in letters written to Hi Simons in 1943, Stevens says canto IV is about the imposition of reason and the operations of the pathetic fallacy (*L* 433, 444) and then asked to comment upon the ways in which the actual diction, intonation, rhythms, and figurative usages in this poem inflect the treatment of these themes (even senior English majors may have to do some research on "the pathetic fallacy" for this one); and an especially capable student or group may be asked to explore canto IX, taking into consideration its pivotal position between VIII and X in developing "major man" as "exponent" of "the idea of man," the poem's "major abstraction" (*CP* 388). While a few red herrings are likely to be dragged across this or that page, I most often find myself encouraged by the perceptivity and cogency with which these student readings are advanced; and I am sometimes exhilarated by fresh disclosures of Stevens's poetry. However this may be for a given class, the students' readings nevertheless provide points of departure, grounded in the particulars of the text, for an exploration of the different notions of abstraction at work in this first section of "Notes," from the root sense of a fresh perception taken out of, or removed from, any accumulated tradition of conceptualizations or interpretations ("How clean the sun when seen in its idea" [*CP* 381]), to the more usual sense of that which lacks particular embodiment or form ("Give him / No names. Dismiss him from your images" [*CP* 388]); for a consideration of the centrality of "the idea of man" (or, as we would say, the human) to Stevens's project here in "Notes"; and, most important, for an exploration of ways in which these concerns are inflected, deflected, and otherwise affected by the very language of the poem.

My own participation in class meetings is played out according to three principal roles: first, I try to provide continual reformulations of the thematic and structural generalizations that guide our readings of particular passages of text; second, I play the role of footnoter, providing the kind of information (lexical, intertextual, biographical, historical) that might be found in the editorial apparatus of scholarly editions of more "classical" texts; and, finally, I offer my own explications of the detail of Stevens's text as part of the ongoing activity of the class in working out readings of given cantos. In each of these roles, the teacher is fortunate in having at hand so distinguished a tradition of scholarship and criticism as has emerged in response to Stevens's work generally, and especially, to "Notes" itself. In this tradition, "Notes" has become a principal site of confrontation among Stevens's strongest readers, and the teacher has thus been provided with a wealth of speculation about the argumentative dialectic of "Notes" and about the rhetorical play of Stevens's language upon this dialectic, as well as a rich repertoire of readings of specific passages of text from which to draw in order to direct and enliven class discussion. A familiarity with this tradition can provide for the teacher the kind of solid grounding from which the spontaneous (though by no means impromptu) play of an improvisational classroom must spring.

If the jazz musician's fake book serves as an apt metaphor for the preparation the teacher brings to the improvisational arena of the classroom, perhaps the assembling of a jigsaw puzzle best figures the actual activity of the class: the closest possible scrutiny of the precise contours of individual pieces (here, phonemes, accents, words, sentences, denotative and connotative significations, images, all manner of figures and tropes) in relation to at least the hypothesis of an overall purpose or design. Though it won't do to press one's metaphor too strenuously in this case, the teacher's initial speculations about the overall character of "Notes"—and, as the class works through the three major divisions, focusing on individual cantos, about each section and any given canto—are loosely analogous to the picture on the puzzle box; only, here, the "picture" is subject to revision at any given moment in the process.

Let me illustrate my point here with reference to canto I of "It Must Be Abstract," since I have already indicated a possible assignment for the written exercise that students will bring to class. I will arrive at this class with my own reading of this canto as about the necessity for the aspiring poet to begin by locating himself in a world of immediate sensory perception and outside of any existing conceptions of that world, especially those deriving from notions of divine origins; and I know that I will be interested in exploring how the primary sense of abstraction here as "extracted," "withdrawn," or "drawn away from" intersects with the notion of a mere being that could never, and must not, be given verbal form, or named—at the same time that the poem goes on inventing names. Once I have read the poem aloud and asked the students to read their paraphrase, class discussion will proceed along the lines of a negotiation of whatever distance appears between their sense of what the poem is about and my own—a negotiation that I will want to conduct in terms of a close scrutiny of the language of the poem itself, especially of the central imagery of the sun. Among the items in my repertory of "footnotes" for this poem will be the observation that Stevens had first thought to caption this poem "REFACIMENTO" (L 431), an Italian term for the refashioning of older literary works, which reminds us of Pound's injunction to "Make it new"; the passage from "The Noble Rider and the Sound of Words" where Stevens writes of the poet's "power to abstract himself . . . and also to abstract reality . . . by placing it in his imagination" (*NA* 23); the one from "The Figure of the Youth as Virile Poet" where he compares imagination to sunlight, writing of the imagination that "Like light, it adds nothing, except itself" (*NA* 61); and the figure of the sun in the *Harmonium* poems as it cycles from the nothingness of "The Snow Man" to the fullness of "Tea at the Palaz of Hoon." The point of this class will not be to convince ourselves of the absolute validity of this or that interpretation, but to take delight in the play of language about matters of significant thought and of the profound feeling that still subtends what Stevens himself called "one of the great human experiences" (*OP* 260), modernity's discovery that "The death of one god is the death of all" (*CP* 381).

As we work our way through the first section of "Notes," the class discerns (or, as sometimes happens, is invited to discern) what William York Tindall long ago observed: a poem by Wallace Stevens is not so much the formulation of theory as it is about "the experience of trying to formulate it" (*Wallace Stevens* 32). Too, a deepening recognition comes to the class, one way or the other, of the degree to which the act of the mind in "Notes" dwells upon "fluttering things" (*CP* 18), the ever-changing weather, the flick of feeling, the ebb and flow of desire. And everywhere we discover the play of the very language of "Notes" about its matter of thought and feeling. As we work our way through "It Must Change" (with its hyperconsciousness of the poem's own acts of linguistic covering and uncovering, weaving and unweaving, veiling and unveiling) and on into the affirmations, however qualified, of "It Must Give Pleasure," there is a growing appreciation of just how far our initial observation that "Notes" is, after all, "about poetry" might take us. "It" becomes not so much an idea or set of concepts ("theory") as an *experience* of poetry; this is first and always an experience of language, of course, but Stevens in "Notes" reaches through language to something that touches the larger being of the human organism. Like the weather, to reverse the direction of Harold Bloom's eloquent commentary on canto VI of "It Must Be Abstract," it "is not to be seen and yet can be seen" (*Climate* 188) in its effects: "the strong exhilaration / Of what we feel from what we think, of thought / Beating in the heart." It is this "elixir, an excitation, a pure power" (*CP* 382) that I wish my students and myself to be "shaken by" in our tracings of the contours of "Notes toward a Supreme Fiction" and in our engagements with its particulars. And "It" has everything to do with that illusive *firstness* so much at stake in Stevens's poem and so entwined with "the irrational" that is yet to be "rational," with "freshness" and what is "strange," with that "nonsense" in which the poem might even "Evade us" as it pursues its necessary endeavor to "resist the intelligence / Almost successfully" (*CP* 350).

I would like my students to grasp, of course, what is at stake in "Notes" with respect to ideas, belief, desire, language, etc. Beyond this, however, I want them to experience the "poetry" of "Notes"; and I think this is where teaching comes into its own—and does so, to a certain extent, over and against the achievements of written literary criticism. I suspect that most of us who continue to teach Stevens's long poems to undergraduates do so because, at some point, we ourselves have been touched by a strong teaching tradition. While I stress the value for the teacher of the critical tradition that has risen up in response to "Notes," I do so with a confidence that its increasing mastery over the legendary difficulties of the poem seems unlikely ever to reduce the teaching of "Notes" to any programmatic treatment of its significance. My own experience so far is that "Notes" is sufficiently strong as poetry to continue to outdistance its professional readers, at least for now and perhaps indefinitely. Will what Helen Vendler has called the "fated presences" (*On Extended Wings* 168) of Stevens's nevertheless unique and wholly original personae—the Arabian, the planter, Nanzia Nunzio and Ozymandias, the blue woman, the great captain and the maiden Bawda, Canon Aspirin and his sister and nieces, and the fat girl—ever be reduced to so many interpretive constructs? Will we ever decide what to do with "Cinderella fulfilling herself beneath the roof" so abruptly after a self, for whom "majesty is a mirror," declares, "I have not but I am and as I am, I am" (*CP* 405)? Will the strangeness of "A bench was his catalepsy, Theatre / Of Trope" (*CP* 397) ever dissipate into so many predictable interpretations of a familiar enough figure of speech? I agree with Eleanor Cook when she writes, "We may impose orders if we wish, but Stevens' fluent mundo is likely to resist us quite successfully if we do. It is better to hold her to herself in other ways, as in the play 'in difference' of rhetoric and dialectic" (*Word-Play* 263). Or, I would add, in the spontaneous if accident-prone readings that can take place at any given moment in the charged atmosphere of an improvisational classroom. Among the many pleasures of teaching "Notes" is the way in which, even for one otherwise a dweller in the apartments of the most celestial of Stevens's readers, one's students can provoke a fresh glimpse of the strange unreasoning in any given passage of the poem, "so that we share, / For a moment, the first idea" (*CP* 382).

Here, then, are my three ideas about what has worked for me that might work for other teachers elsewhere in teaching "Notes." First, we must stay close to the text. Here, I not only recommend that the greater share of class time be spent in quite specifically focused textual explication, but also that those passages under consideration first be read aloud by the teacher, whose own phrasing and intonation will contribute immensely to the students' ability to grasp the poetry in its totality of sound and sense. We might find an analogue in the injunction to the ephebe at the outset of "It Must Be Abstract," suggesting that as readers we begin by perceiving the poem clearly in the language of it, attentive to the play of its multiform rhetoric (of its diction and grammar, its many kinds of figures of speech and of thought) against its dialectic of thought and feeling; and, as we move toward the formulations of our own "reading" or "late plural," we do so in a way that constantly goes from the poem to our reading and back again. Secondly, we must be flexible. That is to say, as teachers, we need to foster an open atmosphere within a classroom where spontaneity and improvisation, one's own as well as one's students', might refresh our reading, "bring[ing] back a power again / That gives a candid kind to everything" (*CP* 382). This is the necessity of change to cast off stale constructs in favor of "The freshness of transformation" (*CP* 397). My third idea is of the poem itself as a perennial site of the pleasure we take, teachers and students alike, in coming together for a series of Monday, Wednesday, and Friday mornings, or perhaps Tuesday and Thursday afternoons, over the text of "Notes toward a Supreme Fiction." One aspect of that ubiquitous "unreasoning" about which, as academics, we reason is the way in which its very unreadability may rest at the center of the pleasure we take in this poetry.

Part II. Prosody, Rhetoric, Diction, and Theme

Making Sense of the Sleight-of-Hand Man

MARIE BORROFF

The poetry of Wallace Stevens is, from beginning to end, a theater of changing adversarial relationships: images, symbols, and themes contend, in endless succession, on an endlessly shifting stage, and all resolutions are subject to change without notice. In a programmatic statement in "The Pure Good of Theory" (*CP* 329), Stevens himself puts it thus:

> It is never the thing but the version of the thing:
> The fragrance of the woman not her self,
> Her self in her manner not the solid block,
>
> The day in its color not perpending time,
> Time in its weather, our most sovereign lord,
> The weather in words and words in sounds of sound.

Despite his belief that it should help us to live our lives, poetry, as Stevens conceived of it, is not the portentous expression of eternal verities. Rather, it consists of attempts to capture the "weather," the conditions of light and atmosphere in which we live from day to day, in an ongoing play of words whose sounds are often as important as their sense. Such a program has implications for readers and teachers of Stevens as well. If our students are to arrive at some notion of what his poetry is all about, we must make sure that getting there is at least half the fun.

The adversarial character of Stevens's poetry suggests an opening strategy for teaching him that I have used to good effect. I ask my students, in studying selected short poems, to identify within each a basic conflict or opposition, to devise titles for the contending agents or concepts involved, and to draw up as full an account as possible of the characteristics of each, listing them in two columns. In discussion, we then try to move from the contrasts inherent in a particular subject matter to contrasts of a more general sort that will provide a basis for comparisons between poems. We might, for example, begin with "Disillusionment of Ten O'Clock" (*CP* 66) and "Anecdote of the Jar" (*CP* 76). Obvious names for the two sides of the opposition in "Disillusionment" are "whiteness" and "colorfulness." The former is associated with custom and predictable behavior, the latter with eccentricity ("socks of lace," "beaded ceintures") and strangeness, specifically, with things remote from everyday experience ("baboons and periwinkles," "tigers"). We note that the set of primary colors named in the first half of the poem is completed by the "red weather" in which the old sailor dreams, and that the strangeness of "beaded ceintures" extends to the word *ceintures* itself, which lies beyond the range of the collegiate dictionary. In the poem's concluding lines, the associations of "colorfulness" widen to include drunkenness and mildly indecorous behavior ("asleep in his boots"); the corresponding (though implicit) associations of whiteness are sobriety and decorum. More generally, whiteness is associated with singleness, colors with multiplicity, as white light is refracted into the colors of the rainbow when it passes through a prism. Finally, the poem's opening image, in which those clad in white nightgowns are said to "haunt" the houses of the speaker's fellow citizens, suggests that whiteness is associated with a dead past, colorfulness with a more vital present. Summarizing the adversarial theme in general terms, we might say that its speaker deplores a world whose "whiteness" seems oppressively familiar, monotonous, and predictable, and opts for a "colorful" world offering a variety of new, unexpected, and exciting possibilities.

The conceptual antagonism of "Anecdote of the Jar" is less straightforward and more complex than that of "Disillusionment of Ten O'Clock," and the class will need more guidance from the instructor in identifying some of its aspects and putting them into words. The artifact that is the successful antagonist of the Tennessee wilderness has many explicit attributes. First of all, it is "round." Set on a hill, that is, a high place from which the landscape can be viewed in every direction, it exerts a dominating or taming force, serving as a focal point that the formerly "slovenly" wilderness, now "no longer wild," "surrounds," as the periphery of a circle surrounds its center. It thus introduces a single unifying design where no such design was present, so that the action of the poem can be thought of, more generally, as the imposition of order on disorder. The jar is further described as "tall and of a port in air." The relevant definition of *port* here is "the manner in which a person carries himself" (*American Heritage Dictionary, port*[5]). The jar has a distinctive manner, or bearing, and because it is "tall," and makes the wilderness rise up to it, we can infer that its bearing is dignified—that it has *hauteur* in both the literal and the metaphorical senses of that word. In the next stanza, the additional attributes of grayness and bareness suggest a simplicity that is also somewhat austere. Finally, we are told that the jar, unlike anything else in Tennessee, does not "give of bird or bush." We can interpret this, in context, as meaning that the jar holds itself aloof; it is "self-possessed" or "self-contained," differentiating itself from its surroundings. As for the jar's defeated antagonist, the wilderness, its corresponding attributes, by implication, include greenness, as opposed to the jar's grayness, and lushness and fecundity of foliage and vegetation, as opposed to the jar's bareness and self-sufficiency. The fact that the jar is brought into the wilderness by a human agency suggests a still more general opposition between nature and artifact, or nature and art, or primitive nature and civilization.

Once "Disillusionment of Ten O'Clock" and "Anecdote of the Jar" have been explicated in some such fashion as the above, the class may be invited to consider some general questions about the two poems taken together. First of all, what about the plausibility, or validity, of the point of view expressed in each? The speaker of "Disillusionment" seems clearly to be a spokesman for Stevens himself; the poem tries to induce its readers to share his point of view, to long, as he does, for temporary relief from the oppression of invariably white nightgowns and tame dreams. "Anecdote" is more problematic. The fictional speaker of the poem is clearly pro-jar, and witnesses the jar's victory with satisfaction: "It made the slovenly wilderness / Surround that hill" has the ring of "I showed them a thing or two." But it is not clear that the grayness and bareness of the jar, or its refusal to "give of bird or bush," are attractive or desirable qualities, or, particularly in this day and age, that wildernesses deserve to be called "slovenly," or are improved by being "no longer wild." After allowing some time for the expression of contending interpretations, the instructor might make the point that something is gained by the imposition of jar on wilderness, and something is lost.

There is also a more profound, and more interesting, contrast to which the discussion should finally address itself. At the highest level of generality, the values endorsed by the speakers of the two poems can be seen as contradicting each other. That is, the speaker of "Disillusionment" turns from an oppressive sameness to imagine a somewhat disorderly variety; the speaker of "Anecdote," through his surrogate, the jar, corrects a "slovenly" and wild overabundance by imposing on it a single unifying force.

Which of these programs represents "Stevens's view"? In leading a discussion of this question, the instructor might eventually draw the attention of the class to certain signs in each poem that the action represented in it is in fact remedial, a counteraction prompted by the speaker's state of mind at a particular time or in a particular place. "Disillusionment of Ten O'Clock" is explicitly tied to a certain time of day, or rather of night. The action of "Anecdote of the Jar" is limited to "Tennessee," a locality less vast and formidable to contemplate than, say, Alaska or Africa. The word *anecdote* itself must be understood partly in terms of its root meaning in Greek, "something unpublished"—that is, something that has not necessarily been cast in definitive form. One longs for colorful nightgowns when one has seen too many white ones; one sets a dominating jar in the center of a landscape when one feels its unruliness to be excessive. What the two poems have in common is the impulse to turn from a given mode of being toward its opposite, from one "version of the thing" to another.

Stevens's rejection of any fixed "version of the thing" accounts for his attitude toward revealed religion in general, and toward the Christian church in particular. The poems that set a secular view of the world against the teachings of Christianity lend themselves readily to an analysis in adversarial terms. Among these, I like to begin with "Waving Adieu, Adieu, Adieu" (*CP* 127):

> That would be waving and that would be crying,
> Crying and shouting and meaning farewell,
> Farewell in the eyes and farewell at the centre,
> Just to stand still without moving a hand.
>
> In a world without heaven to follow, the stops
> Would be endings, more poignant than partings, profounder,
> And that would be saying farewell, repeating farewell,
> Just to be there and just to behold.

To be one's singular self, to despise
The being that yielded so little, acquired
So little, too little to care, to turn
To the ever-jubilant weather, to sip

One's cup and never to say a word,
Or to sleep or just to lie there still,
Just to be there, just to be beheld,
That would be bidding farewell, be bidding farewell.

One likes to practice the thing. They practice,
Enough, for heaven. Ever-jubilant,
What is there here but weather, what spirit
Have I except it comes from the sun?

The instructor leading a discussion of this poem might begin by presenting the class with the well-known lines from the song "Imagine," by John Lennon, asking us to imagine that there is no hell below us and only sky above. Though "Imagine" is Stevensian as regards its underlying theme, it is utterly banal in execution—something we hope the students will discover, eventually if not immediately, for themselves.

I emphasize, in teaching "Waving Adieu," the adversarial character not only of Stevens's thought but of his language. For example, there are invisible italics in the first two lines that must be brought out in a dramatically expressive reading:

> *That* would be waving and *that* would be crying,
> Crying and shouting and *meaning* farewell. . . .

In analyzing the contrast between the sort of farewell the poem repudiates and the sort of farewell that would result from such a repudiation, the class may first note that "*meaning* farewell" has its implicit opposite in "*not* meaning farewell." "Not meaning farewell" in turn should be explained in terms of the Christian belief in "a world *with* heaven to follow," in which the bereaved can console themselves by looking forward to an eternal reunion in the afterlife. In considering the second stanza, the class should explore the opposition between "stops" that are "endings" and those that are merely "partings," and ask in what sense the former are more "poignant" and "profound." (Here some consideration, guided by the instructor, of stanza VI of "Sunday Morning" [*CP* 66]—"Is there no change of death in paradise?"—might be useful.)

The language of the last three stanzas of "Waving Adieu" is somewhat cryptic, but their underlying message seems clear: a life in which one's imagination accepts the finality of death, and thus the necessity of a final parting with everything one loves, is in fact more worth living, as well as more admirable, than a life in which false comfort is derived from belief in personal immortality. The instructor might ask in what sense nonbelievers are their "singular" selves, and in what sense those who have turned for comfort to the idea of life beyond the grave can be said to have "yielded . . . little" to the real world, and "acquired / . . . little, too little to care." He or she ought also to make sure that the speaker's remark that "They [Christian congregations] practice, / Enough, for heaven" is understood as ironic in tone; this, in turn, depends on an understanding of what is meant by "practicing for heaven."

If there is time for further discussion, the instructor may call the attention of the class to certain details of language whose expressive force they are unlikely to recognize without help. In trying to persuade his readers of the validity of his secular vision, Stevens draws on the power of at least one image and one word that have figured importantly in traditional Christian language. The image of sipping one's cup alludes to a number of biblical metaphors in which "cup" stands for one's destiny or lot, whether in terms of blessing or affliction, as in "My cup runneth over" (Psalm 23.5 in the Authorized Version); Jesus' question to the disciples, "Are ye able to drink of the cup that I shall drink out of [i.e., the Passion]?" (Matthew 20.22); and his plea to God in the Garden of Gethsemane, "Let this cup pass from me" (Matthew 26.39). *Jubilant,* in the adjective "ever-jubilant," comes from Latin *jubilans,* the present participle of the verb *jubilare* "to rejoice." In the Latin version of the Old Testament, the words "Jubilate Deo" begin two well-known Psalms (65 and 99 in the Latin version, 66 and 100 in the Authorized Version; the latter translates the phrase "Make a joyful noise unto God"). Psalm 100, in fact, has traditionally been called "Jubilate" in English. The words *jubilant, jubilation,* and *jubilee* have long-standing associations with the rejoicing of Christian believers in the various praiseworthy attributes of God. Stevens's use of the expression "to sip / One's cup" with reference to the lot on earth of a nonbeliever, and of the adjective "ever-jubilant" with reference not to the worship of the Divinity but to the weather, the mere day-to-day circumstances of our life on earth, can thus be understood as underscoring the diametrical opposition between Christian attitudes and the attitudes the poem seeks to inculcate.

The instructor might then go on to ask the class whether they think it matters that the poet is trying to have it both ways. Is the poem weakened or strengthened by exploiting the power of words drawn from the rhetorical armory of the very institution against which it is directed as a polemic?

Other short poems ("The Death of a Soldier," "Evening without Angels," "Flyer's Fall," even "A High-Toned Old Christian Woman") can provide additional material for a discussion of contending secular and Christian values. Once the students understand what Christian belief means to Stevens, and what aspects of it he views with disfavor, they can go on to consider poems directed against more general targets: the sentimental, the doctrinal, the habitual, all that is preestablished and preformulated.

In "On the Road Home" (CP 203), for example, the giving up or casting out of "'the truth,'" that is, of belief in a single, unchanging truth, is followed by an experience of vital apprehension in which perception is enhanced ("the grapes seemed fatter") and the world comes to life in images of motion and color.

> It was when I said,
> "There is no such thing as the truth,"
> That the grapes seemed fatter.
> The fox ran out of his hole.
>
> You . . . You said,
> "There are many truths,
> But they are not parts of a truth."
> Then the tree, at night, began to change,
>
> Smoking through green and smoking blue.

So too, in "The Sense of the Sleight-of-Hand Man" (CP 222), reality manifests itself, and gives pleasure, as our senses respond to unforeseen

changes in the weather which "Occur as they occur" and would continue
to occur if we ourselves were not present:

> . . . So bluish clouds
> Occurred above the empty house and the leaves
> Of the rhododendrons rattled their gold,
> As if someone lived there. Such floods of white
> Came bursting from the clouds. So the wind
> Threw its contorted strength around the sky.

At the end of the poem, Stevens tells us that "the ignorant man, alone,"
that is, the man whose unencumbered mind leaves him free to see things
as they are, can experience those "weddings of the soul" when consciousness and world become one. In the passage from "The Pure Good of
Theory" that I quoted at the beginning of this essay, all attempts to grasp at
the permanence underlying change, to know the essential "self" of a woman
rather than being content with particular experiences of her, or to conceive of "time" as perpetual in its "perpending" rather than as momentary
"in its weather," are seen as inimical to the workings of the imagination,
that is, to the writing of poetry.

The final stage in the movement from one "version of the thing" to
another described in that passage—the turning of words into "sounds of
sound"—involves an aspect of poetry which is of the utmost importance
for Stevens, and which we must not omit when we teach him at the introductory level. I mean "wordplay" in the fullest sense—the activity that
"Piece[s] the world together," as Stevens puts it in "Parochial Theme" (*CP*
191), by linking groups of words in such a way that meaning, though
present, seems a pretext for the generation of conspicuously repetitive
sound patterns. This idea, in all its unpretentiousness, is beautifully expressed in the final stanza of "The Owl in the Sarcophagus" (*CP* 431): "It
is a child that sings itself to sleep, / The mind, among the creatures that it
makes." A number of the short poems of *Harmonium* illustrate this sort of
child's play, and the student should be encouraged to take time out to relax and enjoy them in a willing suspension of analytical modes of inquiry.

One can in fact discover in Stevens's poetry a sort of "code" whereby
certain sounds and kinds of sounds are thematically associated with certain

aspects of the perpetually evolving life of the mind (see Borroff, "Sound Symbolism"). A conspicuous illustration of its workings can be found in the language of an early poem entitled "The Plot against the Giant" (*CP* 6):

First Girl

When this yokel comes maundering,
Whetting his hacker,
I shall run before him,
Diffusing the civilest odors
Out of geraniums and unsmelled flowers.
It will check him.

Second Girl

I shall run before him,
Arching cloths besprinkled with colors
As small as fish-eggs.
The threads
Will abash him.

Third Girl

Oh, la . . . le pauvre!
I shall run before him,
With a curious puffing.
He will bend his ear then.
I shall whisper
Heavenly labials in a world of gutturals.
It will undo him.

We are presented here with a fairy-tale plot in which three protagonists pit themselves against a huge, boorish, and menacing adversary. They plan three different strategies, all of which involve confronting him with objects of sense perception whose qualities are the opposite of his. The first girl will "check him" by diffusing the "civilest odors" of flowers. The second girl will "abash him" by waving cloths on which "small" and delicate colors are "besprinkled." The weapon of the third girl—and we remember that in the realm of the fairy tale "the third pays for all"—will "undo" him by whispering "Heavenly labials" in the "world of gutturals" to which he belongs. The terms "labial" and "guttural," or "lip-sound" and "throat-sound" (the latter is now more usually called "velar") belong to the realm of articulatory phonetics. In the language of the third girl, four labial consonants appear conspicuously, in words that occupy metrically stressed positions and are important carriers of meaning. They are the sounds of the letters *p, b, f,* and *v.* We hear them in *pauvre, puffing, bend, whisper, heavenly,* and *labials* itself. These consonants also occur in the preposition *before.* Two "guttural" consonants, the sounds of the letters *g* and *k,* appear in the speeches of the first and third girls in the words *yokel, hacker,* and *guttural.* To put it somewhat oversimply, velar, or "guttural," consonants are associated in the poem with an unarticulated, brute, undifferentiated version of reality (the giant never speaks), while labial consonants are associated with the "civilizing" of this version of reality as it is transformed into the particular language and imagery of a poem.

So far, the thematic code values of consonant sounds as Stevens uses them are in accord with phonetic terminology. But the whispering speech of the third girl also makes conspicuous use of the sound of the consonant *l* in the words *la, le,* and *labials.* The pronunciation of *l* before vowels calls the front of the tongue into play, and Stevens seems to have associated this variety of *l,* along with the labials proper, with the act of articulation. One might say that in the third stanza of "The Plot against the Giant" it becomes a kind of honorary labial. Two important words in the poem beginning with the sound of the consonant *h,* namely, *hacker* and *heavenly,* should also be noted; the first expresses an aspect of the "guttural" world of the giant, the second, an aspect of the "labial" world of the third speaker. Stevens seems sometimes to have associated this consonant (though it is called an "aspirate," it does originate in the throat) with inarticulate or prearticulate reality, along with the gutturals proper, *g* and *k.* But it also appears in images of breathing as an ongoing vital activity; thus, in section VIII of "An Ordinary Evening in New Haven," we are said to "inhale a health of air / To our sepulchral hollows" (*CP* 470).

It is a profitable exercise to look at certain of the short poems in *Harmonium,* if only for the nonce, as interactions among groups of words contrasting in terms of sound. The instructor can heighten the students' awareness of this sort of interplay by asking them to make lists of important words linked by consonant repetition in "systems" representing thematic oppositions or interactions. "Bantams in Pine-Woods" (*CP* 75), for example, can be enjoyed as a little skirmish between a *k/h* group (*Iffucan, Azcan, caftan, henna, hackles, halt, cock, blackamoor, hoos*) and a *p/f* group (*fat, personal, -foot, poet, pines, points, Appalachian, fears, portly*). Most of the words in the latter are associated with the self-assured, indignant, and highly articulate speaker of the poem, most of the former group with a crude, gaudy, and corpulent adversary whose one utterance, so far as we know, is "Hoo." A supplementary *b*-system is associated with this adversary and the speaker's defiance of him; it includes *blackamoor, blazing, begone,* and *bristles,* not to mention *bantams* itself.

Sound patterning in the form of a *p*-system seems to govern the assemblage of descriptive details in the exemplary narrative that opens "Parochial Theme":

> Long-tailed ponies go nosing the pine-lands,
> Ponies of Parisians shooting on the hill.

(The word *parochial* itself is retrospectively linked to this system, since the imagined scene represents one small part, or "parish," of the world of possible descriptions.) One might with some justice argue that the "ponies" are traversing "pine-lands" rather than "grasslands," and belong to "Parisians" rather than "Virginians" simply because these words, like *pony,* begin with *p;* the phonic link has the playful or "magical" force of those we make up in series like "I love my love with an *a*"; "I love my love with a *p* because she is Parisian." The first eight stanzas of "Parochial Theme" also develop an *h*-system that thematically supplements the *p*-system, and which includes *hunters, heavy, inhuman, health, holy,* and *halloo.* After an interval, this system recurs conspicuously in stanzas 11 and 12:

> The spring will have a health of its own, with none
> Of autumn's halloo in its hair. So that closely, then,
>
> Health follows after health.

With the second of the above statements, the poem shifts from its opening narrative or parabolic mode to a more discursive, gnomic mode; from that point on, we are made less aware of repetitive sound patterns as such. The initial *h* of the words *hanging* and *hands* in the final stanza, for example, seems present incidentally, as a result of the poet's choices among words, rather than by design.

Numerous other poems and passages derive part of their expressive power from conspicuous sound systems. I shall point out a few examples briefly. In the first half of "Poem Written at Morning" (*CP* 219), linkages among words in a *p*-system, including *Poussiniana, paint, pineapple, pewter,* and *palmed,* correspond, on the level of sound, to some of the linkages among ideas created by metaphorical description. The second half of the poem, as in "Parochial Theme," becomes more discursive, and its final statement, "Green were the curls upon that head," is almost conspicuously lacking in phonic play. In "Of Hartford in a Purple Light" (*CP* 226), a *p*-system including *petty, Pasadena, plaster, purple, parasol,* and *Opera,* is associated, uncharacteristically for Stevens, with a sentimental, "feminine" landscape viewed by the speaker with distaste ("as in an amour of women / Purple sets purple round"). A more desirable "masculine" alternative is associated with *h*- and *m*-systems, the former including *hands, heroic, hi,* and *hunks,* the latter *moment, masculine, Master, male,* and *muscle.* Only the word *poodle* remains exempt from the undesirable associations of the *p*-system; it is introduced in an opening image of playfulness and prodigality, and reappears in the final apostrophe, symbolizing these same qualities, as the speaker calls on the imaginary creature to dispel the oppressive "purple" of the cityscape. In "Landscape with Boat" (*CP* 241), a hypothetical turn, from an overly abstract and hence unrewarding mindset to a satisfying one that yields sensory pleasure, takes place at the end of the poem. This change is accompanied by the emergence of repetitive phonic patterns that make us conscious, as we read, of the sounds of words, including the *m*- and *p*-systems to which *Mediterranean, emerald[s], palms, hum, appears, rhythm,* and *pantomime* belong.

If we teach our students to hear and take pleasure in the sound effects that occur throughout Stevens's poetry, while freeing them temporarily from the bafflements and anxieties of discursive analysis, we enable them to share in a "gaiety that is being, not merely knowing" ("Of Bright & Blue Birds & the Gala Sun" [*CP* 248]), a gaiety attendant, for Stevens, upon vital states of consciousness. I have found that many young people, when they read Stevens for the first time, welcome this invitation to "imagine" the scene around them, to take it in from moment to moment with their eyes and ears, and thus to enlarge their experience beyond the numbing, repetitive pressures and responsibilities that, as in "Gubbinal" (*CP* 85), make the world seem inescapably "ugly" and "sad." There is a sense in which every one of Stevens's poems has as its subject some phase or part of the great enterprise of freeing and invigorating the imagination, and thus helping people to lead their lives. With this in mind, I tell my students that when they read through the list of assigned poems they need not feel duty-bound to wrestle each one in turn to the ground. Rather, they should read on, ignoring obscurities and difficulties, on until they find a poem to whose verbal surface of diction, imagery, and sound they can respond with pleasure, and whose general purport, at least, seems clear. Or a passage, or even a sentence or phrase—even if it be no larger than a cricket's horn, let them mark it in the margin, so that they can return to it, read it again, commit it to memory. At the very least, they will in so doing add some elegant verbal furniture to their minds.

Years ago, I met on the streets of New Haven, on a gray day, a tall young man whom I recognized as one of the students in my twentieth-century poets course. He stopped to talk, bubbling over with his excitement about Stevens, whose poems he had never read before. "All the people I know are so depressed all the time," he said, "but when I hear them complaining, it doesn't bother me a bit. I just say to myself, 'Have it your way. / The world is ugly, / And the people are sad.'" The sleight-of-hand man would have liked that.

Stevens's Prosody

GEORGE S. LENSING

When Wallace Stevens was fifteen and vacationing with his two brothers, he sent home an account of his older brother's wooing in a letter to his mother: "At present he is on the top of the house with his Rosalie . . . and while they together bask[,] Buck's kaleidescopic [*sic*] feelings have inspired the keen, splattering, tink-a-tink-tink-tink-tink-a-a-a that are gamboling off the hackneyed strings of his quivering mandolin" (*L* 6). Those tinks of his brother's mandolin are replayed in the younger sibling's arch and be-mused commentary. Fourteen years later, when Stevens was doing some courting himself, he sent off to his future wife another account of his own delight in oral expressiveness:

> Bechtel told me a good story to-night. It was about a Pennsylvania Dutchman that went to the World's Fair. When he had been there a day he wrote a post-card to his wife; and this is what he said:
>
> > Dear Maria: -I-yi-yi-yi-yi! I-yi-yi-yi-yi!
> > I-yi-yi-yi-yi!   Sam.
>
> That's the best story I've heard for a long time. (*L* 784 n. 1)

Both of these accounts occur years before Stevens began writing his mod-ernist poetry, but they anticipate the later poet's constant fidelity to the pleasure of sound in poetry.

It is perhaps that element of pleasure in prosody, indulged so openly by Stevens in these early letters, that escapes the notice of many of his readers, and it is that same pleasure that can be tapped when the poet is presented in the classroom. Seamus Heaney has spoken of the "magical incantation" of poetry, its "power of sound to bind our minds' and bodies' apprehensions within an acoustic complex" (109). In allowing our students such an apprehension, we teach not just how a poem differs from prose, but what poetry is in its own right. While many students today shrink from poetry as arcanely inaccessible, they invariably are absorbed with their own music. From the steady pounding of rap music to the thrumming rhythms of MTV, the insistent measures of popular music obtrude on every part of the subculture of the youth. American students at the end of the twentieth century understand rhythm; they can perhaps begin to understand poetry through the pleasure to be derived from verbal rhythms and sounds. Speaking of such basic pleasure in reading poetry, Stevens once exclaimed, "People ought to like poetry the way a child likes snow" (*L* 349).

Meter and diction, separated out for the purposes of this essay, are always complementary for Stevens as aspects of verbal expressiveness. Rhymes, perfect and partial, are more prevalent in his poetry than has been generally acknowledged. But after moving from his earliest experiments, Stevens quickly began to adapt or violate "rules" of prosody for the sake of the poem's stylistic effect—never constricting "effect" to "rules." Students may have to be alerted to the nature of such "rules"—a task for which they will likely need assistance—but they can be encouraged to decide for themselves how the poet modifies them and why.

I

> The truth is that there comes a time
> When we can mourn no more over music
> That is so much motionless sound.
>
> There comes a time when the waltz
> Is no longer a mode of desire, a mode
> Of revealing desire and is empty of shadows.

Stevens was keenly aware, as these lines from "Sad Strains of a Gay Waltz" (*CP* 121) suggest, that he was writing at a time in which the music of poetry was being transformed. "[N]o longer a mode of desire," the waltz has become a cliché, but the need for a new mode of revealing desire is urgently impressed. These lines, first published in 1935, followed a long period of gestation, of trial and error, in which Stevens moved slowly but steadily toward his own new mode, and it is helpful for students to have some sense of the differences between the old mode and the new. Starting with a series of sonnets that were written and published while he was a student at Harvard, Stevens began under the tutelage of Keats, Wordsworth, Sidney, and Rossetti. Most students will be aware of some examples of these sonnets and can connect Stevens's earliest works to those popularly established norms. Other exercises by Stevens, not sonnets, betrayed the imitation of Herrick, the *Rubáiyát,* and others. Later, Stevens remembered, "When I was here at Harvard, a long time ago, it was a commonplace to say that all the poetry had been written and all the paintings painted" (*OP* 225). Only his poem "Ballade of the Pink Parasol," published just before leaving Cambridge, gives evidence of a premodernist Stevens beginning to find a new diction if not a new rhythm.

In order to understand Stevens's exceptionally long apprenticeship as a poet, students will need to know that in the thirteen years or so that followed his undergraduate years, when Stevens was in New York as a reporter, law student, and unsuccessful lawyer, his writing of poems took a second place in his life. And there are numerous passages in his letters and journal entries that—read aloud or reproduced—will give the class an appreciation of his view of poetry during this period. For his journal, during the middle of that time in his life, he wrote: "Sonnets have their place . . . but they can also be found tremendously out of place: in real life where things are quick, unaccountable, responsive" (*SP* 80). When writing a series of short lyrics for his fiancée's birthday in 1908 and 1909, he shunned the sonnet but seemed no less aware of the limitation of his latest efforts. To Elsie Moll, his fiancée, he wrote: "I read, and then I said, 'I'll write poetry. Young men in attics always write poetry on snowy nights, so—I'll write poetry.' I wrote, 'Only to name again / The leafy rose—' To-to-te-tum, la-la-la. I couldn't do another line—I looked at the ceiling, frowned at the floor, chewed the top of my pen, closed my eyes, looked into myself and found everything covered up" (*L* 120). The young poet mocks himself in these lines but ironically proceeds to compose the very poem about a "leafy rose" in the predictable rhythm of "To-to-te-tum." In so doing, he succumbs to the conventions he otherwise scorns but for which he has, as yet, found no alternatives:

> Only to name again
> The leafy rose—
> So to forget the fading,
> The purple shading,
> Ere it goes. (*SP* 230)

I point out to my students that the poet was a few months from his thirtieth birthday when he composed the lines, and that, in a sense, the development of the poet from "Ballade of the Pink Parasol" (1899) to "Only to name again" (1909) is retrograde.

Altogether different specimens began to appear in the ensuing decade— partly anticipating and partly influenced by the imagists. In pursuing this stage of development, students will have to be provided a context that includes not only the imagists but the Fauves and Cubists (that Stevens in all likelihood saw at the Armory Show in 1913), Verlaine and other French symbolists, and the work of friends like William Carlos Williams, Walter Arensberg, Donald Evans, and others. Absorbing these influences and perhaps, most important, trusting the instincts that made him suspicious of the sonnet and self-mocking about the "leafy rose" poem, he emerged a new poet. To understand Stevens's transition into a modernist poet, the class might discuss briefly an imagist poem by Hulme or Pound and then a poem like "Disillusionment of Ten O'Clock"—or they might examine a reproduction of a painting like "Nude Descending a Staircase" by Duchamp (whom Stevens knew personally as early as 1915) and the third stanza of "Floral Decorations for Bananas."

Almost simultaneously, Stevens developed two different prosodic voices, which students should be able to distinguish after looking at some early examples that show their divergence. I have elsewhere defined these voices as the "ironic mode" and the "prophetic mode" (109-10). The poems of the former tend toward a highly self-conscious tone of flippancy and playfulness, in which impressions are quick and spontaneous. The poet's seriousness is submerged in inventive sounds, highly irregular meters, and witty opacity. The prophetic mode, on the other hand, is a remaking of the tone of the undergraduate sonnets in a voice that remains formal and elevated but resists preciosity and mannerism. Its diction is largely Latinate and the measure is a highly pliable blank verse. Later the two modes tended to merge into one more dominantly prophetic and elegant, but never mis- placing altogether the devices of irony and mockery.

"Depression before Spring" (*CP* 63), an early example of the playful voice, is a tour de force, an exercise by a poet who has finally and success- fully found an idiom within the ironic mode in which his confidence is complete. In introducing the poem in class, I ask one or two students to read the poem out loud, asking them to mark the syllables that they would be likely to stress. I make it clear that there is room for variation in this, just as there are degrees of stress; each student may hear the rhythm some- what differently:

> The cóck cróws
> But nó quéen ríses.
>
> The háir of my blónde
> Is dázzling,
> As the spíttle of cóws
> Thréading the wínd.
>
> Hó! Hó!
>
> But kí-kí-rí-kí
> Brings nó rou-cóu,
> Nó rou-cóu-cóu.
>
> But nó quéen cómes
> In slípper gréen.

In beginning the discussion, I ask the class to examine the contrast be- tween the sounds of the present cock and the absent dove and to speculate on the reasons why Stevens has created the contrast. The dove is, of course, royally feminine ("queen"), while the cock is rudely masculine. The last vestige of winter is already yielding to the softer pleasure of spring—even as "Depression" gives way to enjoyment and self-mockery ("Ho! Ho!"). But the debate is preeminently aural: a contrast between the velar plosives of the cock ("ki-ki-ri-ki") and the elongated vowels of the doves ("rou-cou-cou": from the French *roucouler:* to coo). The cock's sound (*k*) is captured in his name and the sound he makes, "cock crows," while the same *k*-sound of "queen" yields at once to the glide of the softer *w*-sound (*k-ween*). At the end, the poem gently echoes "queen" with "green," the only rhyme of the poem. Though literally absent from the scene ("no queen comes"), the dove is installed in the poem by the very cooing that the speaker both yearns for and recreates. The triumph of the queen-dove over the staccato of the rude cock is complete. A similar setting is used in "The Paltry Nude Starts on a Spring Voyage" (*CP* 5), as the "paltry nude" prepares to yield to another royalty, the "purple stuff" of a "goldener nude."

"Depression before Spring" everywhere resists the urge toward soothing iambs. The notable exception occurs in the ninth and tenth lines through the recreation of the dove sounds: "Brǐngs nó rŏu-cóu, / Nó rŏu-cóu-cóu." Trochees and spondees otherwise dominate. (The iambic and anapestic rhythms of the second stanza lure us into the expectation of dovelike beauty and solace with the feminine image of "my blonde." But the blonde's hair described as cows' spittle is followed by the poet's own reductive spondees, "Ho! Ho!," checking abruptly the lull of such deceptive rhythms.) To read "Depression before Spring" without attention to its self-conscious prosody is, of course, to miss the poem entirely. As a result, it serves as an especially resourceful exercise in training the student's ear to hear how phonemes and stresses contribute to content—not decoratively or after the fact—but organically and intrinsically.

"Sunday Morning" (*CP* 66), published three years before "Depression before Spring," is a quite accessible example of the prophetic mode. In place of irony is the voice of exhortation and rumination cast in the more traditional rhythms of blank verse. In a sonnet composed during his undergraduate years, Stevens had begun, "If we are leaves that fall upon the ground" (predestined to a brief earthly life), "Then let a tremor through our briefness run" (*SP* 31). It is the same presentiment to which he returned in "Sunday Morning." Once again, we are leaves. If death, in fact, "strews the leaves / Of sure obliteration on our paths," then life remains to be savored with heightened intensity. Death causes, not a "tremor," but a "shiver": "She [death] makes the willow shiver in the sun." "Sunday Morning," however, demonstrates for students a voice altogether superior to that of a decade and a half earlier. One cause of that advance is the poet's greater musical versatility with the same iambic pentameter rhythm as the undergraduate sonnets. Students might first be asked to hear and examine the contrast between the regular blank verse of a line like "The holy hush of ancient sacrifice" and the variation on it in a line like "Complacencies of the peignoir, and late." The "measures" of poetry itself, as the poem declares, are—like "All pleasures and all pains"—"destined for her soul." The men who chant their devotion to the sun in stanza VII

> . . . shall know well the heavenly fellowship
> Of men that perish and of summer morn.
> And whence they came and whither they shall go
> The dew upon their feet shall manifest.

Students will recognize in these lines the biblical cadences from something like the Psalms and will quickly appreciate that Stevens is rewriting his own secular scripture of the earth. In a different mode, the laconic syllables of mockery in "Depression before Spring" are fashioned here in alliterative "*m*'s," as Stevens mocks the motherless Jove, the first and totally inhuman god: "No mother suckled him, no sweet land gave / Large-mannered motions to his mythy mind. / He moved among us, as a muttering king, / Magnificent." (An oral rendering of the lines is obviously helpful here.)

The most subtle modulation of rhythm and sound in the poem, however, occurs in the poem's conclusion:

> Déer wálk upón our móuntains, and the quáil
> Whístle abóut us their spontáneous críes;
> Swéet bérries rípen in the wílderness;
> Ánd, in the ísolátion of the ský
> At évening, cásual flócks of pígeons máke
> Ambíguous úndulátions as they sínk,
> Dównward to dárkness, on exténded wíngs.

These familiar lines are full of action and motion (walk, whistle, ripen, make, sink), which, as we might expect, are captured in the poem's rhythm. Counterpoint replays the lines of blank verse, as the students will begin to recognize. In the line above, "Ănd, ín thĕ ísŏlátiŏn óf thĕ ský," for example, the musical variation redefines the rhythm from regular blank verse to "Ánd, in the ísolátion of the ský." The line itself is a parenthetical aside significantly without the action or motion otherwise defined. With this exception, the sequence is steadily marked by trochees and spondees: Déer wálk, quáil / Whístlĕ, Swéet bérrĭes rípĕn, úndŭlátiŏns, Dównwărd tŏ dárknĕss. The rhythm is in the fall of the trochee rather than the rise of the iamb, another kind of sinking downward. Though action is vigorous, the pace is retarded, appropriate to the poem's final diminuendo approaching cessation. The motion downward toward finality is complemented by the images themselves: autumnal berries, isolation of the sky, and evening yielding to darkness. Deer, quail, berries, and pigeons are caught up in their own emanations ("*their* spontaneous cries") but we are drawn into the scene because they hover about and upon "*our* mountains"; the quail whistle their sounds "about *us*" (emphasis added). Indeed, "walk," "Whistle," "cries," and "Sweet" are all appropriate to human action and sensation. In the plenty of life is the "Ambiguous" presence of imminent death into which human life is included. But for the poem's last three words, its ending would attain a climactic somberness. "[Ŏ]n ĕxténdĕd wíngs" returns us ever so briefly, however, to the rise of the iamb, just as the vowel sounds of the stressed syllables rise in pitch in opposition to the emphatic lowering in pitch of "Dównwărd" and "dárknĕss."[1] The extended wings are themselves ballasted, if only momentarily, against the sinking downward of the birds' flight, mitigating the poem's stern finale in a brief, final respite. The poem's last line is an especially useful classroom exercise to demonstrate the role of intonation in poetry.

In following the development of Stevens's prosody after *Harmonium,* students will discover a familiar base—the blank verse line of "Sunday Morning." Donald Justice has noted of Stevens's metrical evolution that it seems to have grown directly out of his own experiments with the blank verse line: "Pound, early in his career, working from the common iambic toward looser rhythms, took his descent in part from Browning . . . , and

Eliot from the minor Elizabethan and Jacobean dramatists, as he himself suggested; but the later Stevens, following along the same path of loosening the common iambic, seems to descend from no one so much as from the younger Stevens himself" (65). As early as 1921, two years before *Harmonium,* Stevens in a letter to Ferdinand Reyher set forth an account of his prosodic goals that demonstrates for students the importance he placed on aesthetic theory: "The fact is that notwithstanding the large amount of poetry that is written over here at the moment there is practically no aesthetic theory back of it. Why do you scorn free verse? Isn't it the only kind of verse now being written which has any aesthetic impulse back of it? Of course, there are miles and miles of it that do not come off. People don't understand the emotional purpose of rhythm any more than they understand the emotional purpose of measure. I am not exclusively for free verse. But I am for it" ("Letters to Ferdinand Reyher" 390). By free verse, Stevens may have been thinking of a poem like "Depression before Spring" and justifying his own right to abandon regular verse. I think it is equally likely, however, that he had begun to discover the range of new freedoms *within* traditional forms—freedom from the metronome. It was the "emotional purpose of rhythm" that was more important than counting stresses. Neither was he "exclusively" for free verse. Paramount for him was the "aesthetic impulse back of it." In 1921, however, he was only beginning to see how his own poetry might fully embrace such pliability without confining himself to the exercises of free verse and imagism. ("Not all objects are equal. The vice of imagism was that it did not recognize this" [*OP* 187].)

Stevens's own growth as a poet would require more than the reductions of the dimeter or trimeter line. The conduits between self and world, imagination and reality, required a wider field of play. Stevens must have seen that poems like "The Snow Man," "The Paltry Nude Starts on a Spring Voyage," "Anecdote of the Jar," "Infanta Marina," and dozens of others (including "Depression before Spring") could be rewritten in a mode different from the minimal compression of image and form. This, of course, is precisely what he set out to do, as can be demonstrated in having students compare *Harmonium* poems with poems of the thirties. The versatility of the heroic line became increasingly apparent in subsequent poems like "Autumn Refrain" (1932), "The Idea of Order at Key West" (1934), and "Owl's Clover" (beginning in 1935). The tetrameter of "The Man with the Blue Guitar" in the late 1930s, with its thirty-three cantos, must have convinced him that meter, too, was subject to all sorts of inventiveness:

> Tom-tom, c'est moi. The blue guitar
> And I are one. The orchestra
>
> Fills the high hall with shuffling men
> High as the hall. The whirling noise
>
> Of a multitude dwindles, all said,
> To his breath that lies awake at night. (*CP* 171)

After "The Man with the Blue Guitar," students will see clearly that the prophetic mode predominated. Poetry eavesdropped on thought—not as stream of consciousness or dreamlike surrealism—but as self-conscious interior discourse put to a rhythm successfully freed of set stresses and syllables per line. At the same time, the roomy lassitude that the blank verse lines of "Sunday Morning" had provided now became the paradigm on which such freedom could evolve. These lines from "Credences of Summer" (*CP* 372) show the direction of that evolution:

> It is the nátural tówer of áll the wórld,
> The póint of súrvey, gréen's gréen ápogee,
> But a tówer more précious than the víew beyónd,
> A póint of súrvey squátting like a thróne,
> Áxis of éverything, gréen's ápogee. . . .

The rhythm of Stevens's later verse is everywhere influenced by his pattern of appositional elaboration, the penchant to redefine, refine, and refashion. Ideas unfold in a fluidity like the waves of the sea, each like its predecessor but subtly different. Syntax and rhythm necessarily expand in an unfolding that seems to have no set limitation or end. In the lines above, apposition is reinforced by repetition, and this is not uncommon in Stevens. Because of the prevalence of appositional thought in Stevens, it is useful to invite the class to plot the progress of apposition from an example like the lines above. How, one might pose, is the *It* (line 1 above) defined within these five lines? The word is united by copula with *tower,* the principal noun-source of the sequence. *Tower,* in turn, becomes, *point, apogee, tower* (repeated), *point* (repeated), *axis, apogee* (repeated), and, by simile, *like a throne.*

"Credences of Summer" is also useful in demonstrating Stevens's variations on traditional meters that students pick up most readily. The fourth line quoted above sets the cadence to five stresses with regular iambs, but the sequence pulls toward a tetrameter, as I have indicated in the scansion. The pentameter boldly asserts itself in the second line, concluding with the rare molossos (´ ´ ´) of "gréen's gréen ápogee." Vocalic rhyme in these three words and the balance between "survey" and "apogee" on each side of the caesura heighten the line's climactic sense. Three lines later, the line is rewritten where "survey" becomes "every" (from "everything") and "green's apogee" is restated following the same caesura. The fifth line, however, is set to the steadily falling rhythm of dactyls ("Áxis of éverything, gréen's ápogee"). I have found that students are keenly interested in hearing a recording of the poet's own reading. "Credences of Summer" is available on the Caedmon tape of Stevens's reading. Here we can hear the poet's own choice of stress. The first line might have a stress on the first syllable ("It"), but I have interpreted it as Stevens reads the line. The first three syllables, unstressed, of the first line then balance with the three syllables, stressed, toward the end of the second. Students can appreciate here the great range of versatility with which Stevens has now adopted an accentual verse rooted in the heroic line to the fluidity of appositional discourse. The iambic pentameter is merely a point of departure, and the iamb itself as a defining pattern is all but lost. As Justice says, "From about the midpoint of Stevens' career on, practically any trisyllabic substitution imaginable can be found" (69). As I suggest, even an occasional quadruple foot ("Ĭt ĭs thĕ nátural . . .") occurs.

It was only by thoroughly mastering the iambic pentameter line (quite fortunately, for teaching Stevens's prosody, the line most familiar to college students) that Stevens found its hidden resources for a poetry that sought to reproduce "the rapidity of thought" (L 319). At the end of his life Stevens told Edwin Honig, "Now I never worried about the line. I've always been interested in the whole thing, the whole poem" (12). By then, I think that Stevens meant he had no need to count syllables or stresses. The rhythm had become as natural to him as thought itself. Many poems were written as he walked the two-mile route in Hartford between his home on Westerly Terrace and the office. "Walking helps me to concentrate," he told a correspondent, "and I suppose that, somehow or other, my own movement gets into the movement of the poems" (L 844). Harvey Gross, Donald Justice, and Dennis Taylor are correct when they note Stevens's unique contribution to the prosody of modernism by extending the heroic line toward accentual verse, and perhaps even free verse (Taylor 209). But Stevens never went as far as Whitman or H.D., as students can see in comparing poems by the three. The difference lies in Stevens's retention of the *framework* of blank verse, however skeletal the remnant: "My line is a pentameter line," he said in 1942, "but it runs over and under now and then" (L 407). For a mind and temperament that liked the extension of ideas, the elasticity of thought, the modes of repetition (nuances, thirteen ways, decorations, variations, extracts, two versions, two illustrations, prologues, etc.), cadences relaxed and indeterminate inevitably prevailed.

II

One is always writing about two things at the same time in poetry and it is this that produces the tension characteristic of poetry. One is the true subject and the other is the poetry of the subject. The difficulty of sticking to the true subject, when it is the poetry of the subject that is paramount in one's mind, need only be mentioned to be understood. (OP 227)

The "poetry of the subject" and its subversive influence upon the poet's "true subject" engages to some extent the hand of every poet. For Stevens such rewritings in prosody were especially "paramount," and the task of leading students to hear Stevens's poems as patterns of sound and to focus on his gaudy language is made easier once they recognize the emphasis that Stevens placed on sound and diction as elements of the poem more engaging than mere "meaning." He put the issue this way in one of his "Adagia": "There are two opposites: the poetry of rhetoric and the poetry of experience" (*OP* 187). In the poems of *Harmonium,* he told Ronald Lane Latimer, a kind of "pure poetry" had made a strong claim upon him: "I liked the idea of images and images alone, or images and the music of verse together. I then believed in *pure poetry,* as it was called" (*L* 288). Four years later, in another letter, he revealed that he had not abandoned that preference: "I am, in the long run, interested in pure poetry. No doubt from the Marxian point of view this sort of thing is incredible, but pure poetry is rather older and tougher than Marx and will remain so" (*L* 340). In spite of these acknowledgments, Stevens never practiced *la poésie pure* in its absolute sense, even in *Harmonium,* but his pleasure in the sounds of language, what he called the "sensuous reality" of poetry (Lensing, "Wallace Stevens and Stevens T. Mason" 35), never took a secondary importance, a point that many students who seem to share these values in their devotion to popular music should appreciate. Stevens preferred, among his own poems, "The Emperor of Ice-Cream" because of its "essential gaudiness" (*L* 263). "Gubbinal," he told another correspondent, was "purely stylistic" (*L* 287). He described "The Curtains in the House of the Metaphysician" as "a poem of long open sounds" (*L* 463). The "sole purpose" of "Domination of Black" was "to fill the mind with the images & sounds that it contains" (*L* 251). Bernard Heringman remembers Stevens's remark that in writing "Peter Quince at the Clavier" "he was thinking in terms of musical movements—sort of libretto" (Brazeau 200). "The Comedian as the Letter C," Stevens later explained, consisted of the "sounds of the letter C" and "all related or derivative sounds" that accompany Crispin as he "moves through the poem" (*L* 351). In an interview at the end of his life, Stevens summarized his work: "Communication is more a showing of the pleasure which the poet felt when he wrote his line than an understanding of the sense he was intending" (Culbertson 11–12). It is reassuring to students as readers to learn that for Stevens himself the way a poem sounded was at least as important as what it meant. To read with the ear as much as the eye is an essential act of interpretation.

Robert Frost spoke more than once of the need to train the ear to the sound of music in poetry, recommending that "the best place to get the abstract sound of sense is from voices behind a door that cuts off the words" (*Letters* 80). In a poem like "Depression before Spring," the competition in sounds between the cock's "ki-ki-ri-ki" and the absent dove's "rou-cou-cou" is just such an exhibition, while, in a different way, the drop and rise in pitch in the vowels at the end of "Sunday Morning" replay another competition between descent to death and ascent to life, as students have little difficulty in seeing. Roland Barthes refers to the sensuous reality of all texts: "Due allowance being made for the sounds of the language, *writing aloud* is not phonological but phonetic; its aim is not the clarity of messages, the theater of emotions; what it searches for (in a perspective of bliss) are the pulsional incidents, the language lined with flesh, a text where we can hear the grain of the throat, the patina of consonants, the voluptuousness of vowels, a whole carnal stereophony: the articulation of the body, of the tongue, not that of meaning, of language" (66-67).

Of course, Stevens's diction is sometimes difficult, and it is helpful for students to understand that much of its difficulty can be traced to its *provisional* nature, its attempts to articulate a world in motion, where no description is definitive. The range of Stevens's lexicon, from rabbinical formality to colloquial slang, from Latinate self-consciousness to native (Germanic) idioms and clichés, creates a surface tone in his poetry where diction constantly highlights itself. Students must be frequently reminded that the diction of Stevens's poetry goes in pursuit of "an always incipient cosmos," while the poet-speaker necessarily remains a thinker "without final thoughts" (*OP* 140). He is also an utterer without final words, but for whom there is nothing else: "It is a world of words to the end of it, / In which nothing solid is its solid self" (*CP* 345). The effusion of language within a poem is a relentless quest of a world in constant flux. On the one hand, "Poetry / Exceeding music must take the place / Of empty heaven and its hymns," but so lofty an aim may be realized "Even in the chattering of your guitar" (*CP* 167). The poet "mumbles" (*CP* 443), even as he speaks "the poet's hum" (*OP* 101). At times, he is more successful, but modestly so: "A few words of what is real or may be / Or of glistening reference to what is real" (*CP* 309). More triumphantly, "the characters [both poets and their alphabets of language] speak because they want / To speak, the fat, the roseate characters, / Free, for a moment, from malice and sudden cry, / Complete in a completed scene" (*CP* 378). Stevens's diction is one of constant gradations, every utterance a fresh assault upon the real, every articulation at once obsolete and in need of immediate re-statement. The world itself passes in a kind of appositional succession. Even when most successful, such capturings in language are only "for a moment."

The same principle of apposition that students will have seen in Stevens's development of the heroic line applies to his choice of diction as well. The succession of words and phrases in lengthened apposition often accompanies a heightening intensity building toward a climactic stop:

> Desiring the exhilarations of changes:
> The motive for metaphor, shrinking from
> The weight of primary noon,
> The A B C of being,
>
> The ruddy temper, the hammer
> Of red and blue, the hard sound—
> Steel against intimation—the sharp flash,
> The vital, arrogant, fatal, dominant X.

The "weight of primary noon" is the finality of pure being from which metaphor shrinks and makes evasions in this conclusion to "The Motive for Metaphor" (*CP* 288). "[P]rimary noon" is itself a metaphor that is recast in a succession of appositives. Once again, the class can be invited to identify them: "ABC of being," "ruddy temper," "hammer," "hard sound," "sharp flash," and, finally, "X." Because each of these designations is a word of Germanic origin (or a minimal character of the alphabet), the poem here becomes a valuable exercise in introducing to the class a brief insight into the history of the language: the contrast in English between native Germanic words and the later, borrowed Latinate ones. In a poem like "The Motive for Metaphor" Stevens constructs the poem upon the contrast and conflict between these two lexical traditions. In this case, the starkness of "primary noon" is redefined in the hard sounds of Anglo-Saxon nominals. The sound-drama is played out succinctly as "hard sound," and such sound is itself identified as "Steel against intimation": the Latinate "intimation" is literally resisted by the *stele* of Old English. Only in the final line is the "X" itself identified by a succession of four Latinate adjectives: "vital, arrogant, fatal, dominant," as if, in the end, the "noon" of being cannot be denied or shrunk from but submitted to as a powerful, commanding force, both living and deadly. The final irony remains that being ("primary noon"), from which metaphor is said to shrink, is itself and in its appositives presented as a succession of metaphors, a truth that Stevens's breathless crowding of phrases in apposition almost camouflages.

To appreciate Stevens's mastery of sound and language at the end of his career, students may be introduced to "Long and Sluggish Lines" (*CP* 522), a late poem (1952) told from the perspective of a poet "so much more / Than seventy." The title connects the sluggishness of the lines to the debility of the aging poet, and so the first two couplets recount the monotony of the wood-smoke rising through the trees: "But it has been often so." The trees themselves emit a squalor in their own repetitiveness. Suddenly, however, they give way to "an opposite, a contradiction," as the aging poet reawakens to life:

The trees have a look as if they bore sad names	5
And kept saying over and over one same, same thing,	6
In a kind of uproar, because an opposite, a contradiction,	7
Has enraged them and made them want to talk it down.	8
What opposite? Could it be that yellow patch, the side	9
Of a house, that makes one think the house is laughing;	10
Or these—escent—issant pre-personae: first fly,	11
A comic infanta among the tragic drapings,	12
Babyishness of forsythia, a snatch of belief,	13
The spook and makings of the nude magnolia?	14

These middle five couplets set up for Stevens a competition of sounds and words as "wakefulness" makes combat with sluggishness and newly found youth with age, and it is useful for students to locate the oppositions in both words and sounds.

The first two couplets of the poem (not quoted above) are perfectly rhymed (*more/before, flow/so*), appropriate to a pattern of endless repetition ("it has been often so"). Line 6, the one that is, in a sense, the longest and most sluggish, is a congeries of rhymes: "And kept saying over and over one same, same thing" (*And/and, over/over; say/same/same; -ing/-thing*). The reader, too, almost nods. Even so, a subtle "contradiction" is already happening: the final words of each line of the couplet (lines 5 and 6) are no longer perfect rhymes (*names/thing*) and in all the succeeding couplets such rhyming is abandoned in the face of the poet's obtruding "opposite."

The trees, in fact, are not swaying in dreary and droning repetition but are "enraged" in an "uproar" of resistance to the as yet unidentified "opposite" and "contradiction." It should be pointed out that internal rhymes linger ("uproar" in line 7 echoes "bore" in line 5) and recur (in "enraged them and made them want to talk it down"). Students may come to see that the "talking" of the trees in long and sluggish lines is the talking of the poem itself, and the talking down lowers the vocalic pitch from "want" to "talk" to "down." The resistance of the trees to change is a verbal, poetic one.

What exactly is the "opposite," the "contradiction," of lines 7 and 9? This is also an issue that the class can be invited to probe. Through what images is it defined? Students needn't rush to a symbolic interpretation, but rather they can examine closely the words themselves. They will quickly identify the "yellow patch" on the side of the house, giving the house the appearance of a laughing face and canceling the "sad names" from line 5. That patch of light is a mere incipiency of spring, preliminary "escent— issant pre-personae." The Latin suffix *escent* in English denotes a general state of being, as *pubescent* or *adolescent,* for example, defines states of being as kinds of "pre-personae." The French *issant* is a present participial suffix. But the action is not yet captured in a complete word. From these inchoate "pre-personae" Stevens again aligns a succession of appositives: "first fly," "comic infanta," "Babyishness of forsythia," "snatch of belief," "spook and makings of the nude magnolia." The voluptuous sibilants and succession of unstressed syllables in "Babyishness of forsythia" (the flower picks up the color of the patch on the side of the house) are reined in and balanced in the same line by the terse "a snatch of belief." All are fresh "makings," the creations of the contradictory force of spring, youth, and vitality. The word *makings* is itself a translation of the Greek word for poet and poetry, as Stevens was well aware; once again we are reminded of "lines," "names," "saying," and "talk" as reflections of the poem itself. In the face of such beginnings and freshenings, the aging poet is "not born yet," and he indulges a new "wakefulness inside a sleep."

As both "The Motive for Metaphor" and "Long and Sluggish Lines" demonstrate to students by now perhaps attuned to the prosodic virtuosity of his poems, Stevens delighted in the play of sounds between the decorous, sensuous Latinate sounds and the earthier directness of the Anglo-Saxon. Marie Borroff has shrewdly noted some of the exercises of this tendency throughout the poetry:

> Odd verbal combinations were identified . . . as a hallmark of his [Stevens's] style; among these, we can single out one type as especially worthy of note: that in which Latinate (*L*) and sound-symbolic (s–s) words appear side by side. The examples "A syllable (*L*), / Out of these gawky (s–s) flitterings (s–s), / Intones (*L*) its single emptiness"; "addicts (*L*) / To blotches (s–s), angular (*L*) anonymids (*L*), / Gulping (s–s) for shape"; and "the honky-tonk (s–s) out of the somnolent (*L*) grasses" . . . were cited earlier. (*Language and the Poet* 71)

Stevens defines this prosodic pattern himself—referring to "Heavenly labials in a world of gutturals" in "The Plot against the Giant" (*CP* 6) or his wish "To compound the imagination's Latin with / The lingua franca et jocundissima" (*CP* 397) in "Notes toward a Supreme Fiction." Without being skilled linguists, students can delight in identifying and playing off labials versus gutturals, imagination's Latin versus lingua franca.

To his Cuban friend José Rodríguez Feo, Stevens once defined his own "frivolity": "All the interest that you feel in occasional frivolities I seem to experience in sounds, and many lines exist because I enjoy their clickety-clack in contrast with the more decorous pom-pom-pom that people expect" (*L* 485). Students, like all readers and like the poet himself, should participate in the carnival of the poem, the entertainment of rhythm and sound. At the conclusion of his essay "The Noble Rider and the Sound of Words," Stevens refers to the imagination as a "violence from within," not unlike the "rage to order words" in "The Idea of Order at Key West" (*CP* 128). Such violence and rage are necessary, he argues; such words "have something to do with our self-preservation; and that, no doubt, is why the expression of it, the *sound of its words,* helps us to live our lives" (*NA* 36; emphasis added). The expressiveness of language, its being heard as well as seen, almost the tactility of its surfaces, delighted Stevens all his life and defined him as a poet, and students who are deaf to Stevens's prosodic effects have missed something essential to his art. The fund of language and the cadences into which it was cast were for him inexhaustible, never to be hoarded but spent at once, "Engaged in the most prolific narrative, / A sound producing the things that are spoken" (*CP* 287).

Note

1. For this observation, I am indebted to Karen Helgeson.

Teaching Stevens's Poetry
through Rhetorical Structure

P. MICHAEL CAMPBELL AND JOHN DOLAN

One of the problems in teaching Stevens's poetry is that teachers tend to focus on the poetry's philosophical content—"what Stevens is saying"—at the expense of its poetics—the manner in which Stevens "says" what he does. A teacher's attempt to provide students with an adequate grasp of the philosophical content of Stevens's poems often devolves into a time-consuming and unproductive remedial course in twentieth-century theories of perception, at the end of which students may be capable of discussing such theories, but are often not especially proficient readers of poetry.

We have discovered, in the course of several years of teaching Stevens's work to students at many levels, that focusing on the dominant rhetorical structures of Stevens's lyrics provides an effective alternative to paraphrasing philosophical content. Requiring students to uncover the rhetorical structure rather than the "meaning" of the poem lessens the students' tendency to paraphrase and speculate, and requires instead that they read the poetry closely, attending to its strategy and design. Such close reading results in a quick, effectual entry into even the most complex of Stevens's poems. In addition, demonstrating the importance of basic argumentative structures to Stevens's work reassures students that poetry is not the occult realm they fear, but a discourse constructed, to a large degree, on familiar argumentative structures.

Stevens's work is especially suited to such an approach because, despite his stunning verbal invention, Stevens's repertoire of basic rhetorical structures is fairly limited. In fact, the structure on which we will focus in this paper recurs in hundreds of Stevens's poems. This structure, perhaps the most basic and illuminating of all Stevens's models, is the one we have chosen to call "praeteritic antithesis." Antithesis has usually been defined as a rhetorical move in which a thing or concept is defined by negation—that is, divided in two, with one part elevated and the other denigrated, e.g., "Not life but death." A praeteritic antithesis would be one in which the ostensibly denigrated or rejected term becomes dominant. We take *praeteritic* from the trope *praeteritio,* traditionally defined as the device of talking about something in the process of promising not to talk about it (the most commonly used example is the politician's promise "not to cheapen the campaign by mentioning my opponent's felony convictions"). A praeteritic antithesis, then, differs from a typical antithesis in that "the rejected thing, the thing denied" (to borrow a phrase from Stevens) ends up becoming the focus of attention, with the ostensibly endorsed term fading into the background. Such a device, it may well be imagined, is particularly suited to the depiction of the sort of wistful or embittered ambivalence in which Stevens specialized.

Stevens's poems built around this structural trope are numerous. Since most teachers still focus on *Harmonium* and Stevens's early work in general, we have chosen two early poems, "Disillusionment of Ten O'Clock" and "Gubbinal," to illustrate the trope and the ways in which we would teach it. To demonstrate the pervasiveness and persistence of this basic rhetorical move, however, we close by demonstrating its importance to one of Stevens's last and most touching poems, "A Clear Day and No Memories," written shortly before his death.

"Disillusionment of Ten O'Clock" (*CP* 66), a relatively simple early poem, is a good way to introduce the model of the praeteritic antithesis:

> The houses are haunted
> By white night-gowns.
> None are green,
> Or purple with green rings,
> Or green with yellow rings,
> Or yellow with blue rings.
> None of them are strange,
> With socks of lace
> And beaded ceintures.
> People are not going

To dream of baboons and periwinkles.
Only, here and there, an old sailor,
Drunk and asleep in his boots,
Catches tigers
In red weather.

The poem is very simple, largely composed of a list of colors. These colors are placed within the context of a very clear, simple antithesis between "white"—a bland, flat color—and the bizarre, gaudy combinations that do *not* adorn the inhabitants. This is what is praeteritic about the antithesis—the fact that almost all the lines in the poem are devoted to detailing what is *not*—the colors that are not present. Thus, the antithesis turns in a way very different from most other antitheses; it leaves the reader with a very vivid sense of the *rejected* term. In fact, the reader is left with a sense of regret that the ostensibly positive term of the antithesis, "white," has managed to overpower the much more appealing color combinations that are iterated only to be denied.

Students should be able to grasp this basic antithetical form fairly soon, as long as the instructor insists on focusing closely on the *form* of the poem, rather than letting students speculate fruitlessly (as they will, if permitted to do so) on the possible significance of the color symbolism (e.g., "I think red stands for passion, and blue stands for depression"). Once students have grasped the basic praeteritic/antithetical form that grafts onto the bulk of the poem, the instructor may usefully ask them to consider the effect of the last four lines, in which this antithesis is modified by the "old sailor" who *does,* somehow, manage to create color. Students will eventually grasp that this presence modifies the negative tone of the poem, suggesting that one may, by a powerful imagining, transcend the "white" facts.

"Gubbinal" (*CP* 85), a somewhat later poem, presents the praeteritic/ antithetical strategy in an oblique, polemical form. "Gubbinal" might effectively follow "Disillusionment of Ten O'Clock" in a discussion of this form because, though essentially similar, it is more demanding—in fact, it often strikes students as enigmatic, elliptic, and too arcane to grasp. In our experience, however, "Gubbinal" becomes more transparent, more readily accessible to students, when the underlying rhetorical structure is glimpsed.

That strange flower, the sun,
Is just what you say.
Have it your way.

The world is ugly,
And the people are sad.

That tuft of jungle feathers,
That animal eye,
Is just what you say.

That savage of fire,
That seed,
Have it your way.

The world is ugly,
And the people are sad. (Emphasis added)

The key to getting students to grasp this poem, which often strikes them as utterly obscure at first reading, is to ask them to imagine the *argumentative context* in which it occurs—or, more graphically, to ask them to imagine first the tone of voice in which it is spoken, the emotional state of the speaker, and so on—that is, the rhetorical situation in which Stevens has located it. The key, repeated phrase "Have it your way" often provides the beginning of such an understanding. We ask students to categorize the contexts in which this phrase may be used in American English conversation. They soon realize, by class consensus, that this is a phrase with an extremely specific context—it can be spoken only by someone who is petulantly abandoning an argument without conceding defeat. Since the phrase is used to describe someone's view of the sun, the students soon realize that the central antithesis in the poem must be between two competing ways of perceiving the sun. The only oddity is that the view of the other, yet triumphant, speaker is *unheard*. Yet, by understanding the rhetorical structure—the antithesis between views of the sun—we can easily reconstruct this opposing view. We can do this by looking at the praeteritic, defeated view of the speaker (the italicized lines in the poem cited above). These lines stand out as highly metaphorical and eloquent ("That tuft of jungle feathers, / That animal eye"), praeteritically arguing for a sacramental, prescientific view of the sun.

And so the structure of the poem begins to emerge, since students sensitized to the argument implied in the poem can easily discern the pattern whereby these mystical, metaphorical lines are followed by a sullen concession, first the sarcastic ". . . is just what you say" and then the telltale idiom "Have it your way." And, in an argumentative sequence that will seem familiar to most students, these concessions are in turn followed by an angry focus on the consequences of the "other," nonmystical view of the sun: "The world is ugly / And the people are sad."

Seen thus, as the relic of an argument, the poem, in our experience, will suddenly become not merely comprehensible but enjoyable for most students, who can now *hear* the lines—the sad implications of the praeteritic "tuft of jungle feathers," the petulant contempt of "Have it your way," and the bitter resignation of the repeated conclusion, "The world is ugly / And the people are sad." Students who have once grasped the rhetorical structure and situation implied in "Gubbinal" quickly gain mastery of the fairly subtle aspects of its poetics; for example, once the basic rhetorical structure is clear, we usually ask students to see if there is any division within the diction of the poem. They invariably recognize that there is a sharp antithesis in diction, following the argumentative antithesis, between the "poetic" metaphors of the praeteritic lines and the determinedly flat, low diction of the "realistic" view, which reaches its comic extreme in the concluding couplet.

This diction can give students the clue necessary to reconstruct the "missing" term in the antithesis—the term that opposes the mystical view of the sun, and that has extracted the grudging capitulation of the speaker. The low, flat, "realistic" diction, the sharp antithesis to the mystical view— all this leads students to the realization that the "missing" voice must be that of a "realistic," nonmystical view of the sun. The praeteritic twist Stevens gives this antithesis—the way the "losing" term, the sacramental, primitive reverence the speaker would like to be able to feel for the sun— wins by losing—that is, the victory of the "realistic" term leads clearly to the consequence that "the world is ugly / And the people are sad."

This way of introducing students to Stevens's view of the sun—which is, after all, a central term for most of his poems—seems to us much more effective than the traditional lecture/paraphrase of the intellectual debts of "Sunday Morning." Indeed, we generally introduce Stevens via a poem like "Gubbinal," and only after students have mastered its rhetorical structure do we ask them to read a longer poem like "Sunday Morning." After deciphering "Gubbinal," many students find "Sunday Morning" and other such works easier to read, and need not be guided through them line by line by the instructor.

Perhaps, in fact, we should consider whether the "content" of any Stevens poem may be effectually taught without the inclusion of the rhetorical structures in which this "content" is couched. In the case of "Gubbinal," paraphrase *must,* it seems to us, include mention of the praeteritic antithesis. Stevens is not "saying," in "Gubbinal," that we should embrace a mystical, rather than a scientific, view of the sun; rather he *dramatizes* the moment in which a defeated holder of such a view concedes loss. The difference is a vital one, and one that can lead students back toward a love of poetry, by showing them that Stevens's works are not just purposely muddled *essays* but rather highly dramatic soliloquies in which a divided and eloquent mind makes difficult decisions.

The dramatization of such moments is in fact the reason for the prevalence of praeteritic antitheses in Stevens's work. Stevens's middle period, the era of *Parts of a World,* which Stevens himself considered his best work, abounds in poems based on this rhetorical structure. A poem that provides an excellent introduction to the period is "Dezembrum," a textbook example that is unfortunately not included in *The Palm at the End of the Mind* but can be found in the *Collected Poems.* For a better-known example, consider using the opening quatrain of "Study of Two Pears" (*CP* 196), which includes some interesting variations on the basic rhetorical effect of the praeteritic antithesis:

> Opusculum paedagogum.
> The pears are not viols,
> Nudes or bottles.
> They resemble nothing else.

This quatrain comprises a praeteritic antithesis. The antithesis makes a division, which at first seems clear and sharp, between perception that is objective and clear (cf. "The Snow Man," "The Poems of Our Climate," and "Dezembrum") and the subjective, associational descriptions that influence traditional descriptive forms (in this case, the genre of painting called "still life"). Students will discern this basic antithesis quickly enough, once they have been introduced to the praeteritic structure; the point is to get them to notice the changes Stevens puts this basic antithesis through in the course of six quatrains. First, he says that the pears are *not* "viols, / Nudes or bottles." Ask your students why Stevens would even bother to say this; if it's not the case, why mention it? Ask them how a pear *might* resemble "viols, / Nudes or bottles," and they will soon realize the basic similarity in shape. Then ask them the effect on the reader of mentioning such a similarity *only to deny it*. They will soon realize that, as in the experiment in which a subject is told, *"Don't* think about a red horse," the effect is to cause the reader to think of exactly those similarities that have ostensibly been denied. The *praeteritic* term—the term being ostensibly denied, refuted—comes through after all. This is the effect of the entire poem as a whole, as well as most of its component quatrains. And, as often in Stevens when the praeteritic term wins out, the poem ends in a statement of defeat: "The pears are not seen / As the observer wills." The praeteritic, associative terms overpower the clear, hard perception desired by the speaker, just as they do in "The Poems of Our Climate" (*CP* 193), a poem of the same period. It is useful, in fact, to go from a case study in perception like "Study of Two Pears," to "The Poems of Our Climate," which makes the point in more general, abstract terms:

> Say even that this complete simplicity
> Stripped one of all one's torments, concealed
> The evilly compounded, vital I . . .
> Still one would want more, one would need more. . . .

From this poem, a sort of manifesto of the praeteritic-antithetical view of the world, one might go on to poems that make a similar point: "Dezembrum" (*CP* 218), which ends, "The reason can give nothing at all / Like the response to desire," or "The Well-Dressed Man with a Beard" (*CP* 247), which concludes, "It can never be satisfied, the mind, never."

Perhaps the purest example of the praeteritic-antithetical form in all of

Stevens's work occurs in the very late poem "A Clear Day and No Memories" (*OP* 138). Here the essential pathos of the form is developed in a deeply touching manner:

> No soldiers in the scenery,
> No thoughts of people now dead,
> As they were fifty years ago:
> Young and living in a live air,
> Young and walking in the sunshine,
> Bending in blue dresses to touch something—
> Today the mind is not part of the weather.
>
> Today the air is clear of everything.
> It has no knowledge except of nothingness
> And it flows over us without meanings,
> As if none of us had ever been here before
> And are not now: in this shallow spectacle,
> This invisible activity, this sense.

Here, in deeply moving form, Stevens presents a tour de force for the praeteritio. The entire first stanza discusses *what is not*—the aged speaker bravely tries to deny his memories, just as the speaker of "Study of Two Pears" tries to deny the inevitable associative processes of his mind. And, as always in Stevens, what is denied wins out. The denied memories come flooding in—to the reader's as well as the speaker's mind. The second stanza then takes the praeteritic-antithetical form one step further by denying *everything*—denying even that the speaker exists. Since emotion is so clearly driving the praeteritic form here, the instructor can simply ask students *why* the speaker tries to deny all the warm memories he mentions in the first stanza. This stanza's praeteritic denials are so poignant that students, especially those who have already been exposed to earlier versions like "Disillusionment" or "Gubbinal," will readily grasp that the memories are too painful for the speaker to bear; thus, the attempt to deny them.

We have concentrated here on Stevens's use of a particular trope, what we are calling the praeteritic antithesis. We do not, however, mean to suggest that this is the only rhetorical move that Stevens makes (or that it is the only trope worth considering when teaching Stevens's poetry). On the contrary, we have found Stevens's poems to be virtual training seminars on the effective use of forms and figures, and we regularly assign a rhetorical handbook to help students pick out the various figures Stevens employs. (Arthur Quinn's brief but eloquent *Figures of Speech* has, in this regard, worked well for us over the years.) By closely reading Stevens's poems and identifying his rhetorical strategies, students not only learn to read Stevens better but also become adept at recognizing the various tropes employed by other writers.

We could easily compile an article similar to this one considering Stevens's use of various forms of repetition, or his use of expeditio, or gradatio, or correctio. For example, Stevens's use of expeditio (a trope in which a number of alternatives are considered and usually rejected in favor of a particular counteralternative) resembles in many ways his use of the praeteritic antithesis. In class, we often consider poems such as "On the Road Home" and "Metaphors of a Magnifico," which test three "failed" logical propositions against a landscape. In "Metaphors of a Magnifico" (*CP* 19), for instance, Stevens opens with what sounds at first like a logical proposition: "Twenty men crossing a bridge, / Into a village, / Are twenty men crossing twenty bridges, / Into twenty villages." However, such a proposition "will not declare itself" (it involves too many terms and finally contradicts itself) and is rejected, ostensibly for a more carefully worded counterproposition: "Twenty men crossing a bridge, / Into a village, / Are / Twenty men crossing a bridge / Into a village." This proposition, however, involves too few terms and is finally a tautology that must also be rejected on logical grounds. A third proposition is considered, but it is of a very different sort, stated in a much different diction and tone: "The boots of the men clump / On the boards of the bridge. / The first white wall of the village / Rises through fruit-trees." With the introduction of the "fruit-trees," the speaker of the poem seems to lose his place ("Of what was it I was thinking?") and the meaning again escapes; the introduction of a less rigid, more subjective perspective, while perhaps more aesthetically pleasing, leads inevitably to a flood of sensory perceptions and a loss of the original subject and hypothesis.

As with the praeteritic antithesis, we ask students to consider why Stevens has chosen to record three "failed" attempts at describing a particular instance and why he offers no "solution" or counterproposal. They usually conclude that the three attempts are presented for much the same reason that the rejected side of the antithesis is considered in other Stevens poems: because he is trying to depict dramatically the process of considering the unconsiderable, of speaking the unspeakable.

Stevens makes similar use of correctio (the self-correction trope) in a number of poetic meditations (for instance, in the all-equating statement/restatement form of "The House Was Quiet and the World Was Calm") and of gradatio (the step or gradation trope) in poems such as "The Well Dressed Man with a Beard" and "The Latest Freed Man," where the imagination rises (depicted usually in a sort of rising diction) only to trip finally on reality and tumble back to earth. It is in the depiction of these attempts to rise above day-to-day experience that Stevens finds poetry "The poem of the mind in the act of finding / What will suffice" (*CP* 239).

And this, finally, is what we believe an emphasis on rhetorical form brings to the study of Stevens's poems. This approach, by getting students to focus on the poetics of the work, the strategic decisions Stevens makes in constructing his poems, clearly demonstrates that Stevens is not a writer of blurred philosophical essays but a dramatic poet of the first rank—a poet whose specialty is the dramatization of the moment in which a mind in flux chooses between equally painful, demanding modes of perception.

Wallace Stevens in the Classroom: "More Truly and More Strange"

ALISON RIEKE

As teachers of literature, we are fortunate that Wallace Stevens "Found his vicissitudes had much enlarged / His apprehension, made him intricate / In moody rucks, and difficult and strange / In all desires . . ." (*CP* 31). This complex, powerful, and sustaining poet constructs language that, at its most intricate and expansive, embodies the whole world of words. His approach to language and his play with the conventional boundaries of expression had to be inclusive, not exclusive, if he were to invent a poetics that could accommodate his desire for "supreme fictions." Out of this very expansiveness, the remote and strange figure of Hoon (who?) in his "Palaz" describes poetic utterance: "Out of my mind the golden ointment rained," for "I was myself the compass of that sea: / I was the world in which I walked . . . / And there I found myself more truly and more strange" (*CP* 65). Hoon's mind sounds suspiciously like that of Stevens himself, and indeed Stevens's canon is hardly ever a house "haunted / By white night-gowns" in which "None of them are strange." His habit, from *Harmonium* forward, is to combine "socks of lace" with "baboons and periwinkles" (*CP* 66).

With his wide range of tones and moods, disruptions of verbal logic, surprising conjunctions of abstraction and concretion, enigmatic wordplay, resistance to closure, among other deviations from straightforward speech, Stevens's verbal complications are notably myriad. Marie Borroff shows us, for example, that Stevens uses radically "different qualities of style," from "discursive, difficult language," to "solemn simplicity," to "elevated rhetoric," to "eccentricities," to "colloquial phrasing" (*Language and the Poet* 42–43). Readers know all too well that these features are troublesome to sort out and describe—much less to integrate and organize in the activity of making meaning. While his gamut of poetic surprises may delight scholars and devoted readers, these same eccentricities, as my experience has borne out, do not always fascinate under-graduate students. Certainly Stevens's quirkiness makes him one of the tough-est poets of the twentieth century to teach in college classrooms.

Taking his canon as a whole, we still have not adequately come to terms with his puzzling verbal boundaries; finding and agreeing on Stevens's range, and on a poetic theory that would settle opposing views of his work, has been problematic (Leggett, *Wallace Stevens and Poetic Theory* 1-4). Of course, Stevens does not exercise his "intricate" and "expansive" range in every poem. Nevertheless, we characterize Stevens by his richness, not his leanness, and we remember him most for his ability to mix diction and modes of discourse in uncanny combinations. "Three Academic Pieces," an exercise pertinent to academics, expresses his own inclusiveness and ec-centricity as a "habit of the truth" in which

> The scholar, captious, told him what he could
> Of there, where the truth was not the respect of one,
> But always of many things. He had not to be told
>
> Of the incredible subjects of poetry.
> He was willing they should remain incredible,
> Because the incredible, also, has its truth. . . . (*NA* 85)

Stevens's mind is "captious," intentionally perplexing, bent on entrapping and confusing the reader. His drive toward strange verbal inclusion, or, alternately, his rejection of conventional utterance that would identify him with one tradition or limit him poetically, is forcefully expressed in his vast linguistic variety. Yet some forty years after his *Collected Poems* appeared in 1954, we continue to limit Stevens's range in order to present an academic version of his achievement.

If we are to do justice to Stevens's poetry in the classroom, we must, I think, capture something of his eccentricity, represent him as he is when in an "enlarged" and "captious" frame of mind. As teachers we might be tempted to introduce Stevens to undergraduates—in courses on twenti-eth-century poetry and surveys of American literature—by sidestepping his most conceptually obscure verse. I would guess that, like me, teachers who faithfully cover Stevens rarely assign poems as verbally "enlarged" as "The Comedian as the Letter C." Even the ever-anthologized but unyielding

"Emperor of Ice-Cream" is a piece I slide around, except to illustrate that Stevens's uses of language are so strange that they resist intelligent explication with almost complete success. The exquisite, abstract music of "The Idea of Order at Key West" (*CP* 128)—also routinely anthologized—is equally difficult to convey to students lacking familiarity with Stevens's sophisticated uses of poetic language. This poem's setting and speaking subject are available for paraphrase (Ramon and I heard a woman singing by the sea; we listened; then we turned back toward town), but its subject, theme, and meaning must be articulated as song representing sound and then as song about poetic speech. Its "ghostlier demarcations, keener sounds" are poetically "true" but incredibly tricky to talk about. Yet we also perpetuate an overly simplified view of Stevens's range by continuing to assign "The Snow Man" (*CP* 9) as an autonomous lyric. As an early version of a poem he kept rewriting with increased obscurity and lack of closure, it introduces a subject the poet turned to repeatedly while in his "mind of winter." An almost straightforward representation of regional realism and a neat exercise in paradox, "The Snow Man" perhaps goes down *too* easily with students. With its wintery New England landscape, "The Snow Man" even invites comparison with the one American poet who always seems to satisfy them, Robert Frost.

Since much of his best and most characteristic poetry is baffling and opaque, teachers need to develop strategies for helping students grapple with the mysteriousness at the heart of Stevens's poetic achievement. We must carefully evaluate and even overhaul our traditional methods of pedagogy if we are to present Stevens as he is, "more truly and more strange." Frank Lentricchia's introduction to *Ariel and the Police* offers a useful and provocative discussion of "Anecdote of the Jar" which can help us with this evaluation (3-27). His remarks amply demonstrate that even the apparently teachable short lyrics in Stevens's canon have the notorious habit of breaking down under close scrutiny and formal analysis.

In his examination of "Anecdote of the Jar," Lentricchia points out that this devilish little poem forces readers "at the outset into confronting the inadequacy of the modernist literary theory of aesthetic autonomy" (6). He also reminds us that "The American New Criticism . . . remains in force as the basis (what goes without saying) of undergraduate literary pedagogy" (6). No doubt, our version of Stevens for the classroom lags too far behind our understanding of his work. It is perhaps tempting to allow the now "old-fashioned" New Critical interpretative practices to dominate our approaches to Stevens: New Criticism facilitates pedagogy, especially when poets are difficult. Teachers continue to feel satisfied when students successfully extract brilliance from small packages of words. Not surprisingly, then, the long, wandering, indeterminacies of "Notes toward a Supreme Fiction," "Credences of Summer," and "An Ordinary Evening in New Haven" are virtually impossible to teach in the undergraduate setting. Some of Stevens's short lyrics are quite teachable, especially those that develop around a consistent metaphor, wrap up with a neat paradox, or achieve some kind of recognizable and conventional poetic closure. Yet how many of Stevens's poems, long or short, rise up as "well-wrought urn[s]"? More typically they are "The rudiments in the jar, farced, finikin, / . . . flatly there, unversed except to be, / Made difficult . . . intricate" (*CP* 452).

When Stevens works at the limits of his verbal motley, he can be exceedingly remote and impersonal, much more so than the average poet in the lyric tradition. As teachers we routinely work to overcome alienating literary conventions. Reading "God Is Good. It Is a Beautiful Night" (*CP* 285), one of my students, unaccustomed to poetic apostrophe, registered a protest: "No one talks to the moon!" However, as Jonathan Culler points out in *Structuralist Poetics,* poetic language is inherently remote: "The specific features of poetry have the function of differentiating it from speech and altering the circuit of communication within which it is inscribed" (162; see also Riffaterre 1–5). Stevens intensifies the remoteness of an already remote mode of speech, and his particular brand of "strangeness" results from stylistic saturation, from a high concentration of verbal incongruities and calculated barriers to reading, comprehension, and restatement. As Tzvetan Todorov has said in *Introduction to Poetics,* verbal style "is never a matter of an absolute presence or absence, but of quantitative predominances (which, furthermore, it is extremely difficult to measure: how many metaphors must there be to a page before we can qualify a style as 'metaphorical'?)" (21). More often than not, Stevens's poems resist reconstruction as coherent enunciative acts. He toys with all the vehicles we employ in "our attempt to order and naturalize the text" (Culler 170).

Culler outlines the ways in which reading, in the process and progress of interpretation, works to overcome the remote and impersonal—indeed, the strange—quality of poetic language. I have become convinced that explaining these interpretative practices to students helps immeasurably in derailing wild misreading and overreading. First, we humanize poetic language and make it approximate more closely other kinds of familiar speech: "Our major device of order is, of course, the notion of the person or speaking subject, and the process of reading is especially troubled when we cannot construct a subject who would serve as source of the poetic utterance" (Culler 170). Culler goes on to say: "The second fundamental convention of the lyric is what we might call the expectation of totality or coherence" (170). He then covers the demands of meaning and significance and the drive toward "theme and epiphany" in the lyric tradition, which is "closely related to the notion of unity":

> To write a poem is to claim significance of some sort for the verbal construct one produces, and the reader approaches a poem with the assumption that however brief it may appear it must contain, at least implicitly, potential riches which make it worthy of his attention. Reading a poem thus becomes a process of finding ways to grant it significance and importance, and in that process we call upon a variety of operations which have come to form part of the institution of poetry. (Culler 175; see also Riffaterre on unity and significance, 1–22)

These points are especially crucial in coming to terms with the deviations from meaning and linguistic expectation habitual in Stevens's "captious" poetics.

Students of literature, particularly those without a specialist's concern for what is uniquely literary about a writer, often sustain their interest in the work by humanizing it. The "human" ingredient (hopefully one close to their own lives, as they perceive them) allows them to identify with and recognize the thoughts, conflicts, feelings of the speakers and "characters" of literary texts. In understanding poetry, they benefit from discussions that articulate the troubles and conflicts of its speaking subjects. Conflict, the "stuff of life," makes poems more human. No wonder, then, that beginning with speaker, setting, and situation effectively brings what is remote and strange closer to a student's experience. In this area, teachers can introduce Stevens by making shrewd selections from among his poems with reasonably well-delineated speakers and settings.

His aesthetic concerns and his modes of expressing them emerge out of deep human desires, needs, pleasures, insecurities, failures, and successes. Having said that, we must admit that he tends to be impersonal and distanced in expressing human feeling, and he incessantly takes up aesthetic conflicts not touching most students. Mark Halliday, in *Stevens and the Interpersonal,* even claims that "Stevens' poetry largely tries to ignore or deny all aspects of life that center on or are inseparable from interpersonal relations" (3). I do not share the need some apparently have for a more human Wallace Stevens who would write out of "the suffering of others, the humanity of desirable women, the sheer presence of others" (Halliday 5). This kind of thinking, I would assert, gives dangerous sanction to our own students' unwillingness to accept writers on their own terms. All too frequently my students express, in less sophisticated ways, the assessment made by Halliday: "Poetry, if it is, as I believe, a means of understanding our most profound and essential human problems, may thus be expected to address the issues of social life" (6).

Often it will be impossible to humanize the utterance of his speakers, and students will perhaps fall silent when encountering such figures as "Lady Lowzen," who lived "In Hydaspia, by Howzen" ("Oak Leaves Are Hands" [*CP* 272]), or the "Secretary for Porcelain," who makes an aesthetic observation "That evil . . . / If neatly glazed, becomes the same as the fruit / Of an emperor, the egg-plant of a prince." This idea of "evil" in "Extracts from Addresses to the Academy of Fine Ideas" (*CP* 252) will not resemble anything familiar to our students, and, surely, grappling with such textual intricacies is a task for seasoned readers. Yet to talk in classrooms of Stevens as he is, teachers must resist the tendency to domesticate his eccentricity. Our task is to approximate more closely a description of these qualities—human or inhuman—in Stevens's odd meditations on the world of words. Description must precede and may altogether replace meaning.

Even when he is being linguistically playful and comical, Stevens's speakers and central subjects can be inhumanly strange. However, the enigmatic, musical, noisy short lyrics should be among our choices in presenting Stevens at his most eccentric. Many exemplary poems of this type are rarely, if ever, anthologized, though his devoted readers know them well because they startle, surprise, and delight. "Jouga" (*CP* 337), for example, is characteristic of Stevens's writing at its most intriguingly playful. Through poems such as this one, we can bring students closer to the linguistic fun running throughout his canon. His wordplay, as strange and obscure as it often is, makes him one of the most appealing poets to puzzle through, an activity that students enjoy. The speaker of "Jouga" observes strange "Ha-eé-me, who sits / And plays his guitar. Ha-eé-me is a beast." The central figure of the guitarist is remote, without question, so much so that the name "Ha-eé-me" may be unrecognizable to students as a verbal riddle or pun. Yet they are intrigued by the notion of listening to this odd, beastly guitarist "Who knocks out a noise." The impenetrable name of the guitarist presents itself as a word in need of explanation. Such words teach students that Stevens works beyond limits of linguistic familiarity and that he has a good bit of fun in the process. "Jouga" bangs out a kind of verbal clatter for which Stevens is famous. Read beside "Bantams in Pine-Woods" (*CP* 75)—who is "Chieftain Iffucan of Azcan in caftan"?—students encounter the truly strange limits of Stevens's "lingua franca et jocundissima" (*CP* 397).

The fact that Stevens's speaking subjects and figurative "characters" routinely stand in for the poet himself, or for some aspect of the artistic process, may increase the distance between the poem and the average student. Not surprisingly, the noisy, "imbecile" guitarist "Ha-eé-me" plays poetry; he is a personified figuration of the speaker's attempt to reproduce a particular "meaningless" sound: "The physical world is meaningless tonight"; "This afternoon the wind and the sea were like that—." While creative writing students might appreciate the abundance of poet/speakers and figurative renderings of the poetic process in Stevens's canon, the general run of humanity may well find his aesthetic preoccupations compulsively rarified, self-indulgent, exaggerated. Why must he always envision "the poet as / Eternal *chef d'orchestre*" (*CP* 136)? Nevertheless, students can learn much about poetic sound and sense from one who plays an insistent, perplexing musical nonsense—"Poet, be seated at the piano. / Play the present, its hoo-hoo-hoo, / Its shoo-shoo-shoo, its ric-a-nic" (*CP* 131).

Returning briefly to the conventions of the lyric outlined by Culler, we as teachers should be especially careful in the undergraduate setting to clarify the ways in which Stevens habitually defies "the expectation of totality or coherence" and of "significance and importance" (Culler 170-75). In these areas, Stevens's poetry often disrupts expectations of closure and completion in poetic speech (on closure in the lyric tradition, see Smith). In resisting unity, he in turn resists significance and final, settled meanings; he tends less toward the neat, organized, and explicable than the baffled, mysterious, and open. Since he frequently begins poems *in medias* process, closes them in states of partial resolution, and allows them to drift toward anticlimax and failed effort, students should be made aware of traditional biases toward unity and coherence in the lyric. Stevens's poetic accomplishment, teachers must insist, does not depend upon neat closure and finished ideas. Typographically, stanzaically, and grammatically his poems may suggest closure and completion in the lyric tradition. However, Stevens's intratextual cross-referencing, which operates across his whole canon, fights with the conventional "shape" of his verse—the term "intratextual" describing how one part of his canon consciously designates another; the term "cross-referencing" indicating a method we use to unmask obscurities by reading poem against poem.

Of course, Stevens does not altogether avoid the conventional realm of closure, meaning, and significance. Some well-taught poems as complex as "Sunday Morning" meet all the expectations of poetic significance and unity. Yet as he progressed through his canon—certainly from *Parts of a World* until his last volume—Stevens became increasingly enigmatic and obscure (see Leggett, *Wallace Stevens and Poetic Theory* 110-41). He defies intelligibility with as much vigor as he asserts it, or, in the convoluted paradoxes saturating his verse, he negates meaning even while he asserts its presence. Stevens may use enigmatic language so involuted that it virtually shuts the reader out of the realm of poetic significance. Some may feel reluctant to introduce unsolved enigmas to undergraduates, but asking why "The Man on the Dump" (*CP* 201) closes with "The the" or why "Man Carrying Thing" (*CP* 350) is finally unintelligible opens up important questions about the poet's baffling poetic range.

Fortunately, students are just as receptive to absence of meaning, order, and coherence as they are to its reverse, once these concepts have been framed and illustrated with solid examples. Since Stevens tends to work on both sides of the question of meaning, its absence and its presence, his canon offers contrasting examples on single subjects. From his many versions of a poem of snow and "deep January" (*CP* 294), for instance, teachers can make selections showing Stevens's degrees of resistance to closure and finality, his alternate affirmations and denials of meaning. "The Snow Man" undoubtedly still receives more attention than others, and *Harmonium* continues to dominate our coverage of Stevens in the undergraduate classroom. Supposedly, "the postmodern appropriation of Stevens . . . demanded a critical strategy which not only would wrest the author from the New Critical hold but would venture farther in addressing all of Stevens' works" (Schaum 100). Yet I surveyed the selections in seven current editions of anthologies and found that 43 percent of the total number of poems available in this format still come from *Harmonium:* ten of twenty-five total in the *Norton Anthology of Modern Poetry,* second edition; ten of nineteen in the *Norton Anthology of American Literature,* third edition; seven of ten in the *Heath Anthology of American Literature;* ten of twenty in *Heritage of American Literature;* six of nineteen in the *Harper American Literature;* eight of thirty in *American Literature: A Prentice Hall Anthology;* eleven of twenty in the *American Tradition in Literature,* seventh edition.

Reading beyond *Harmonium,* we discover that Stevens's various rewritings of his poem of winter are not as neatly rounded off as "The Snow Man," but they are just as worthy for classroom use. One of Stevens's most intriguing versions of winter's "single emptiness" is "No Possum, No Sop, No Taters" (*CP* 293). The poem is based on a something/nothing paradox, as is "The Snow Man," but in its expression of "winter-sound" it moves beyond "the nothing that is." Its rich and strange title peculiarly prefaces what follows. Its Ovidian personification of "broken stalks" that "have heads in which a captive cry / Is merely the moving of a tongue" carries overtones of "mal" that are crucial in Stevens's ongoing exploration of evil. These suggestions lead the speaker to a recognition of a bleak, broken tree of knowledge, which finally distills out of "this bad . . . / The last purity of the knowledge of good." The outcome of "No Possum, No Sop, No Taters," in terms of discovery and potential closure, is more complex than "The Snow Man." At the close of the poem, the speaker notes the presence of a crow and the arrival of its companion sitting "at a distance, in another tree." This ending forecasts something about to occur, a reemergence out of "the nothing": in the coming of a new season, the "rusty" crow will rejoin its companions.

This poem and others related to it in subject and theme—for instance, "Snow and Stars," "The Plain Sense of Things," "Long and Sluggish Lines," "A Quiet Normal Life," "Not Ideas about the Thing but the Thing Itself"—are not as textually autonomous as "The Snow Man." Yet, taken together, these poems effectively illustrate Stevens's constancy to a particular subject; they also facilitate a contextual reading that acknowledges his persistent revisions of a poem of winter. If we continue to pretend that "The Snow Man" is a discreet, autonomous lyric, and put aside its revisions, then we domesticate the poet's strangeness.

In teaching the "enlarged," "intricate" mind of Wallace Stevens, it is abundantly clear that we must use the richness and depth of his entire canon to cross-reference his treatment of subjects, motifs, ideas, moods, images, and figures. As critics we link poem with poem as an effective route into his baffling word-world. As teachers we will more closely approximate Stevens's poetic accomplishment if we examine poem against poem, image against image, even word against word. This method has long been with us. In 1932, R. P. Blackmur stated that "Mr. Stevens' difficulties to the normal reader present themselves in the shape of seemingly impenetrable words or phrases which no wedge of knowledge brought from outside the body of Mr. Stevens' own poetry can help much to split. The wedge, if any, is in the words themselves, either in the instance alone or in relation to analogous instances in the same or other poems in the book" (202). Particular poems estrange themselves from us until we link them to others of their kind, but systematic cross-referencing within Stevens's canon overcomes many linguistic and conceptual eccentricities.

Of course, this method of reading challenges us because it broadens boundaries of possible interpretation. New puzzles and enigmas result from placing one complex poem beside another; the second one may not settle down as easily as the first. Stevens's revisions of an idea may well be more remote and strange than his first try. Yet they teach students that only through the intricacy of revision does he express his incredible brand of truth, in an ongoing engagement of "Life's nonsense" (*CP* 383). In his reworked versions of an idea, it is hoped that students will find a "strange relation" (*CP* 383). Stevens's concerns are "captious," perplexing; his diction, wordplay, sonic and figurative devices are unfamiliar and intentionally enigmatic. If our students feel inclined to ask of such writing, "Was it that—a sense and beyond intelligence?" (*CP* 331), we should reply "Yes!" and explain the particular ways in which Stevens writes "beyond" our limits of verbal expectation. In teaching Stevens's oddities, we hardly ever risk sounding like "nincompated pedagogue[s]" (*CP* 27), and once encouraged to solve such verbal puzzles, students can become welcome members of Stevens's strange "Academy of Fine Ideas."

Learning Stevens's Language:
The Will & the Weather

JOAN RICHARDSON

The great sail of Ulysses seemed,
In the breathings of this soliloquy,
Alive with an enigma's flittering . . .
As if another sail went on
Straight forwardly through another night
And clumped stars dangled all the way.

"The Sail of Ulysses" (*OP* 131)

Teaching Stevens, I tell my students, is like teaching about the weather to those who want to sail offshore. Sharpening attention is crucial. The more exposure, the more practiced the observation of patterns, forms, casts of light and changes of air, the greater the possibilities for successful passages, for interpretation. But nothing is ever fixed, certain or precise—except that at a particular moment all of the variables arrange themselves to produce a specific effect or condition, arrange themselves into a poem. If we have been astute, we will find ourselves, too, "arranged," so that even if we come upon major weather, we will come through. This is "momentary existence on an exquisite plane" (*OP* 228). It is as if through the experience of "learning Stevens"—as we would learn another language, which is, in fact, what we are doing—we have ourselves fashioned a craft (a particular network, a habit of mind) that can carry us through this new strange sea of thought. This makes sense. The different shapes of ships and boats derive from various weather and sea conditions—how long or short the waves, how steep their troughs, for example. While we can learn to recognize stars and so navigate, we can never know all about the weather, however, only develop, from being keenly and constantly alert, a feeling for it that helps us get it right. Stevens was writing and he was going to write.

Hearing a new language sets us adrift in the pure sound of words. Stevens knew this and knew, too, that to discover oneself amidst the slap and sigh of this aural sea is to know again the originating human situation, hearing what we have always heard but as though we had never heard it before, in its first idea. The poet, knowing this, who makes a language that entices us to attend to its concupiscent words, nudges us along to reawaken our earliest skills. We come to recognize (re*cognize*) them with profound wonder. This is the first thing I communicate to my students about Stevens's poetry. I then read aloud, selectively, "The Emperor of Ice-Cream," sections of "The Comedian as the Letter C," or "Domination of Black," and close the reading from Stevens with "Human Arrangement." I follow with this observation from William James's *Principles of Psychology:* "in music the whole aesthetic effect comes from the manner in which one set of sounds alters our feeling of another" (228).

This introduction serves as a prelude to the class's beginning to learn Stevens. I encourage them to play with, and on, the feelings that have been prompted. From feeling, at first, lost, at sea, the crescendoing announcement of feelings provides points from which we can select those on which we will take bearings. At this juncture my greater expertise with the body of Stevens's work and secondary material, as well as my involvement as a biographer, enters the conversation and offers guidance in that selection.

In locating ourselves, we initially distinguish contrasts, opposing or distanced points, so to speak, that we need to plot the triangulation of Stevens's experience through time and our following course. The "set[s] of sounds" resonating with the vigorous yet balanced power of the poet's middle age are set against the sounds of slowly silencing advancing age in "Human Arrangement." Talking about how the later set of sounds alters our feelings about the earlier sets and vice versa opens up the general discussion of music and poetry—for Stevens, particularly, the late-nineteenth-century symbolist hope to have all art attain the condition of music. I ask students to describe what they understand as musical form, symphony, in what ways the understanding of music differs from, or is the same as, the understanding of other humanly shaped forms. I touch on Mallarmé here, too: on the French poet's creating words to fit certain line sites on the basis of a needed sound alone; on his incorporation of, and play with, the central notion of chance in composing words on the page, as in *Un Coup de dès;* on the idea of the poet's creating *l'oeuvre complète* and Stevens's idea for "The Whole of Harmonium" so that the title of his first published volume would have appeared as *The Whole of Harmonium: Preliminary Minutiae.* In this aesthetic frame any one poem means in the context of the whole, just as, following Mallarmé's example, a jewel is best seen and appreciated in a setting in which it is enhanced by the design and scintillations of other stones. This last perception is then connected back to the larger project of "learning Stevens," and I observe that I still, after almost twenty-five years of study and practice, am learning Stevens, that there are today lines, passages, entire poems whose soundings I have not yet fathomed, and perhaps never shall, and that that is part of the wonder of experiencing major poetry, like major weather.

Alerting students to this comforts them at the same time that it points out how demanding makers of new languages are. I urge them to feel encouraged by their puzzlement and comment that this is the optimal condition in which to find themselves, and that this—in spite of recent critical injunctions—is precisely what the poet intended, that finding themselves, especially in the context of America's new world experience, is what it is all about, as Stanley Cavell reminds us in his discussions of Thoreau and Emerson. The problem of intention is mentioned but put on hold. I do observe, however, that Stevens, as one exquisitely attuned to the turnings of words, tried to untie the same set of linguistic and syntactical knots that Darwin himself described in his journals concerning certain phrasings in writing *On the Origin of Species.* He was stopped again and again in revising and rewriting the *Origin,* he noted, by the realization that in the record he had set forth, the idea of intention was implicit, while what he had come to understand from all the evidence he had collected was that there is no intention or purpose in the universe we inhabit. Our language, however, preserves in its grammar and syntax an older world view of the great chain of being. This fact is one of the dominant forces of Stevens's weather, the weather of a post-Darwinian world.

As students become more comfortable expressing their befuddlement in questions, I gradually bring in more and more of what I have come to recognize, as a biographer, of the wind and weather of Stevens's experience. I indicate that the various things I have to say represent the bearings that I took in order to navigate my way in Stevens, but that there are, if not an infinite number of points, at least as many as there are visible stars that can be used to plot a successful course. The questions they ask are their stars, their guides in this celestial enterprise. Anecdotes enter as illustrations.

I usually relate, for example, how preoccupied I became early on in my reading of Stevens with the demonstrative adjective "that," pointing to a very particular November through five headlined repetitions in each of the five sections of "Sea Surface Full of Clouds" (*CP* 98). Other critical readers of the poem generally agreed with John Crowe Ransom's 1938 characterization of it as the purest of "pure poems," the product of a poet descended directly and exclusively from the symbolists and "art for art's sake" aesthetes; here is Ransom:

> The poem has a calculated complexity, and its technical competence is so high that
> to study it, if you do that sort of thing, is to be happy. That it has not been studied
> by a multitude of persons is due to a simple consideration which strikes us at once:
> the poem has no moral, political, religious, or sociological values. It is not about "res
> publica," the public thing. The subject matter is trifling. (59)

Ransom introduces his discussion of the poem with "Time and place, 'In that November off Tehuantepec,'" but, in the purest New Critical manner, fails to follow the pointing, and so is able to go on and complacently finger this poem as the prime example of "modernity" and its style, emptied of anything but formal, "objective" concerns. The modern poet Stevens, Ransom observes, "cares nothing, professionally, about morals, or God, or native land. He has performed a work of dissociation and purified his art" (58).

I read Ransom in 1970, I tell my students, long before I had even thought of reading William James, who in the key "Stream of Thought" chapter of his *Principles of Psychology* (1890) significantly directs attention away from substantives and precisely to words like "that" and other seemingly innocuous shifters as the sites where real meaning/feeling is expressed:

> If there be such things as feelings at all, *then so surely as relations between objects exist in*
> *rerum natura, so surely, and more surely, do feelings exist to which these relations are known.*

There is not a conjunction or a preposition, and hardly an adverbial phrase, syntactic form, or inflection of voice, in human speech, that does not express some shading or other of relation which we at some moment actually feel to exist between the larger objects of our thought. If we speak objectively, it is the real relations that appear revealed; if we speak subjectively, it is the stream of consciousness that matches each of them by an inward coloring of its own. In either case, the relations are numberless, and no existing language is capable of doing justice to their shades.

We ought to say a feeling of *and,* a feeling of *if,* a feeling of *but,* and a feeling of *by,* quite as readily as we say a feeling of *blue* or a feeling of *cold.* Yet we do not: so inveterate has our habit become of recognizing the existence of the substantive parts alone, that language almost refuses to lend itself to any other use. The Empiricists have always dwelt on its influence in making us suppose that where we have a separate name, a separate thing must needs be there to correspond with it; and they have rightly denied the existence of the mob of abstract entities, principles, and forces, in whose favor no other evidence than this could be brought up. But they have said nothing of that obverse error . . . of supposing that where there is *no* name no entity can exist. All *dumb* or anonymous psychic states have, owing to this error, been coolly suppressed; or, if recognized at all, have been named after the substantive perception they led to, as thoughts 'about' this object or 'about' that, the stolid word *about* engulfing all their delicate idiosyncrasies in its monotonous sound. Thus the greater and greater accentuation and isolation of the substantive parts have continually gone on. (238-39)

Stevens had been sensitized to this and other of James's central insights into the workings of language and perception while he was a student at Harvard (1897-1900) during the long period when these ideas agitated the thinking *about* thinking of those concerned with the power of words—George Santayana, Josiah Royce, Barrett Wendell, Robert Frost, Gertrude Stein. Later in his career, Stevens, in a quiet rhetorical attempt at recall, asked, "Where was it one first heard of the truth? The the" (*CP* 203), still pondering the kinds of linguistic questions addressed by James. Richard Poirier has most recently in *Poetry and Pragmatism* elaborated on this important line of development through William James at Harvard. As Poirier correctly and significantly indicates, James was working out the implications of what Emerson had a generation before set down in the intricate maze of his writing. Stevens had himself come to Harvard carrying his Emerson with him. His mother had given him a complete set of Emerson's works as a gift on his graduation from high school. The young Stevens began annotating certain of the essays and lectures then. He continued and returned many times to some lines and passages; along the way he was introduced to James and his *Principles*.

I followed Stevens's pointing to "*that* November off Tehuantepec" and discovered that "Sea Surface Full of Clouds" was, contrary to what Ransom perceived, a poem deeply stirred by moral concern. The subject matter was hardly trivial. "In that November off Tehuantepec" Stevens's only child was conceived, after fourteen years of marriage, on the first extended holiday he and his wife had taken since April 1910, when they last traveled together for a few weeks as they had on their honeymoon. It was fortunate for me that Holly Stevens had in 1966 published her edition of her father's letters. Perusing them in 1970, looking for clues as to what could have happened "In that November off Tehuantepec" that prompted a poem— *not* that the poem could be reduced simply to an account of that occasion—I realized, as I tell my students, the limitations of a strict New Critical approach and, I see now, began working on Stevens's biography. When I came across Stevens's comment in a letter to an inquiring reader of his poems that he "believe[d] in pure explication de texte" as an interpretive method, indeed, as his "principal form of piety" (*L* 793), I understood what he meant. *Explication de texte,* originally an eighteenth-century method, was phrased in the nineteenth century by Hippolyte Taine as considering the work at hand with *race* (as culture), *milieu,* and *moment* in mind. From that point, I immersed myself as fully as possible in Stevens's "fluent mundo," following his indications, reading what he read, trying to recreate some similar network of references and echoes. I was embarked, learning Stevens.

The voyage begun, odd, seemingly chance findings presented themselves—"The acquisitions of poetry are fortuitous: trouvailles" (*OP* 195)— or, if they were not chance, I had indeed, it seems, begun to think/perceive "in Stevens" (as "in Greek" or "in French" when we realize that we have begun to internalize the language we have been studying). For example, in a used bookstore one day in the early 1970s, my eye was caught by a title, *The Jade Mountain;* its full title, as I discovered on taking it from the shelf and opening it, *The Jade Mountain: A Chinese Anthology, Being Three Hundred Poems of the T'ang Dynasty, 618-906,* translated by Witter Bynner from the texts of Kiang Kang-Hu. Witter Bynner was one of Stevens's classmates and close friends at Harvard, with whom, after graduation, he maintained a correspondence. During Stevens's years in New York City, 1900-1916, Bynner, returning from travels abroad, to the Orient, en route to Boston or to the Southwest, would visit with Stevens. I ask students to imagine what they would talk about with old friends if they found themselves in similar situations. They answer, invariably, that they would describe the "newnesses" they had come across, and especially select points of common interest and central concern. I then relate that the remaining letters to and from Bynner indicate this kind of thing to have characterized the relationship between the two poets. I go on to note that in the introduction to *The Jade Mountain* Kiang Kang-Hu remarks that this classic eighteenth-century selection from the 48,900 existing poems of the T'ang Dynasty—made by an anonymous editor who signed himself with what could have become a title of a Stevens poem or a character in the third section of "Le Monocle de Mon Oncle," "A Retired Scholar at the Lotus Pool"— like the Confucian Classic of Poetry, numbers "about" 300 poems—an odd number added to bring the total to 301 or 311, suggesting open-endedness. This choice "was based upon a common saying: 'By reading thoroughly three hundred T'ang poems, one will write verse without learning'" (xxvi). The Chinese editor goes on to note that such an anthology served as a "household reader"—much like the Bible in American households up until the beginning of the twentieth century—and that it would be read from aloud so that even the illiterate members of the household could enjoy the sound and play of words and meanings. I remark to my students that after coming upon this information, I promptly went home and counted up the number of Stevens's *Collected Poems,* and still wonder whether the total of 301 is accidental. "Begin, ephebe, by . . ." (*CP* 380).

Because I want students to have their own first ideas and use and sharpen their skills in "learning Stevens," I emphasize the importance of vagueness, both in Stevens's aesthetic and in my approach. I connect this to the development of a post-Darwinian consciousness where possibility and probability replace determined certainties. Mallarmé's description of a rose as the absence of all *bouquets* epitomizes the symbolist understanding that emerged out of this shift. Similarly, William James's seemingly oxymoronic focus on "vagueness" itself as the central mode of thinking grows out of this naturalized perception of the human place in the order of things. I suggest to students that this is Stevens's constant as well, the understanding of the mind as "a place of perpetual undulation" (*CP* 60). This understanding underscores his strong affiliation with Emerson, whose volumes—as is evident from going through them at the Huntington Library, where they are part of the Wallace Stevens Collection—served him in much the same way as their classic anthologies served the Chinese. Emerson's perception of society as a wave was an extension of his careful attention to what was being uncovered about the forces of nature during his lifetime, in the work of Michael Faraday and Alexander von Humboldt, for instance:

> Society is a wave. The wave moves onward, but the water of which it is composed does not. The same particle does not rise from the valley to the ridge. Its unity is only phenomenal. The persons who make up a nation to-day, next year die, and their experience with them. (II, 91)

Emerson charged his language with his apprehension and tried to make each of the words in his sentences an infinitely repellent particle, each sentence, then, a solar system in which the sun is the reader. Stevens "learned Emerson" and did not wince at taking in his law: "Society is a sea" (*OP* 195). And, as Richard Poirier has most recently elaborated, this kind of "grammar" or language management, which William James later incorporated into the work of what he called radical empiricism, "would make us aware that the relations between things are as important to experience as are the things themselves. It is necessary to stay loose." For James, he goes on to say, this "ideal grammar leads to his politics, and not the other way round. The grammar he proposes is already anti-imperialist, antipatriarchal, while never becoming directly focused on political or social structures" (152). Exactly the same thing can be said about Stevens's grammar. It sets us adrift, out to sea/see, and then teaches us how to navigate and survive in the waves—the *vagues* ("French and English constitute a single language"

[*OP* 202]). The only thing definite is the indefinite: *It Must Change;* "Uncertain certainty" (*OP* 127). When language is experienced as indefinite and in constant motion, thinking, the selection of temporary resting places, is understood to be the ultimate, and perhaps the only, moral activity. This is something that Emerson and William and Henry James knew and that Stevens knew as well. We are "made out of words" (*CP* 355), and we can make ourselves, but only as well as we can handle and shape our material. Stevens teaches us to recognize our singularly human skills. "To 'subtilize experience' = to apprehend the complexity of the world, to perceive the intricacy of appearance" (*OP* 201), like Henry James's advice to "Try to be one of the people on whom nothing is lost!" (53), is to become receptive and responsive to the trembling rhythms and resonances of the waves we inhabit and are. Stevens would have us become expert sailors who, sensitive to the hum and rush of wind and wave and craft, *feel* when to come about. Only those who have paid the most careful attention to the facts of weather and vessel can do this.

In paying attention to the facts of Stevens's life, I was struck innumerable times by how these facts were occasions of poems—"The poem is the cry of its occasion, / Part of the res itself and not about it" (*CP* 473). The accompanying cry, the *innuendo* haloing the *inflection,* as it were, records the complex turns the poet took around these moments. Stevens noted that the order of his poems was chronological; the poems, then, could be regarded as entries in the vast log of the life of his mind as it surveyed the course of his particular. It is important to be reminded of the concreteness of Stevens's anchorages of thought. Good examples for students include relating how as a young man living in New York Stevens was, like a prototype of the James Stewart character in Alfred Hitchcock's *Rear Window,* fascinated by night images of ladies in nightgowns moving around their rooms while he observed them unseen from across the brownstone courtyard (*L* 68); this recollection insinuates itself into "Disillusionment of Ten O'Clock" (*CP* 66): "The houses are haunted / By white night-gowns." Similarly, the peacock-patterned bathroom rug in one of the poet's first apartments in New York, that Holly Stevens figured (*SP* 73) as connected to "Anecdote of the Prince of Peacocks" (*CP* 57), also mingles with the other details set down in the opening of "Sunday Morning" (*CP* 66) to become "the green freedom of a cockatoo / Upon a rug." In speaking of "Sunday Morning," it is useful, too, to note that in the years when the poet as a young man kept a journal he had inscribed this pair of words more often than any other as he came to replace observing the Sabbath in church with weekly excursions into the countryside where, he found, "The sun . . . , an occasional sight of the sea, and thinking of blue valleys, and the odor of the earth . . . make a god of a man" (*L* 96). Later, poems came to replace journal entries. Again, it must be stressed that grounding the poems in "occasions" does not reduce their meaning to simple memorializings of those occasions. Reading in this way provides, rather, a deeper understanding of the poet's mental processing of experience, looking not "*at* facts, but *through* them" (*L* 32), as Stevens observed to himself in the journal he kept as a young man.

Following the poems written between 1937 and 1942 gives an especially sharp sense of Stevens's use of occasions. Through the images he sets down in his lines we see his repeated movement through the seasons of poetry writing: details from letters he wrote or received; reports of the news and weather; stray lines from popular songs (as he noted years later to Renato Poggioli in connection with section XV of "The Man with the Blue Guitar" [*CP* 165], its "Good-bye, harvest moon" line had the song of this title as its source [*L* 783]). Overlays such as this are numerous. In May 1937, for example, in a letter to Ronald Lane Latimer, he described how he had rearranged his room: "One side of my bed there is nothing but windows; when I lie in bed I can see nothing but trees"; he reported that this change made him more attentive to the sounds of a rabbit that in the morning delighted in digging out the bulbs he and Elsie had carefully planted (*L* 321). A few months later "A Rabbit as King of the Ghosts" (*CP* 209) appeared in the October 1937 issue of *Poetry*. His worrying about the rabbit, which had assumed comically monumental proportions, is echoed by the way the rabbit in the poem becomes gigantic, growing "higher and higher, black as stone." Contributing to this as well was the memory of his reaction, years earlier in 1916, to hearing Easter hymns. He had expressed then in a letter to his wife his belief that Easter carols represented "a religious perversion of the activity of Spring in our blood" that went together with the bishops' even having adopted the poor rabbit as one of their symbols (*L* 193).

At around the same time he composed this poem, Stevens reiterated his feelings about Christianity in the "Materia Poetica" notebook. "Loss of faith is growth" (*OP* 198), he wrote (and later included as one of his "Adagia"), and followed it, after several entries, with "Christianity is an exhausted culture" (*OP* 202). This was cramped in two lines written in one space beside a seemingly unrelated entry: "The theory of poetry is the life of poetry" (*OP* 202). The antithetical connection between "life" and "exhausted" seems to have prompted this linking, which had all to do with Stevens's attempt to establish with his poetry a new canon to replace the outworn religious faith that loomed like a ghost, like the ghost of the rabbit, the bishops' symbolic pawn, which, nibbling away at his bulbs, disturbed his sleep. Significantly, a group of poems entitled "Canonica" appeared in the autumn 1938 issue of the *Southern Review;* these became the first twelve poems of *Parts of a World.*

Illustrating how another fact of his experience was worked into poetry, "A Weak Mind in the Mountains" (*CP* 212), which appeared originally titled "Force of Illusions" in the 10 July 1938 issue of the *New York Times,* elaborated on the powerful hold the idea of Ceylon had recently taken on the poet's imagination. Stevens's relationship with Ceylon began with a request he made of Leonard van Geyzel to purchase necklaces or carved boxes for Elsie and Holly and some tea for himself to arrive in time for Christmas 1937. Stevens's interest grew as van Geyzel became a worthy correspondent to whom the poet in turn sent books and subscriptions to the *New Yorker* and other "odds and ends" (*L* 332). Van Geyzel not only continued to send long descriptive letters about all aspects of life in Ceylon, sharing with Stevens his strong socialist commitment as the years passed into war, but also continued to send things that delighted Stevens, Elsie, and Holly: brilliantly colored saris; broad-brimmed sun hats; jellies; volumes of Singhalese poetry and other books about Ceylon; collections of photographs that particularly fascinated Stevens; and figures of Buddha in different positions. These last he prized. After choosing for his own out of the first Christmas 1937 box one Buddha "so simple and explicit [he had] to have it in [his] room" (*L* 328), he wanted others: one seated and one reclining. He was willing to incur "any reasonable expense" (*L* 333) to have them. His desire for these was so insistent that he repeated his request to van Geyzel in the form of reminders well into the spring of 1939: "I shall be most grateful to you if you will continue to bear the Buddha in mind. Somehow or other, with so much of Hitler and Mussolini so drastically on one's nerves, constantly, it is hard to get round to Buddha" (L 337). He reiterated that van Geyzel should not hesitate at this point about the expense and that he would reimburse him promptly.

The situation Stevens symbolically pointed to in "A Weak Mind in the Mountains," with the "wind of Iceland" gripping his mind and grappling with the metaphorical black wind of Ceylon, was one he imagined his Buddha experiencing as he sat on the windowsill of his room: "At night, when my windows are open and the air is like ice, this particular Buddha must wish that I put a postage stamp on him and send him back to Colombo" (L 328). Both the Buddha and details of life in Ceylon that he received from van Geyzel, details that he wanted about other places in the East as well (he asked his correspondent-friend if he knew of others in Java, Hong Kong, or Siam who would write to him in the same spirit), provided Stevens with strong imaginative centers that functioned as contrasts to the world in which he actually lived and to the religion in which he had been reared. The oppositions he set up echoed the structure he became conscious of imposing while writing the poems of *Ideas of Order*. Projecting himself into the figure of Buddha sitting on his windowsill, he imagined himself in Ceylon and the East. As events in the West became more violent, his early interest in the East became keener and less purely aesthetic.

Stevens was in Virginia when the "unbelievable catastrophe," as he referred to World War II, broke out in September 1939. It was the end of a summer unusually full of travel and unusual, too, in that the whole family spent their time together, moving from place to place. Toward the middle of July the Stevens family left for Maine to stay for a few weeks at Christmas Cove in a hotel, the Holly Inn, managed for the season by Peter Schutt, who had been manager of the Casa Marina Hotel in Key West, where Stevens had stayed with his friend Arthur Powell on their many visits. From the summer of 1939, Stevens sent out and later collected two poems, "Bouquet of Belle Scavoir" and "Variations on a Summer Day."

These, together with the following four as they appear in the *Collected Poems*—"Yellow Afternoon," "Martial Cadenza," "Man and Bottle," and "Of Modern Poetry" (*CP* 236-40)—reflect the operation of Stevens's imagination on reality over the summer into fall and winter of 1939-40. This sequence is important both because it covers a particularly significant moment in history and because it illustrates that Stevens did indeed write poems the way he had once written entries in his journal. They were records of the movement of his intelligence through the days and seasons of his life.

In each of these poems Stevens was careful to place either a spatial or a temporal marker that allows, when it is noted in the context of other poems and of details reported in letters, his passage through time to be perceived. This device seems to reflect at least a surface understanding of the basic law of quantum mechanics, the Heisenberg uncertainty principle: if the speed of an electron is known, its location is not, while if its location is known, its speed is not. Since Stevens read in physics, it is not unsafe to suggest that he might have wanted to integrate an application of this revolutionary concept into his work (just as John Donne had incorporated into his poetry an understanding of the scientific discoveries of his day). In poems where a specific location is indicated, time is not; conversely, in poems in which time is indicated, location is either generalized or not given. This is in marked contrast to a poem like "Sea Surface Full of Clouds," for example, in which both time and place are indicated: "In that November off Tehuantepec." This is not surprising since the earlier poems are, in terms of how Stevens apprehended the physical world, transitional. They reflect his ties to a Newtonian universe where apples fell predictably and obediently, like everything else and "serve[d] as well as any skull / To be the book in which to read a round" (*CP* 14). In the poems of this later period when *both* time and place *seem* to be specified, the reality described is wholly imaginary, as in "Forces, the Will & the Weather" (*CP* 228), where "It was at the time, the place, of nougats," candies he conjured from the ever-changing colors of dogwoods.

In "Variations on a Summer Day" (*CP* 232), time is specified: it is a summer day, and the variations reflect the passage of longer and shorter moments in the poet's consciousness. That it is Maine is known from particular references to Monhegan and Pemaquid, but it is impossible to locate a fixed position from which the poet observed. One moment he could see Monhegan; another, the "last island"; another, "Everywhere" around where there were "spruce trees." Close attention to what seem at first to be imagistically connected improvisations, however, reveals that there is a precise movement charted: Stevens's approach to Christmas Cove in a ferry.

In section I the real facts around which his imagination spun were the gulls following the ferry still at sea; in II, the distant rocks, appearing small, like letters fringed by waves; in III, closer, the rocks' attachment to the cliffs now seen in enough detail to resemble the heads of dogs; in IV, the evening star rising over Monhegan; in V, the trees onshore, at this point near enough to be seen, that prompted the waves-as-leaves metaphor; in VI, the shore, even closer so that the stones at its base could be particularized; in VII, a last look back at the sea—a *reflexion*—that produced the reflection that he was engaged in an "exercise in viewing the world"; in IX, clouds gathering over land—the "world"—in the diminishing daylight; in X, the "natures" of things and people seen around; in XI, the "timothy at Pemaquid" very close by, "silver-tipped" as the moon rose; in XII, the place where Hugh March was killed, one of the facts gathered from the history he had read about the place he was visiting; in XIII, another view of the open sea, Pemaquid passed, now rose-colored in the sunset; in XIV, the "mica" and "dithering of grass" of another island passing; in XV, the "last island" passed before the ferry's arrival at Christmas Cove and the disembarkation of Stevens's family; in XVI, the bell buoy marking the harbor entrance, through portals of pines on the shore in XVII; in XVIII, the low tide perceptible in the harbor, its flat water unruffled by waves in its haven; in XIX, a boy swimming under an old "tub" and another boy sitting on top, greeting the "man-boat" that carried the man-poet; in XX, the brass on a sailing ship, just adjacent now as the ferry approached its berth, the poet having to look up to see the top of her mast taper to nothing (like the tops of distant steeples that had once helped him find his way through the streets of New York). In this record of movement through time, from midafternoon, when the air was "light blue," until early evening, each moment was particularized by its perception. The subject is the process of perception itself.

Moving our consideration to a later period in the poet's life, we read about "The Westwardness of Everything":

> . . . as if
>
> There was an end at which in a final change,
> When the whole habit of the mind was changed,
> The ocean breathed out morning in one breath. (*CP* 455)

We are given a bearing in Stevens's actual world when we know that all through his childhood his bedrooms faced west and that in later life, as he related, whenever he found himself at the end of a day in a room not facing west, he kept trying in his imagination to turn the house where he was on its axis so that its entering light would conform to the earlier imprinting. Details such as these enliven. They make us sensitive to the motive behind Stevens's wanting to add as a fourth section to his "Notes toward a Supreme Fiction," *It Must Be Human.*

In this vein, I never fail to share with students, too, some of the informing joys of having worked on the Stevens material at the Huntington. His scrupulous attention to and playing with words were not limited to his work as a poet. Almost every day of his life as an executive for the Hartford Accident and Indemnity Company, Stevens composed and dictated the equivalent of at least three single-spaced pages of sharply reasoned paragraphs; some days there were two or three such documents. Personal letters were in addition to these, and even seemingly trivial matters, such as the sizing and thread count of undershirts he had ordered and found wanting, were dealt with in the most detailed precision. There was never an aspect that was not considered. It was as though Stevens held each and every object of thought still in his mind and walked around it, slowly considering, for a long time. He made the quotidian an exquisite meditation. When he took a companion with him on one of his mental rounds, he was always attentive to sweeten the tour. Because of this, I was the only scholar who more than occasionally broke the silence of the Rare Book and Manuscript Room at the Huntington with peals of laughter when, after, say, going through Stevens's four-page, single-spaced description to the manufacturers of his undershirts of the inadequacies of the last order, and being amazed at the poet's almost microscopic analysis of materials and workmanship and how these differed from earlier orders, finding, in the penultimate paragraph, "After all, it is undershirts I am trying to buy, not necklaces!" followed by an uproarious depiction of how these last shirts looked on his corpulent form. More than any other one feature, it was this constantly erupting, though delayed and early-disguised, humor that emerged as the unexpected element for me in doing the work on Stevens's biography. While he was courting Elsie Moll, he noted to her in one of the richly beautiful letters he sent during their five-year engagement, when he was in New York and she in Reading, that he aspired to what the motto "'Angelic hilarity with monastic simplicity'" (*L* 101) described. Temperamentally shy, Stevens was comfortable hidden in the leaves he left behind, Professor Eucalyptus.

The most important practical lesson I impress upon students is to learn to read aloud. Again and again I stress the centrality to Stevens of the sound of words. The sounds intoned complete the requisite physiological effect William James makes so much of in *Principles of Psychology* as what, in fact, etches a neural pathway into the brain's subtle circuitry. This is the physical basis of pragmatism and real understanding, taking on the identity of another in the flesh. Relinquishing ourselves to Stevens's complicate harmonies, we escape the limited syntax of outworn inherited forms, and learn to hear, to feel another kind of reasoning and must decide for ourselves how to inflect out of innuendo.

Out of this practice, we grasp what prayer used to do or could do. I tell students that if they succeed in learning Stevens, they will find that at unexpected moments a line or phrase will repeat itself insistently in their mind's ear. Trusting this mantric oracle will lead them to discover what they didn't know they remembered—when, for example, the rest of the poem builds itself out and around this seed—or will lead them to ask questions of themselves that they could not have thought of posing before. They will, in short, find themselves more truly and more strange in the new world of their own intricate syntax—"By reading thoroughly 300 Stevens poems, one will write verse without learning."

The Poles of Imagination and Reality:
An Introduction to Wallace Stevens
in the College Classroom

DAVID C. DOUGHERTY

Most of us who teach Stevens's poems to undergraduates have already developed an intense appreciation for his unique synthesis of the aesthete who sees beauty as the appropriate end of poetry and the pragmatist who sees poetry as a special way to address complex intellectual and especially philosophical issues. During my first few semesters of presenting this material to reasonably sophisticated junior and senior English majors, however, I was often disappointed that only the very brightest shared my enthusiasm for this poet's finely honed adaptation of Horace's depiction of art as simultaneously an occasion for delight and a source of truth.

Yet the majority of these students were neither illiterate nor insensitive to the delights of poetry. With only a little coaxing, most had made sense of, and had often delighted in, poems by William Butler Yeats, William Carlos Williams, Ezra Pound, T. S. Eliot, Marianne Moore, John Crowe Ransom, e. e. cummings, and some of the British poets of World War I by the time they encountered the insurance executive. If they could deal with the multilingual obscurity and sometimes inflammatory rhetoric of Pound, the sophisticated and densely allusive cultural carping of Eliot, and the private, arcane, mythic systems of Yeats, why should Stevens, whose work was assigned as the culmination of a course in modern poetry, give them trouble?

The answers are probably familiar to most experienced teachers of modern poetry. For one class, Stevens's poems are perceived as simply too "difficult." Although most of the words, in contrast to the densely multilingual vocabularies of some of his contemporaries, are at least in English, the language is put to exotic and therefore unexpected rhetorical purposes. For another set of readers, the elegance and unabashed joy in "the sound of words" (part of the title of an important essay by Stevens) smack of the decadence of an art for art's sake movement.

For by far the largest group, however, the complexity and unfamiliarity of the themes, with their emphasis on post-Kantian epistemology, constitute a major obstacle. Whether or not we teachers like it, most students educated during the final decades of this century have little grounding or interest in philosophy or logic, both of which are important aesthetic as well as thematic components of Stevens's poems. We have little choice except to be patient with the increasing number of our students who question (either loudly or silently) whether poems like "The Idea of Order at Key West" or "Sunday Morning," to say nothing of more complicated texts like "Notes toward a Supreme Fiction" or "An Ordinary Evening in New Haven," should not be prose treatises—whether the attraction of such poems is not their aphoristic bent or their facility in expressing some warmed-over meta-Lockeanism or neo-Kantianism or post-Hegelianism.

As teachers we have two obvious but equally problematic options. We can insist that students digest the spoon-fed synopses of Locke or Kant we find useful in unraveling the content of Stevens's poems, in which case the best we can hope for is that our students will be motivated to learn enough diluted epistemology that they will be able to read Stevens intelligently. In the worst case, this practice could lead to our giving students compelling proof that there is indeed something to their suspicion that "The Auroras of Autumn" might as well be a prose essay. This worst case indicates more about poor teaching than about any inherent quality in Stevens's poems, but an insistence that students must confront the difficult philosophical issues in the major poems without adequate preparation can involve a serious risk of reducing great art to philosophical paraphrase or even parody.

A tempting alternative is to abandon altogether the philosophical enterprise as unteachable and to concentrate on the beauty of Stevens's rhetoric. Poems should, after all, be read for their beauty and students should not be encouraged to substitute watered-down epistemology for real elegance. Yet abandoning this element of the poetry has hazards, too. We strip the art of much of its content and thereby inadvertently support the notion that Stevens's romanticism is closer to Oscar Wilde's than to Wordsworth's, of the decadent rather than of the meditative type.

Moreover, Stevens often indicated that for him much of poetry's appeal is the degree to which poets have a special opportunity to relate difficult content to their readers. In "The Noble Rider and the Sound of Words," he insists several times on a fundamentally pragmatic definition of the poet's unique role, one consistent with that in Horace's "Epistle to the Pisos" and with the celebrated "medicine of cherries" metaphor coined by Lucretius and appropriated by Sir Philip Sidney for his "Apologie for Poetrie": "I repeat that his role is to help people to live their lives. He has had immensely to do with giving life whatever savor it possesses. He has had to do with whatever the imagination and the senses have made of the world" (*NA* 30). One of the aphorisms in "Adagia" expresses a very similar thought: "The poet is the intermediary between people and the world in which they live and, also, between people as between themselves" (*OP* 189). "Notes toward a Supreme Fiction" contains an eloquently similar statement on how poems originate and what they can do:

> From this the poem springs: that we live in a place
> That is not our own and, much more, not ourselves
> And hard it is in spite of blazoned days. (*CP* 383)

This notion of the poet as intermediary or surrogate does not, of course, mean that the poet's function is didactic. On the contrary, Stevens feels that the poet's role is explicitly not to tell us what to think; he rather gives us a working example of one individual's imagination creatively encountering an unfamiliar reality and making sense of it.

Is there a middle ground that recognizes the importance of content without risking an epistemological snow job? In other words, is there a practical way for us to teach students what they need to know in order to read Stevens creatively? Several years ago, responding to my disappointment that only a few students appreciated what Stevens was up to in his poems, I tried this experiment, and since then it has seemed that a much higher percentage of them understand and appreciate the unique relation of genre to content in Stevens. Through a gradual approach to the canonical or inevitably anthologized poems that begins with selected minor texts, it is possible to prepare students for the complex issues behind "Notes toward a Supreme Fiction" or "The Man with the Blue Guitar," all the while keeping in focus that we are dealing with poems, not metaphysical treatises.

To introduce Stevens, I find it worthwhile to devote the entire first class to a dialogue among some minor poems, with emphasis on what I label "the poles of imagination and reality." This class occurs, usually, immediately after students have concluded their study of either Williams or Moore. The session will be followed up by a discussion of Stevens's notion of the fiction-making process, supported by close readings of "A High-Toned Old Christian Woman," "The Emperor of Ice-Cream," and "Anecdote of the Jar" arranged in a dialectical order similar to that of the initial class (thesis-antithesis-synthesis). This portion of the Stevens study, which will be followed by at least a week of studying selected larger texts, culminates with a session devoted to a dialectical reading of "The Idea of Order at Key West" as an integration of the aesthetic and philosophical concerns. For the sake of brevity I shall in this description skip over the second class, which takes up predominantly aesthetic issues, and describe how the first and third sessions prepare students to read Stevens with confidence and in many cases authentic delight.

Taking a cue from the opening stanza of "Connoisseur of Chaos," I mention early in the first class that Stevens's poems play with propositional logic and meditate on the need for synthesis in any either/or proposition. For pedagogical purposes, I reduce the basic epistemological issue in Stevens's poems to these excluding propositions:

A: The World Is What You Make of It.
B: You Are What the World Makes of You.

Proposition A deliberately suggests an imaginative approach to the world, one that leads almost inevitably to subjectivity. If reality exists only because a perceiving subject creates it, those errors and misconceptions to which all individuals' perceptual apparatus are subject may be given free reign. At the extreme of this approach to reality is solipsism, which at least one student can usually explain as a belief that all anyone can know is the self in the process of knowing. Proposition B, on the other hand, implies an objectivist approach to reality in which the external world dictates to the perceiver not only what can be known, but how one can know it. At its extreme this approach leads to paralysis, for one cannot influence, but can merely be influenced by, the external reality one encounters.

To illustrate Stevens's poetic meditation on Proposition A, I read "Tea at the Palaz of Hoon" (*CP* 65) aloud even though it has been assigned along with several other short poems. From the title and the overall tone, the students correctly infer that we are entering an exotic world, where palaces not only exist but are named in romance languages. More directed questions about diction (I usually carry a dictionary to this class) will reveal that Hoon's landscape is enchanted with purple aureoles or costumes in which one descends through the "loneliest air." The speaker (one of the many advantages of treating this poem as an introduction is the degree to which it repudiates the lyric mode and uses a speaker created for the occasion) asks grandiose questions about ointment on his beard, hymns in his ears, and the sea "whose tide swept through me there." Some students may discover for themselves that Hoon's questions are exotic and Whitmanesque. I usually have to tell them that his conclusions are virtually solipsistic, and sometimes cite Frank Doggett's quoting the fourth and fifth of these lines as examples of solipsism (Doggett 113):

> Out of my mind the golden ointment rained,
> And my ears made the blowing hymns they heard.
> I was myself the compass of that sea:
>
> I was the world in which I walked, and what I saw
> Or heard or felt came not but from myself;
> And there I found myself more truly and more strange.

Students who have studied American literature may be amused to learn that Joseph Riddel once equated Hoon with an Emersonian "I" at his fullest potential, or a transcendental "I" in turn-of-the-century costume (Riddel, *The Clairvoyant Eye* 64-65). Most important to my class strategy is helping students see that Hoon believes that his imagination, by perceiving, has actually created the world around him and that his created world is little more than a tribute to the ego that produced it—a monument to an imaginative process of self-conception.

The next, and key, challenge to this introductory class is what we are to make of Hoon's confident assertion that he not only creates the world he perceives in the act of perceiving it, but that this process leads him to exotic self-knowledge ("there I found myself more truly and more strange"). Is he an early version of the "fictive hero" in many of Stevens's later meditative poems who learns his own nature while creating the world in a sweeping act of perception? Or is he a massive egocentric? The often funny verbal clues indicate the latter. The pun on oneself as a "compass" (both a perimeter and an instrument for finding a direction) seems to me convincing evidence that Stevens is making fun of those who believe their own sense of conceptual direction is as absolute and reliable as a compass's magnetic instinct for true north. To corroborate this ironic reading of Proposition A, I sometimes show the class Stevens's description of "that mountain-minded Hoon" in "Sad Strains of a Gay Waltz" (*CP* 121), "Who found all form and order in solitude, / For whom the shapes were never the figures of men." To stimulate discussion, I occasionally mention that Michel Benamou calls Hoon a "mythical hero, whose palingeneses are among the most exciting features" of Stevens's poems (32). The problem Stevens satirizes in his portrayals of Hoon is a key term in his aesthetic, in his theme, and in the dialogue in which I hope to engage my class. Although it is inevitable that people shape their reality by perceiving it individually, to do this without restraint is to risk an absurdly egocentric view of reality, a point that could easily be corroborated by looking at "Bantams in Pine-Woods" or "A Rabbit as King of the Ghosts."

For this pedagogical purpose, then, Hoon and, by extension, Proposition A ("The World Is What you Make of It") are represented as a thesis. A poem from the same period "The Doctor of Geneva" (*CP* 24) and, by extension, Proposition B ("You Are What the World Makes of You") can be presented as the antithesis. In ways that students should easily discern if we ask the right questions, the poems suggest clear contrasts. "Tea at the Palaz of Hoon" is dramatic, whereas "The Doctor of Geneva" is a small narrative; the character Hoon is egocentric, whereas the doctor seems diffident; Hoon is gallant, exotic, and hubristic, whereas the doctor appears to be a meek academician; Hoon rejoices in dominating the physical world and becomes the "compass" of a sea, whereas the doctor is overwhelmed by an unfamiliar ocean.

Upon the last contrast the class should begin to develop some sense of what is at stake in this dialectic. If they learned that Hoon's error was his asserting himself too confidently and uncritically as the arbiter of his environment, they will discover for themselves that the doctor's error is nearly a direct opposite. As a "Lacustrine" man, or someone who lives in a region of lakes, he is intimidated by the magnitude and power of the Pacific Ocean (clever students will be delighted to catch an irony here; "pacific," of course, means "peaceful"). His perplexity is suggested by two sets of images to which most undergraduates will discover that they can relate. Like a child on the verge of a tantrum, he "stamped the sand" in a futile gesture of control or self-assertion, with a probable pun on "stamp" as to impress or make a mark. Unable to assert himself, he "Patted his stove-pipe hat and tugged his shawl," two funny and anachronistic, but signifying, gestures; both are efforts to tighten, or control, his clothing, which at its most practical level protects one from the elements, a signification Stevens reinforces when the doctor resorts to his handkerchief in the final line. At a slightly more symbolic level, this taking refuge in his clothing suggests his introverted response to being intimidated by a reality as unfamiliar and massive as the ocean (we may be fortunate enough to have a student remind us that Hoon claimed to be the sole creator of the sea). The doctor's initial position thus suggests that he is powerless to influence his world and can only be influenced by what he sees.

But "The Doctor of Geneva" is a narrative poem, and the genre itself implies plot or sequence. Whereas Hoon's experience of the sea is static, the doctor's is dynamic. Once this is pointed out, students will see that this character does not accept defeat easily. He even indulges momentarily and mock-heroically in a Hoon-like enterprise. Having read about oceans and the like in authorities he apparently respects (Racine and Bossuet), he attempts confidently, if unsuccessfully, to apply what he has read in books and what he has learned as a lake-man to this new problem:

> He did not quail. A man so used to plumb
> The multifarious heavens felt no awe
> Before these visible, voluble delugings. . . .

Reasoning by analogy, the doctor tries to apply what he knows about lakes, usually fairly calm and contained bodies of water, and about heavens, usually distant and unreachable abstractions, to oceans. His failure is in part due to his having an insufficient frame of reference to deal with the phenomenon before him; he knows a great deal, but much of it is about irrelevant things.

The failure is also due to his lack of fundamental respect for what he observes (he "felt no awe"). The sea does not yield to the doctor's intellectual paradigms, and the result is mental frenzy. It sets "his simmering mind / Spinning and hissing with oracular / Notations of the wild, the ruinous waste." His mind—not the sea, as many students are likely to construe the passage—"spins," "hisses," and "simmers" with frightening observations about what the sea, and by extension its intransigence to human conceptions, means. In what must be the funniest metaphysical conceit in all of Stevens's poems, the doctor sneezes: "the steeples of his city clanked and sprang / In an unburgherly apocalypse." Just as adverse physical conditions can produce illness in individuals, a lack of flexibility in concept formation can produce mental paralysis. The doctor "sighed," a response that in most students' experience indicates regret and often resignation to a condition one cannot do anything about.

So the point of this first class is that logically any combination of thesis and antithesis requires a synthesis, an approach to reality that accounts for the operation of imagination in a creative way and that recognizes art as a mediator—in short, a way to avoid both the solipsism of Hoon and the paralysis of the doctor. This understanding can lead the class to a comprehension of the fiction-making process and eventually toward a synthesis. An unanticipated benefit of reading "Tea at the Palaz of Hoon" and "The Doctor of Geneva" as preparation for reading "The Idea of Order at Key West" is that having treated these poems as drama and narrative, we can approach the more complicated work with a critical and genre-based, rather than esoteric and metaphysical, set of questions and thereby avoid some of the abstraction problems cited early in this paper. In fact, the dramatic and narrative properties of "The Idea of Order at Key West" may help us to understand its themes and aesthetic qualities much more clearly than an obtuse set of epistemological paraphrases would.

In a narrative poem, the first question we need to ask is "What happens?" After all, there is probably some perfectly good reason that a particular inspiration suggested the narrative mode to the poet. What happens in "The Idea of Order at Key West" (*CP* 128) is surprisingly simple. Someone, an unidentified speaker, hears a woman sing a song and thinks about what he has heard, then acts on it. While my students assimilate such a deliberately reductive paraphrase, I begin to refine it by observing that the woman sings a song while the man thinks about the meaning of her song and its possible applications for his life.

What is fascinating about the poem is how very little anyone knows about its central incident as event. I often challenge my students to list the things they can say about either the woman or her song. What did she look like? Tall and stately, short and demure, plump and sunburned, slim and pale? We know only that she walked by herself ("striding there alone"). What if any gestures accompanied her performance? The stage directions in the poem apply to the sea. How did she sound—alto, soprano, flat, dramatic, clear, resonant? Did she chant, rhapsodize, or merely mumble? Nothing at all describes her voice, which seemed to be the focus of the poem. Most curiously, what on earth *was* her song? We get several hints that it was not "of the sea," but what it was we must guess for ourselves.

The point of discovering what we do not know about the poem, although most students thought they knew all of this before they were asked about it, is that "The Idea of Order at Key West" is not "about" the creation of art primarily, but about our need for art. The importance of the song is not what it said, but the effect it had on an auditor. In fact "she," the singer, virtually disappears from the poem after the fourth stanza, precisely because her existence and her song were never the key issues. The major concerns were the reflections by the unidentified speaker upon the ways in which her song could create order out of a chaotic sea, which is neither self-created as in "Tea at the Palaz of Hoon" nor overwhelming as in "The Doctor of Geneva," but unmistakably there as something to be decoded and interpreted. In the third stanza, the speaker ponders the sound of the sea as merely a sea and concludes that, had they been listening to the sea itself, "it would have been deep air, / The heaving speech of air, a summer sound / . . . And sound alone." This conclusion leads the speaker and us as teachers and students to yet another question, for what was heard was not the sea, but it was "More even than her voice." What, then, was it?

In this poem "it" is primarily the cause for the speaker and the reader to reflect on the relation of art to our living our lives. What they heard, whatever it was, causes the speaker to see that the ocean, formerly "Inhuman," "ever-hooded," "meaningless plungings of water and the wind," can be brought into perspective by the human imagination. She, through her song, transforms this meaningless and menacing reality into a meaningful construction:

> . . . And when she sang, the sea
> Whatever self it had, became the self
> That was her song, for she was the maker. Then we,
> As we beheld her striding there alone,
> Knew that there never was a world for her
> Except the one she sang and, singing, made.

Although the most perceptive students may suggest that this sounds like Hoon's solipsism, the emphasis here is not on her transforming the world by perceiving, but on her need to interpret and articulate her perception. Even more crucially, the emphasis is not on what she learns about herself by "singing the sea," but on what the speaker learns about himself by hearing her song.

The transformation of the sea to "the self / That was her song" produces two results for the speaker, our intermediary with her. First, he finds that hearing someone else's fiction can establish a perspective on what he has up to this moment failed to understand: her voice makes the sky "acutest at its vanishing," or sharpens his perspective on his horizons— figuratively as well as literally. Much more importantly, her song produces in him the need to make his own supreme fiction. This is the meaning of the last, crucial phase of what happens at Key West.

What happens in the last two sections of the poem is something similar to one of James Joyce's epiphanies. The speaker re-sees, and recreates, the sea by seeing it anew. Whereas before hearing her song he felt uninterested in, or perhaps alienated from, the ocean, this "afterglow" of her song brings him a revised, enriched perception of the sea: as he observes the play of lights in the harbor, the sea and the night become *mastered, portioned, fixed, arranged, deepened,* and *enchanted.* Of the six adjectives here, students can be led by simple diction questions to see that four of them indicate control, perspective, mastery, or what Stevens implies by the phrase "idea of order." The final two, however, suggest aesthetic richness and wonder. What these describe, moreover, is not the singer's idea of the sea, for that was something she could describe only for herself and something, significantly, that Stevens as creator chooses not to share with us. The speaker, and Ramon Fernandez, and for that matter we as readers, cannot appropriate her fiction; but what they and we take from hearing her song is the impetus to create our own, to make our own fictions that paradoxically render the commonplace exotic and the fearful manageable.

The song in "The Idea of Order at Key West" and the poem of which it is a key component serve precisely this function. They teach us how to make the world we cannot understand our own. But the poem does not create or order the world for us; it shows us how we might proceed for ourselves, and it shows us one set of rewards that may follow on our efforts. If our students understand, by reading comparatively simple poems like "Tea at the Palaz of Hoon" and "The Doctor of Geneva," just how much can go wrong if we practice excessive subjectivity or passivity in creating our understanding of the world, they should be able to understand and appreciate how art empowers us to form our own fictions in a more complex poem like "The Idea of Order at Key West." With this understanding in place, they, and perhaps we, will be ready to reflect on the great meditative poems.

Part III. Comparative Approaches

Lending No Part:
Teaching Stevens with Williams

LISA M. STEINMAN

Stevens's poetry can be notoriously difficult to teach. As Williams wrote on the occasion of Stevens's death, many of the poems seem to bespeak a man "sticking [his] thumb . . . to [his] nose . . . at the world" ("Comment" 234), or at frustrated readers, as my students sometimes complain. In fact, Williams imagines himself and Stevens together facing the world's contempt for their "mastery in the difficult art of the poem. It is at the contempt of the world for that, that we would be really thumbing our noses" ("Comment" 234). As this comment suggests, Stevens's poems are far more accessible to students when placed back into the literary and other debates to which they respond, most especially when seen as a response to questions that the world of early twentieth-century America posed to its poets and that the poets debated with one another.

Despite Williams's hint that the two poets jointly thumbed their noses at the world, Stevens and Williams were not always in agreement. Yet they were part of the same conversation (MacLeod 77–91; Heinzelman 85–113), a conversation that began in the teens and can be traced in the classroom through Williams's *Kora in Hell,* Stevens's "The Comedian as the Letter C," Stevens's introduction to Williams's *Collected Poems,* Williams's "Comment" on Stevens, or Stevens's late poems with titles that seem to be variations on themes by Williams: "The Plain Sense of Things," "Not Ideas about the Thing but the Thing Itself," and "Reality Is an Activity of the Most August Imagination."

One of the easiest ways to present this conversation to a class is to start with Stevens's sly 1918 response to Williams's 1916 poem "El Hombre." In Williams's deceptively simple-looking, four-line poem, the speaker views a single star at sunrise—Venus or Lucifer, the morning star—and notes that the star "lend[s] no part" to the gathering morning light (*CPWCW* I, 76). Yet in its separateness, the star is said to give "a strange courage" to the speaker. Having asked students to glance at other poems by Williams from the same period (even the same volume), I can count on someone to point out that "El Hombre" is atypical in that it invokes none of the gritty local detail—"old chicken wire, ashes . . . outhouses," or "stinking ash-cart[s]" (*CPWCW* I, 64, 77)—most often found in Williams's short imagist poems. For instance, Williams's "Smell!" contains the following lines: "What tactless asses we are, you and I, boney nose, / always indiscriminate, always unashamed, . . . we quicken our desires / to that rank odor of a passing springtime" (*CPWCW* I, 92). With its deliberate inversion of the poetic tropes of spring and desire, "Smell!" gains much of its power from the poeticisms it invokes and then refuses, as much as from the realistic detail it includes. In context, then, students first read "El Hombre" as a parodic romantic gesture. The Shelleyan star of love stands fast against the hard light of day, as the speaker—presumably the macho "El Hombre" of the title—stands against the world (perhaps thumbing his nose).

Stevens, of course, knew Williams's work: "Smell!" appeared in Williams's volume *Al Que Quiere!* as well as in the July 1917 issue of *Poetry;* Stevens most probably read it in both of these places. "El Hombre" first appeared in the December 1916 issue of *Others* and was reprinted the following year in both the *Others Anthology* and *Al Que Quiere!* Stevens could have read it in any one of these publications, and, again, probably saw the poem in more than one publication. "Nuances of a Theme by Williams" (*CP* 18) may then be taught as a rereading of "El Hombre" through Williams's more usual strategy of thumbing his nose at genteel readers by making poetry of what seems ordinary, even squalid. In "Nuances of a Theme by Williams," Stevens reprints Williams's short poem, and then adds a ten-line commentary on it, in which he tells Williams's star to "shine like bronze, / that reflects neither my face nor any inner part / of my being, shine like fire." In other words, starlight is *not* reflected light, and Williams's use of the star as a mirror of his position (even while he claims the star shines "alone") is questioned in Stevens's transformation of Williams's star from bronze, which does reflect, to fire, which "mirrors nothing." In effect, Stevens uses "El Hombre" to mock

Williams's usual pose as a sharp-eyed (or sharp-nosed) realist, even a muck-raker, catching the sights and speech of urban America for what they are.

To be sure, in poems like "Pastoral," Williams insists that poetry is in opposition to the usual business of "the nation," where men try to "make something of [themselves]" (*CPWCW* I, 64–65). Pointing this out, I can often lead students to the conclusion that the portrait in "El Hombre" of the solitary stargazing artist seems self-conscious about its pathos. Williams's poem, in other words, may already contain the self-consciousness Stevens brings to it. After all, why is it a "strange courage" "El Hombre" is given? On first reading, "strange courage" reads as the courage to stand up in the face of overwhelming odds, knowing one will certainly be eclipsed. On second reading, however, especially in light of Williams's own final image of the star as that which lends no part to anything around it, the speaker's courage seems "strange" just because of his recognition that his relationship to what he sees is problematic. In short, Williams in one word has already recognized the irony of his apostrophic address to the isolate star, a gesture Stevens simply unpacks at greater length: "Lend no part to any humanity that suffuses / you in its own light." And if Williams already knew that his star was "Half man, half star," not the thing in itself he more usually appeared to claim, Stevens may be said to have granted Williams this recognition. Asking my students to reconsider Stevens's title, I can note that Stevens's poem offers "nuances," not revisions, of Williams's theme, suggesting he knew that the shades of meaning to which his poem calls attention were already there in "El Hombre."

At the same time, one can in effect recreate the poets' exchange in the classroom by further noting how Stevens's poem ends with a shift of emphasis that, to paraphrase one of Stevens's epigrams in "Adagia," is tantamount to a change of meaning. Telling Williams's star not to be "an intelligence, / Like a widow's bird / Or an old horse" is like telling someone not to think of pink elephants. The mind, naturally, thinks of just what it has been told not to imagine. Further, widows' birds and old horses are domestic creatures, comforting pets made over in their owners' images just as Williams's star is domesticated when it is said to give his speaker courage. Stevens's point, as in "The Snow Man" (*CP* 9), written three years later, is that we construct even those landscapes that appear to be naturalistic reports containing nothing "that is not there."

More generally, classroom discussions of "Nuances of a Theme by Williams" are most illuminating when the poem is placed in the context not only of Williams's "El Hombre" (read with poems such as "Pastoral" and "Smell!"), but also in the context of other shorter early poems by Stevens like "The Snow Man," "Gubbinal," "Another Weeping Woman," "Thirteen Ways of Looking at a Blackbird," and "Earthy Anecdote." In this light, it becomes clear to students that Stevens is deliberately refusing to give us what, by literary convention, we understand to be realism or a plain sense of things. This refusal is, in part, one side of a conversation with Williams. What is at stake in the conversation is not simply whose style is best, but, ultimately, what poetry can claim to offer its readers, and in particular Americans of the teens, twenties, and thirties.

The conversation, as I tell my students, was long-standing: in response to a 1934 survey that asked, "Do you intend your poetry to be useful to yourself or others?" and "As a poet what distinguishes you . . . from an ordinary man?" Williams stated he wished his poetry to be useful to others and offered "[p]owers of perceptions, synopsis, and expression" as what made him a poet ("An Enquiry" 15–16). Again, Williams claims he concisely expresses what he sees. Stevens, on the other hand, objected to the questions. Asked if he meant his poetry to be of use to himself or others, he said, "Not consciously." Asked what distinguished him as a poet from the ordinary man, he suggested that he shared with ordinary men an inability "to see much point to the life of an ordinary man." Implicit in Stevens's apparently dismissive comment is his insistence that poetry does have a point, but it is not to be confused with practical utility, or portraits of daily life presented as a kind of journalistic realism. Williams was still carrying on the conversation between them in his comments written after Stevens's death, where he gets the last word, pointing out that Stevens was "in the midst of a life crowded with business affairs a veritable monk"; that "the poems themselves [dealt] not at all with the man in the street"; that when Stevens *became a realist it was never in his own person*" ("Comment" 235–36; emphasis added).

Revising Stevens's reaction to the 1934 questionnaire, and reversing Stevens's strategy in "Nuances of a Theme by Williams," Williams repeats much that Stevens said, or might have said, of himself. But Stevens would presumably have protested that the opposite of a businessman is not a monk and that literary realists are no more in touch with reality than anyone else. For Stevens, reality always lends a part to those who suffuse it in their own light, which is to say that it grants a role (or rather lends one), as well as offers a piece of itself, to those who imaginatively invest themselves in it. If we see only what we have already changed, and if we ourselves—our self-identities, roles, or "parts"—are constituted by this interactive process, then no one is a realist "in his *own* person."

Students can also be made aware of other contemporary voices—James Oppenheim's or John Dewey's, found in the pages of the *Dial,* for instance—that enter this conversation between Stevens and Williams. Dewey insisted, for example, that "the locality is the only universal" (Dewey 687). This statement is from a June 1920 article, "Americanism and Localism," in which Dewey argues that neither newspaper reporting nor "local color" count as "locality." Stevens, who briefly tried his hand as a reporter, had reason to agree. For that matter, Williams would have agreed on what did not count as locality. What might count remained a point of contention between the two poets, as the dialogue that began in "Nuances of a Theme by Williams" continued throughout the two men's lives. However, something further is revealed by bringing in Dewey and others (by the thirties, including those who insisted on realism in the *New Masses*). Students can be shown that Stevens is not only engaged in a friendly argument with Williams; both are responding to widespread discussions about what constituted American writing about American reality. To reframe the point: Stevens's and Williams's poems are informed by, as well as forming, a larger cultural dialogue. If Williams at times defends poetry as valuable in twentieth-century America by appeal to realistic, detailed description, Stevens keeps him honest by asking if his landscapes are not, like a widow's bird, personal and social constructions. If Stevens insists that all landscapes are imagined—that there are at least thirteen ways of looking at any bird—Williams forces him to be clear about how his style makes this larger statement.

Reading Stevens in this light, a class can discover just how much is at issue in an apparently simple poem like "Nuances of a Theme by Williams." Seeing how Stevens's insistence on process, as well as his suspicion of literary realism, are embedded in, and responsive to, larger cultural questions also illuminates poems like "Thirteen Ways of Looking at a Blackbird" and "Earthy Anecdote." It is worth telling students that in 1918—the same year he wrote "Nuances of a Theme by Williams"—Stevens wrote to Carl Zigrosser, editor of *The Modern School,* who published a number of Stevens's pieces, that there was "no symbolism in the 'Earthy Anecdote'"; Stevens added, "There's a good deal of theory about it, however" (*L* 204). The theories informing such poetic gestures are, I suggest to my students, theories about realism, about the representation of facts, about place and how we constitute ourselves in places. Further, such theories are forged in dialogue with others, most visibly with Williams.

I also emphasize that there was not always a clear understanding between the two poets, by any means. Indeed, were their agreements clear or their disagreements easily settled, presumably Stevens and Williams would not have continued their lifelong exchange. The complexity of this exchange can be further presented in class by looking at the letters reprinted by Williams in the prologue to *Kora in Hell* (published in 1920) and at Stevens's references to Williams in "The Comedian as the Letter C" (which appeared two years later). In *Kora in Hell,* Williams explains his "clash" with Stevens, quoting a letter from Stevens on how one should not "'fidget with points of view [which] leads always to new beginnings and incessant new beginnings lead to sterility'" (*Imaginations* 14–15). Stevens concludes, "'I think your tantrums not half mad enough,'" and Williams responds: "*What would you have me do with my Circe, Stevens, now that I have double-crossed her game, marry her? It is not what Odysseus did*" (*Imaginations* 16). Williams later reports Stevens's cutting response about those expatriates whom Williams disliked—and half envied—for running to London: "'But where in the world will you have them run to?'" (*Imaginations* 27). Williams grudgingly responds, "Dear fat Stevens, thawing out so beautifully at forty!" (*Imaginations* 27). Students generally enjoy the sharpness of this dialogue, and the exchange, though moderated by Williams, is instructive, since we tend to think of *Stevens* as fidgeting with points of view, at the same time that we associate him with stylistic decorum, not mad tantrums.

Thinking back to "El Hombre" and Stevens's variations on it, however, a class usually can make sense of Stevens's letter: Williams's stylistic experiments may be said to dance around the question of how to understand poetic representation. For example, I ask whether "Smell!" is a piece of American speech, or a verbal description of a "real" world, or whether even the "rank odor" it describes is just another widow's bird. Williams raises such questions, but usually only implicitly insofar as he tries different strategies from poem to poem. Stevens, on the other hand, makes such questions central; indeed, he makes poems out of such questions and asks Williams to do the same. In this sense, "Nuances of a Theme by Williams," for all that the first stanza is Williams's poem, is characteristically a poem by Stevens, while "El Hombre" is only one of many poses Williams strikes.

Often someone in class will mention that Williams unfairly puts words in Stevens's mouth by appropriating his letters (a gesture I point out he may have learned from Stevens's "Nuances of a Theme by Williams"). To rescue Stevens's letter from Williams, I ask *which* poet fidgets with points of view. The answer is not cut and dried, but it becomes clear that the poet "fidgeting with points of view" is not necessarily the one who looks at blackbirds in thirteen ways, although Williams's final "Comment" returns to complain that "Stevens seldom comes down on a statement of fact. It is always, 'thirteen ways of looking at a blackbird,' which cannot but weaken any attack" ("Comment" 236). Stevens's response was already in the letter Williams placed in *Kora in Hell*. It is also more fully in "The Comedian as the Letter C," which, among other things, tackles head on Williams's challenge: *"What would you have me do with my Circe . . . marry her? It is not what Odysseus did."*

It is after my students have grappled with the above-mentioned exchanges between Stevens and Williams that "The Comedian as the Letter C" makes most sense to them, since the poem further confronts and deconstructs Williams's (and Stevens's) desire for "the veritable ding an sich, at last" (*CP* 29), suggesting in that very phrase that things in themselves come to us always already in a foreign tongue . . . or in translation. Although I assign the entire poem, I tell students to concentrate on four passages from "The Comedian as the Letter C" (one in "The World without Imagination," a second in "Approaching Carolina," and two in "A Nice Shady Home"), which can most easily be read in light of the conversation the class has been tracing between Stevens, Williams, and others. On Crispin's world without imagination (a world of things in themselves), Stevens writes in the first passage I assign that the "imagination, here, could not evade, / In poems of plums, the strict austerity" (*CP* 30), which students understand as meaning in part that the world in itself, truly unimagined, truly undomesticated, has nothing to say to us; indeed, we would have no way of constructing ourselves in such a world. The second passage on which I have students focus describes how, as Crispin approaches Carolina seeking a new, unliterary world in America, he has "postulated as his theme / The vulgar" (*CP* 35). Seeking "the essential prose" (*CP* 36), Crispin is surely a parody of Williams (Strom 258–76), as more than one student can be counted on to point out after reading the following lines:

> . . . Tilting up his nose,
> He inhaled the rancid rosin, burly smells
> Of dampened lumber, emanations blown
> From warehouse doors, the gustiness of ropes,
> Decays of sacks, and all the arrant stinks
> That helped him round his rude aesthetic out.
> He savored rankness like a sensualist.
> He marked the marshy ground around the dock,
> The crawling railroad spur, the rotten fence,
> Curriculum for the marvelous sophomore. (*CP* 36)

Having begun with the postulate that "man is the intelligence of his soil" (*CP* 27), as widows are of their birds, Crispin settles down in "The Idea of a Colony" by reversing the hypothesis: "his soil is man's intelligence" (*CP* 36). As "realist," he admits in the third assigned passage that one may "stop short before a plum / And be content and still be realist. / The words of things entangle and confuse. / The plum survives its poems" (*CP* 40–41). Classroom discussion can be led to the idea that the poems of plums here do not evade either reality in itself or the essential prose of American industrial landscapes; one can note that Stevens thus points out to Williams, through Crispin, how to be a realist without the standard sordid subject matter of literary realism. Reality, in any case, survives its poems.

It is in "The Comedian as the Letter C," also, with the building of a nice shady home, that Stevens reconstructs the quotidian, both for himself and for Williams, in the final passage to which I ask students to pay close attention. The passage also allows me to reiterate that the arguments between the two poets are, in part and in each case, arguments with themselves as well as arguments they both have with a world in which poetry is not highly valued.

Stevens writes: "the quotidian saps philosophers / And men like Crispin" (*CP* 42). Students often first read this as simply a statement to the effect that realism—rancid or sweet—has limits, or that, as Williams so astutely pointed out, to marry what enchants one (one's "Circe") is to cease to explore. I propose in class an alternative reading, suggesting that Stevens transforms the quotidian, in part by a redefinition of what it means "to sap" toward the end of the assigned passage:

> But the quotidian composed as his,
> Of breakfast ribands, fruits laid in their leaves,
> The tomtit and the cassia and the rose,
> Although the rose was not the noble thorn
> Of crinoline spread, but of a pining sweet,
> Composed of evenings like cracked shutters flung
> Upon the rumpling bottomness, and nights
> In which those frail custodians watched,
> Indifferent to the tepid summer cold,
> While he poured out upon the lips of her
> That lay beside him, the quotidian
> Like this, saps like the sun, true fortuner.
> For all it takes it gives a humped return
> Exchequering from piebald fiscs unkeyed. (*CP* 42–43)

The sun, of course, makes sap rise and produces fruit (Zinn 86–89). The quotidian works "like this," writes Stevens, and closes with two lines I suggest to students are calculated to set Williams's teeth on edge, using precisely the kind of language that Williams's "Comment" cites as Stevens's weakness in its attention to "the sheer tactile qualities" (236) of words rather than to statements of fact: "giv[ing] a humped return / Exchequering from piebald fiscs unkeyed."

My students often arrive already having read Williams's "This Is Just to Say" ("I have eaten / the plums" [*CPWCW* I, 372]), and I generally assign them "To a Poor Old Woman" ("munching a plum on . . . " [*CPWCW* I, 383]). Quite rightly, they ask if Stevens is not also commenting on Williams's plums. What is interesting is that both of Williams's plum poems appeared in 1934, twelve years after "The Comedian as the Letter C." So to the question of whose plums these are, one must answer that Stevens is the exchequer of the plums. Or, perhaps, "The plum survives its poems." It is illuminating to consider especially Williams's "To a Poor Old Woman" as another round in the exchange between the two writers. But that is to consider reading Williams in light of Stevens, while my topic at the moment is how students might profit from reading Stevens in light of Williams.

Here, then, it is more appropriate to end with the final comment I make to my classes on how Stevens's landscape in "The Comedian as the Letter C" is an American landscape, and on how explicit he is in saying that not just rank lumberyards but piebald fiscs are part of this landscape. Put another way, not just piebald fiscs but rank lumberyards are imaginative and linguistic constructions. Stevens thus again responds to Williams's edgy bitterness about those who ran off to Europe and despaired of there being civilization in the United States (to use the title of Harold E. Stearns's influential 1922 collection of essays). The substance of the response is that in Stevens's treasury, to cite John Barth on another speaker, Scheherazade, "the key to the treasure *is* the treasure" (Barth 8, 11, et passim). The quotidian is "like this," the gestures or language of the mind in the act of finding, an act more easily understood when it is made clear to students that Stevens's is not a solo performance enacted in isolation.

Teaching Wallace Stevens and Marianne Moore: The Search for an Open Mind

ROBIN GAIL SCHULZE

As a teacher of poetry I daily confront a central and disturbing contradiction. Seated in front of a sea of faces I present material that I deem important, asking questions that I find relevant, conducting discussions that I, for the most part, orchestrate. Each day while introducing my charges to my world and my thoughts, I rather didactically implore them to "think for themselves." Ironically, the lesson I try to teach my students is not simply to learn my lessons. Rather than have my undergraduates adopt my words as gospel, I bid them gather as many thoughts as possible, "take their prey to privacy," as Marianne Moore would say, and reemerge with informed, considered opinions of their own.

To grant such power to a sea of nodding heads over notebooks may seem difficult. The very act of "instructing" students to think their own thoughts stands as a contradiction, one that Wallace Stevens himself encountered most memorably at the beginning of "Notes toward a Supreme Fiction" when the poet-narrator "instructs" the novice poet to "become an ignorant man again" (*CP* 380), to see his world for himself and thus presumably to resist the sort of instruction he is being offered. The question of "thinking for oneself" in the face of seductive ideas lies deep at the heart of much modern verse, particularly that of Stevens and his friend and fellow poet Marianne Moore. Throughout their careers, both Moore and Stevens considered the potentially inhibiting effect of strong thoughts, weighing the benefits and pitfalls of intellectual influence in an attempt to maintain individual poetic freedom. In my experience, both Moore's and Stevens's poems strike a chord in undergraduate students who themselves are grappling to find individual voices, struggling to create "more furious selves" in a world of shifting forces that compete daily for their minds and souls. "Why seraphim like lutanists arranged / Above the trees? And why the poet as / Eternal *chef d'orchestre?*" questions a petulant Stevens in one of his many poems dedicated to mental housecleaning, "Evening without Angels" (*CP* 136). Why must poets continually fill the sky with the same stale images that adorn the great vault of heaven dictated by poets past? "Air is air," he grumbles; why clutter it with the same old pictures? Moore, too, questions the wisdom of adopting outworn inflexible systems to govern life and art. Both Moore and Stevens search for ways to challenge comfortable forms and "think for themselves" in the face of inhibiting established perceptions.

Yet, for both Moore and Stevens the act of "thinking for oneself" proves more difficult than it might appear. Both poets remain painfully aware that the tropes we hold dear will eventually age, that ideas that attract will become thoughts that trap. What, then, is a poet to do? If all tropes, all thoughts have the potential to oppress, how does the poet, or, I might add, the professor, keep his or her own work from duplicating the didactic sins of the past he or she wishes to escape? How does the poet, like the professor, avoid becoming the unwitting oppressor in turn—as Stevens puts it in "Esthétique du Mal," "the lunatic of one idea" (*CP* 325)? Stevens's and Moore's responses to such questions speak to the relevance of both poets in a college classroom. Throughout their careers, the two poets developed similar strategies to maintain the open-ended nature of their poetic explorations, stressing the concept of poetry as process rather than product. Teaching Stevens and Moore through the lens of such strategies provides students with an important lesson in keeping an open mind. Rather than construct poems as acts of clear ideological assertion, both poets struggle to discover their artistic selves in provisionalized moments meant to question, not duplicate, intellectual oppression.

As most teachers know, Stevens's verse is filled with tactics designed to downplay the finality of any one poetic event. Stevens writes "anecdotes" rather than manifestos, making "notes" toward the supreme fiction rather than didactically prescribing the whole. Stevens most clearly displays his provisionalizing tendencies, however, in his careful poetic ordering, a fact that points to the importance of teaching Stevens with an eye to original arrangement. Both Moore and Stevens made a habit of publishing poems in carefully organized sets, particularly in pairs in which one poem questions, undercuts, and cycles into the other. In such pairs the space between the poems often proves as important as the content of any single lyric. Reading Stevens's and Moore's pertinent pairs helps students get a textual handle on the ways both poets work to keep their minds open and their poetry alive.

Granted, teaching Moore's work alongside Stevens's may seem to generate a double burden, particularly in an undergraduate class. If Stevens's work has a reputation as a difficult study, many teachers consider Moore's poetry positively impenetrable. Yet, I find that teaching Moore and Stevens side by side makes the job of teaching both poets easier. The similarity between Stevens's and Moore's paired poems gives students the opportunity to think comparatively. Students baffled by Stevens's images may find the same ideas crystal clear in Moore's quirky concrete poems; those perplexed by Moore's allusions may feel more at home with Stevens's metaphors and abstractions. Bringing both poets to class gives students twice the opportunity to understand and enjoy. I also think it important to show students that Stevens did not create his poems in a vacuum. Stevens and Moore were correspondents, colleagues, and sponsors of each other's works. Their poetic conversation positions Stevens in an intellectual community of a particular period for whom certain thoughts were in the air.

I like to begin an exploration of poetic pairs by sending students to our rare-book room to examine a copy of Harriet Shaw Weaver's little modernist magazine *The Egoist*. Whenever possible, I like to familiarize students with the textual package in which modernist poems first appeared. Reading around in a lively, controversial modernist periodical gives students a sense of intellectual and historical context, introducing them to a concrete record of the past that rescues poems from a position as mere stale museum pieces. The 1 October 1915 issue of *The Egoist* contains a pair of Marianne Moore's verses that she published under the heading "Two Poems": "Diligence Is to Magic as Progress Is to Flight," and "To a Steam Roller." After sending my students to the library, I ask them to consider how each poem in Moore's pair depicts the relationship between a designated mind and a set of new ideas. In "Diligence Is to Magic," Moore pictures the progress of a path-clearing female poet who, perched on an elephant, works "diligently" to escape old ideas and outworn tropes. Moore writes:

> With an elephant to ride upon—"with rings on her fingers and bells on
>   her toes,"
>   she shall outdistance calamity anywhere she goes.
> Speed is not in her mind inseparable from carpets. Locomotion arose
>   in the shape of an elephant; she clambered up and chose
> to travel laboriously. So far as magic carpets are concerned, she knows
>   that although the semblance of speed may attach to scarecrows
> of aesthetic procedure, the substance of it is embodied in such of those
>   tough-grained animals as have outstripped man's whim to
>   suppose
> them ephemera, and have earned that fruit of their ability to endure
>   blows,
>   which dubs them prosaic necessities—not curios. (158)

Moore starts her poem by rewriting the popular nursery rhyme "Ride a Cock Horse," and I can always count on a few students being able to recite the original verse and interpret Moore's revisions. The quotation Moore borrows, "with rings on her fingers and bells on her toes," points to the lady's role as an artist ("and she shall have music wherever she goes," ends the rhyme), yet instead of a graceful white horse, Moore puts her lady poet atop a lumbering elephant. The woman who rides may still be "fine" but, in Moore's version, she is not afraid to get her hands dirty; poetry implies work and sacrifice. The ornamental jingle-jangle of verse becomes a matter of life and death for Moore's poet, a means to "outdistance calamity" in a hostile world. Moore's revised nursery rhyme speaks to her vision of a durable new poetic and students are quick to grasp the nature of elephant verse: earthbound, substantive, strong, tough-grained, and prosaic. New ideas must be "earned" and Moore's poet prefers to travel individually, working to outstrip old notions about art.

The elephant poet thus travels a route directly opposed to a purely decorative tradition in verse that Moore pictures in another image readily accessible to undergraduates, the magic carpet. Exotic flights of fancy detached from the every day, magic-carpet poems offer transcendent moments that Moore sees as nothing more than hot air. Students often note that, while elephants are real creatures, magic carpets belong only in bedtime stories. Moore dubs such ephemeral products of the imagination "scarecrows of aesthetic procedure," speedily erected shams constructed only to fool and distract. I make a point of reminding my students that "Diligence Is to Magic" is a war poem. The quest for a new poetry that can endure blows and bear hard witness to disaster rather than offer a frivolous romantic escape becomes particularly poignant in the context of a world blowing itself to bits. Crafting a wonderful thematic pun, Moore ends by insisting that white-elephant poems are not "white elephants." Moore's fine lady may ride a pale pachyderm, but her works are not rummage-sale curios or intellectual knickknacks; they are "prosaic necessities" applicable to the calamities at hand.

After a discussion of "Diligence Is to Magic," my students generally sit back, convinced that they now have a handle on Moore's agenda: modernist lady poet proposes new tough prosy poetry to transform the restrictive tropes of a flighty tradition, granting poems themselves a new place of popular importance. Fine. With such thoughts in play, Moore's companion piece "To a Steam Roller" seems at first to fall easily into place:

> The illustration
> is nothing to you without the application.
> > You lack half wit. You crush all the particles down
> > > into close conformity, and then walk back and forth on them.
>
> Sparkling chips of rock
> are crushed down to the level of the parent block.
> > Were not "impersonal judgement in aesthetic
> > > matters, a metaphysical impossibility," you
>
> might fairly achieve
> it. As for butterflies, I can hardly conceive
> > of one's attending upon you, but to question
> > > the congruence of the complement is vain, if it exists. (158)

Where Moore's "Diligence" poem paints a picture of an individual working to free herself from established ideas, "To a Steam Roller" presents just the sort of restrictive mind that such a lady wishes to "outdistance." Students involved in university bureaucracies, feeling themselves "steam rollered" by a host of autocratic minds like the one Moore describes, their "sparkling" ideas leveled by a need to conform to seemingly oppressive rubrics firmly in place, often respond strongly to Moore's metaphor. I can always count on at least one student noticing the phrase "parent block" and making the connection between the steam roller's crushing demands and the pressure on young thinkers to adhere to the thoughts of their elders. Moore's steam-roller mind cannot admit an individual thought, judging all art and ideas by its own singular set of restrictive utilitarian standards; without an established application, illustrations, the steam roller concludes, are useless. Moore complains that the steam roller's unforgiving judgments leave no room for the simple beauty of butterflies, but she ultimately decides that arguing with a steam roller's ingrained drive to conformity is difficult at best. If a set of "impersonal" abstract rules exists, such as those that create complementary angles in plain geometry, to question "the congruence of the complement is vain." The steam-roller mind views the world through a grid of abstract laws that govern aesthetic value in the same way that abstract laws govern geometry. To question such rules is out of the question.

Reading "To a Steam Roller" on the heels of "Diligence Is to Magic as Progress Is to Flight," students never fail to grasp the easy contrast between the lyrics. Where Moore's female poet atop the elephant seeks to change old outmoded forms in an individual quest for new music, Moore's steam-roller mind oppressively prohibits such experiments, forcing all thinkers to follow a particular line. Where the lady "progresses" and "travels" atop a sensitive living creature, the steam roller stands as the very image of an unfeeling mechanistic intelligence that inhibits all change. Yet, after pointing to the differences between the minds in question, I like to direct students to consider the potential *similarities*. Read in tandem, Moore's steam roller and her piloted pachyderm look tellingly alike. The experimental elephant, like the well-established steam roller, has the power to crush all particles down into close conformity with its heavy stride, smashing all thoughts that get in the way of its mighty poetic feet. Moore's steam roller, the ultimate prosaic mind, becomes the potential mechanized version, unfeeling and unthinking, of Moore's diligent animal, an image of what happens when a new thought becomes an old inflexible rule. One image bleeds into the other.

To cap the discussion, I ask my students to consider the literal space between the poems. "To a Steam Roller" ends with an image out of a geometry textbook, "to question / the congruence of the complement is vain, if it exists"—a bit of mathematics meant to reinforce the imperturbability of ingrained abstract concepts. "Diligence Is to Magic as Progress Is to Flight" begins, in its very title, with a mathematical expression of ratios. In Moore's terms diligence/magic = progress/flight and the poet must take care to keep all terms in balance. As the text of her poem indicates, magic stands in inverse relation to progress—the more magic a poet depends on, the less real progress a poet achieves—and the same relationship holds true for diligence and flight. Expressing her title as a mathematical equation, however, Moore ties the elephant poet inextricably to the workings of the steam-roller mind. The poet atop the elephant runs the risk of picking up where the steam roller left off, dictating rules far too rarefied and restrictive to be applied to poetic production. The oppressed may in turn become the oppressor.

Read together in class, then, Moore's paired lyrics speak to an issue of intellectual liberty and responsibility that radiates beyond the isolated presentation of either poem. Exploring her sense of a new poetic, Moore remains crucially aware that all ideas, including her own, will eventually begin to oppress if they remain static icons. Change is of the essence. Such an idea will certainly sound familiar to those who teach Stevens's verse. Studying a pair of Moore's poems that point to the danger of strong ideas arms students with a helpful set of images to bring to bear on a reading of Stevens. I find that Stevens often confuses students because he is one of those pesky poets who refuses to be satisfied. Students content with a vision of Stevens as a summer poet of pure imagination have a hard time understanding the same poet's argument that "Bare earth is best" (*CP* 137). Students convinced that Stevens longs for a winter world of unadorned actualities find his appeals to "jovial hullabaloo" (*CP* 59) perplexing. Yet, Stevens is not a poet of either the imagination or the actual, but of *both* the imagination *and* the actual, a point made particularly clear in the context of his paired poems. I try to teach students that Stevens's imaginative ideas, like Moore's, have a life span—tropes are born, age, and ossify, calling on the poet to sweep them away and start again in an endless quest for what will suffice. Like Moore, Stevens understands how quickly the mind may be trapped by thoughts it initially finds attractive.

Asking my students to keep Moore's pair in mind, I send them back to the rare-book room to contemplate a copy of Harriet Monroe's little modernist magazine from Chicago, *Poetry*. The October 1921 issue includes a set of Stevens's poems—"Sur Ma Guzzla Gracile"—that contains a series of paired poems well designed to demonstrate Stevens's provisionalizing sensibilities: "On the Manner of Addressing Clouds" (*CP* 55) and "Of Heaven Considered as a Tomb" (*CP* 56), "The Doctor of Geneva" (*CP* 24) and "The Cuban Doctor" (*CP* 64), and "Tea at the Palaz of Hoon" (*CP* 65) and "The Snow Man" (*CP* 9). All the pairs in Stevens's set revolve around the same apparent opposition between the desire for fancy and the need for bare facts. I like to start discussion of Stevens's set with either his cloudy twosome or his pair of doctors, leaving his more complex lyrics for last. The speaker of "On the Manner of Addressing Clouds" longs to find divine presences and adorns the sky with "still sustaining pomps / Of speech," peopling the heavens with stock images that prove attractive, but "stale." The speaker of "Of Heaven Considered as a Tomb" offers an opposing view of the same sky, stripping the space clean of poetic images of divinity and replacing the anthropomorphized clouds with empty "nothingness." Opening conversation with this pair works well in that students quickly recognize that the speaker of "Of Heaven" directly undercuts the speaker of "On the Manner." "What word have you, interpreters, of men / Who in the tomb of heaven walk by night, / The darkened ghosts of our old comedy?" the speaker asks incredulously of the silly poet who sees gods strolling in the sky (or, as one of my students translated the question, "spoken to any good angels lately?"). Given the frank opposition between the lyrics, I ask students which perspective Stevens seems to endorse. The answer they usually (and instructively) propose is "none of the above." Where the heaven filled with "Gloomy grammarians in golden gowns" appears oppressively full, the heaven without presences seems frighteningly empty, an "icy" abyss. Read together, these two lyrics imply that, left unaltered, either of these intellectual states would prove an uncomfortable burden. Each must change and be changed in turn in an endless intellectual cycle.

Stevens's doctors reflect a similar apparent opposition. Stevens's Cuban doctor escapes the actual in a life of imaginative lassitude, reveling in decadent delusions that have become comfortably stale. The Genevan doctor, in contrast, perceives the world through cold, rational categories that inhibit all free play of the imagination. The Genevan doctor prefers northern climes, Stevens's space of imaginative austerity, while the Cuban doctor drifts in Stevens's visionary South. Once more, however, I urge students to notice that neither of Stevens's medicos appears entirely complete or content. Again implying an imaginative cycle, Stevens pictures each doctor as struck by the opposing law. The Genevan doctor cannot resist the "Pacific swell" of a warming fancy that "set[s] his simmering mind / Spinning and hissing with oracular / Notations of the wild," the sonic equivalent of applying imaginative heat to mental ice. The Cuban doctor in turn fears the "Indian," a force that strikes out to disturb his sleep and rouse him from his dreamy and distracted sofa. Stevens insists that each static man of medicine change his mind. Caught by the southern swell of the imagination, the doctor of Geneva will become the drowsy Cuban doctor who will, in turn, be roused into austerity. Restoring their initial context and reading such lyrics side by side shows students that Stevens cannot find any one idea, however initially liberating, ultimately satisfying.

Perhaps Stevens's most famous pair of poems to this point, however, hails from the same *Poetry* set. In the "Sur Ma Guzzla Gracile" grouping Stevens places his great lyric of imaginative extinction "The Snow Man" next to his fiery poem of imaginative opulence "Tea at the Palaz of Hoon." While most teachers present these lyrics separately, I think it key to an understanding of Stevens to bring them into class together and in context, emphasizing that Stevens intended the two as a pair, the extreme poles of his poetic experiment. "Tea at the Palaz of Hoon" and "The Snow Man" are notoriously difficult poems to teach, but I find the context of Stevens's other pairs once again makes my work easier. Through a reading of Stevens's cloud lyrics and doctors, students come to the "Tea"/"Snow Man" pair armed with the knowledge that Stevens equates northern climes and icy states with an absence of the imagination, southern locales and warmth with the play of an active fantasy. Establishing a previous metaphorical connection between the weather, the latitude, and the workings of the mind saves me a good deal of interpretive groundwork on the more complex poems. Through a reading of his other pairs, students also learn to search for apparent images of opposition that in fact imply an imaginative cycle.

Clues to Stevens's intended pairing of "Tea at the Palaz of Hoon" and "The Snow Man" lie throughout both poems, and the search for textual similarities sparks good initial class discussion. Stevens writes both lyrics in triplet stanzas. "The Snow Man" consists of five triplet stanzas of rough iambic tetrameter; "Tea at the Palaz of Hoon" reverses the structure—four triplets of fairly regular iambic pentameter. Stevens not only maintains a similar structure from "The Snow Man" to "Tea at the Palaz," but recasts the same images from poem to poem, and I usually ask my students to pause and make a list of those they find. Students rarely fail to see that both "The Snow Man" and "Tea at the Palaz of Hoon" make prominent use of the sun as a trope for imaginative power. In quest of "reality," the snow poet, like the doctor of Geneva, fights to suppress the imagination's power to warm the mind and set it simmering. The snow man's imaginative sun is a "January sun," a "distant glitter" that provides little light and less heat, low on the horizon and very far away. In "Tea at the Palaz of Hoon," however, Stevens creates a counterconsciousness so expansive that his imaginative sun usurps all experience. Stevens begins "Tea at the Palaz of Hoon,"

> Not less because in purple I descended
> The western day through what you called
> The loneliest air, not less was I myself.

Reveling in the makings of his own mind, the Hoon poet becomes a fire ball, "descend[ing] / The western day" in purple, the very image of a brilliant sunset. Poem to poem, Stevens places two different suns close to the horizon to reflect two different states of the Stevensian imagination—one distant, pale, and weak, the other close, blazing, and potentially obliterating. The "mind of winter" turns to a mind of summer.

Stevens conducts the same recasting with images of sound in the two poems, and I often ask students to interpret the difference between what the snow man and Hoon hear. The snow poet struggles

> . . . not to think
> Of any misery in the sound of the wind,
> In the sound of a few leaves,
>
> Which is the sound of the land
> Full of the same wind
> That is blowing in the same bare place
>
> For the listener. . . .

Where the snow poet "listens in the snow," straining to hear what lies outside the self with an ear to escaping the pathetic fallacy, the Hoon poet listens to a buzzing beside his ears and triumphantly concludes,

> Out of my mind the golden ointment rained,
> And my ears made the blowing hymns they heard.

The snow poet attempts to strip the "blowing" wind of human associations; Hoon, however, does the opposite, transforming the "blowing" he hears into opulent songs of self-worship. In Hoon's palace, all sound becomes a reflection of the singing self. I try to get students to see that Stevens hinges both poems on the same word, recasting the external "blowing" wind of the snowscape as the stuff of Hoon's mighty romantic (in)spiration.

Another useful focus of class consideration lies in the vastly different landscapes Stevens designs for each poet. My sharpest students will often note that, throughout his set, Stevens exploits the contrast between the desire for exterior and interior experience played out in the snow poet's blowing wind and Hoon's blowing hymns. The snow poet mentally wanders as far from recognizable tropes and constructions as possible, into an outdoor white space that implies metaphorical exposure to the elements. As Stevens puts it, to extinguish the imagination and confront the elemental, one must "have been cold a long time," accustomed to an arctic mental landscape without protective images. The Hoon poet, on the other hand, leads an indoor existence, luxuriating in a palace of tropes of his own making that isolates him from the "not me." Where the snow poet works to achieve a point of abject deprivation, to become nothing more than a part of the landscape in a search for "real" sight, Hoon participates in the civilized artifice of high tea, an indoor ritual of pure pleasure. The use of triplet stanzas in the two poems also works to express the difference between Hoon's mental topography and the snow man's. The confident Hoon speaks a dramatic monologue in relatively short sentences that indicate declarative confidence. Hoon asks pointed questions—"What was the ointment sprinkled on my beard? / What were the hymns that buzzed beside my ears? / What was the sea whose tide swept through me there?"—and answers them directly, without hesitation or qualification. Each of Hoon's triplets is end-stopped and plays out a specific assertive step in the expansion of his consciousness. Maintaining triplet stanzas, Stevens examines the snow man's experience in the space of a single tortured sentence filled with nested clauses—a tentative rumination that inches forward denying assertive conclusions. The snow man's triplets creep toward the very edge of conscious connection, spreading and diffusing into the distance like the white landscape they portray, challenging the concept of Hoon's centralized identity.

Point for point, I have found students quick to discern the contrast between the polarized consciousnesses of Hoon and the snow man. Yet, here again, the key to Stevens's poetic approach lies in helping students recognize the cyclic nature of such apparently oppositional states. Pairing the poems, Stevens again implies that Hoon, for all his fiery opulence, will tire of his palace and, casting off his old protective images, become the snow poet. The snow man in turn will yield to the warming sun of other mental seasons until he shines like Hoon. Like Moore in her elephant/steam roller pair, Stevens implies an inescapable cycle in the opening and closing phrases of each lyric. The snow poet's journey of personal extinction moves from the line "One must have a mind of winter" to a glimpse of the "Nothing that is not there and the nothing that is"—from an assertion of individual presence, "One," to an expression of absence, "the nothing that is." "Tea at the Palaz of Hoon" in turn begins with the phrase "Not less." Hoon's journey thus begins where the snow poet's leaves off, at a point where nothing less is possible, a poetic ground zero. Hoon rebuilds from a place of imaginative diminishment, "Not less," to make a world in which he finds himself "more truly and more strange." "One" becomes "nothing" only so that "less" can become "more" in a poetic cycle that implies an endless repetition of making and unmaking in turn. Stevens's pairing suggests that he finds either pole of his imaginative project ultimately static and undesirable. Both the snow man and Hoon, for differing reasons, inhabit "The loneliest air," Hoon trapped in his own perceptions, the snow poet caught in a space that prohibits all access to conscious discourse. Stevens insists that each of these states "must change."

And so Stevens continues to insist throughout his career as a poet. I find that studying the early *Harmonium* pairs establishes a paradigm that students can apply to all periods of Stevens's poetry. From later pairs like "Botanist on Alp (No. 1)" and "Botanist on Alp (No. 2)," "The Brave Man" and "A Fading of the Sun," "Nudity at the Capital" and "Nudity in the Colonies," "Man and Bottle" and "Of Modern Poetry," "Study of Images I" and "Study of Images II," to the numerous paired sections of Stevens's long poems, "The Man with the Blue Guitar," "Notes toward a Supreme Fiction," and "An Ordinary Evening in New Haven," Stevens's poetic life constitutes a sincere attempt to avoid becoming trapped by the seductive nature of strong thoughts. Predicted in part by Moore, Stevens's cyclic groupings remain a staple of his later verse.

Throughout their careers both Moore and Stevens remain keenly aware that all ideas, no matter how initially progressive, will eventually, if static, begin to oppress. In the ordering and content of their verse, both poets imply that blind acceptance and imitation of any one dominant school of thought can lead to cultural and poetic stasis in an empty habit of mind and a collection of stale tropes. The only solution lies in Stevens's assertion that "It Must Change." The snow man will become Hoon only to become the snow man once again. The elephant will age into the steam roller only to be pushed aside by a new elephant. For both Stevens and Moore, then, the joy of thinking lies in questioning what one creates, a concept key to good critical thinking in the classroom. I find that teaching Stevens's and Moore's poems in their intended pairs gives students a clear view of both poets' provisionalizing patterns of intellectual change and charges students to rethink some of their most deeply ingrained beliefs. Both Moore and Stevens challenge all of us, students and teachers alike, to keep our minds open and our thoughts alive.

Teaching Wallace Stevens:
The Relations between Poetry and Painting

CHARLES DOYLE

In teaching poetry, I find that the limiting question "What does this poem mean?" frequently has to be circumvented. A standard educational method of dealing with poetry, it leads into two blind alleys, or at least narrow ways: that a paraphrase may account for a poem, or that a poem necessarily carries a contextual message. I encourage students to ask themselves different questions: "What kind of an experience is this poem?" "What is the experience of the poem?" "What kind of an event is this?" "What is happening here?" If only because words are a tool for communication, implicitly every poem carries a "message," though not at the level usually sought in the kind of teaching I'm referring to here. The "message" of a poem that is experienced as fully as possible aesthetically will emerge inevitably from the experience, even though it may still defy one-dimensional explanation.

For the teacher, it will be a short step from the sort of introduction suggested by the above remarks to establishing the point that a crucial number of Stevens's poems are self-reflexive, i.e., that they are about the art of poetry and "the poet as / Eternal *chef d'orchestre*" (*CP* 136). A variety of examples can be mentioned in support: "The Man with the Blue Guitar," "Man and Bottle," "Man Carrying Thing," "Reply to Papini," and so on. Following this, the teacher can establish that Stevens often proposes other forms of aesthetic experience as ways of talking about poetry (e.g., architecture, theater, music, painting), as in "A High-Toned Old Christian Woman," "Of Modern Poetry," "Woman Looking at a Vase of Flowers," or "Mozart, 1935" (*CP* 131), the last an instance simultaneously offbeat and obvious:

Poet, be seated at the piano.
Play the present, its hoo-hoo-hoo,
Its shoo-shoo-shoo, its ric-a-nic,
Its envious cachinnation.

While this is not Stevens at his best, such a passage is rich in teaching possibilities: typical in its implied analogy between poetry and music, in its deliberate resort to "high" vocabulary in "cachinnation," and then its mocking of each of these elements through the adjacent use of nonsense syllables, which also serve (here as elsewhere) to achieve closer correspondence between word and thing, by minimizing referentiality.

From here, the teacher can go on to show that, like music, painting is a significant preoccupation in Stevens's poetry and that its influence is evident in various ways—as a model, as an analogue, and as a motif (i.e., formalistically, analogically, and metaphorically), and also as a method of abstraction and a literary variation of cubist theory. To pursue these aims, the teacher (and preferably the students) should have some knowledge of the history of painting, and particularly modern painting from French impressionism to cubism.

Evidence of Stevens's interest in painting is easy to find, both in his poetry and prose, and the first question is to decide a starting point, which might logically be the formalist aspect of Stevens's deployment of painting in his poetry. A good approach is to begin from a particular poem, and there's one ready to hand, "Sea Surface Full of Clouds" (*CP* 98). This five-part sequence is frequently cited as an attempt by Stevens to emulate in words the methods of French impressionist painting. But what does this mean, and how does it apply to his work? How may impressionist methods be related to Stevens's poetry? (The poem can usefully be discussed along with selected slides—say Monet's *Water Lilies*.)

Baird calls the sequence "five impressionist paintings in which color is the sole subject" (186). Amending this slightly, to note that the poem features both color and light (as Baird in fact makes clear), the teacher can then point out that each of the poem's five parts begins with an identical line: "In that November off Tehuantepec." This strategy anchors each "impression" in the same time and place, in the transition from night to morning (which is established by the rhymes and variations of the opening stanza in each part) and in a scene that has recurring factors (stanza two in each of the five parts has the same end-words, "chocolate"/"green"/"machine"), and variables, to do with the varying intensities of light, in which "sometimes the sea / Poured brilliant iris on the glistening blue" or, contrastingly, the overcast produces "the macabre of the water-glooms."

Out of a set of color variations (chocolate, gilt, green, yellow, silver, white, black, and the naturally predominant blue) comes the final painterly impression:

> . . . The wind
> Of green blooms turning crisped the motley hue
>
> To clearing opalescence. Then the sea
> And heaven rolled as one and from the two
> Came fresh transfigurings of freshest blue.

Class discussion can establish that the sequence resembles impressionist painting in its apparently passive observing and recording of change. From all this arise possibilities of two kinds of participatory exercise. With a collection of Stevens's poetry as text, students can be asked to find how often, and with what various purposes, Stevens uses color in his poems. This exercise can be done preliminary to a discussion of Stevens's frequently noted color symbolism. The other kind of exercise might be a search to compare the posture of the speaker in this poem with that in other poems, to establish that the same "determining personality" (see *NA* 45ff) manifests different moods (just as the "Sea Surface" does), ranging from a dramatic, dialectical, and characteristically "gaudy" stance to the austerity of the "mind of winter."

In further pursuit of the theme of formalism, the teacher can compare or contrast Stevens's emulative approach to the making of poems with that of his more literal-minded compeer William Carlos Williams, who in some instances attempted to apply theories of painting directly to the techniques of poetry. At least for "Sea Surface Full of Clouds," Baird considers this to be Stevens's method also:

> One may propose that this poem stands unmatched in the English language. It is not only a full demonstration of a principle, that poetry and painting may meet in

compositional use of words and colors. It is also a testament to the ultimate possibility that the afterimage produced by a poem will be of exactly the same kind as that enduring beyond actual sight of a composition in pigments. (187)

In shifting from modeling, or emulation, to analogy, the teacher must make quite plain the sense in which the term is being used. As Bonnie Costello shows, it is a slippery term, one that in his essay "The Effects of Analogy" Stevens himself uses to mean "pictorialization," which, in short, means for him that painting is a less discursive, more imagistic mode, one that evokes presence more immediately than is possible for any verbal medium. A quick example is "Life Is Motion" (*CP* 83), which can also serve to exemplify Costello's notion of analogy in Stevens as "illustration":

> In Oklahoma,
> Bonnie and Josie,
> Dressed in calico,
> Danced around a stump.
> They cried,
> "Ohoyaho,
> Ohoo" . . .
> Celebrating the marriage
> Of flesh and air.

The final two lines here fulfill the same function as the opening two in Williams's "The Red Wheelbarrow." Class discussion, centered on the two poems and perhaps starting from the anomaly that Stevens's verbs are in the past tense, can usefully seek imagist elements in Stevens and relate these to the topic of his painterliness.

When dealing with analogy, it is useful for students to understand that the context in which Stevens sees painting as analogous to poetry is holistic, in terms of a "fundamental aesthetic . . . of which poetry and painting are manifestations" (*NA* 160), which in turn informs a "universal poem" (in this discourse, "poetry" and "art" become synonyms). By cooperating with the students to locate examples, the teacher can show that Stevens's writing is permeated with painting allusions and painterly postures, so that many critics have seen parallels between the methods of his poetry and those of art movements such as cubism, fauvism, expressionism, surrealism, and even dadaism, but on the whole these links are most usefully treated by the teacher as animating associations.

In his essay "The Relations between Poetry and Painting," Stevens quotes with approval the art critic Leo Stein's desire "'to see anything as a composition'" and also Braque's cubist aphorism "'The senses deform, the mind forms'" (*NA* 162, 161); on his own account, he once remarked to Williams, as quoted in the prologue to *Kora in Hell:* "'One has to keep looking for poetry as Renoir looked for colors in old walls, woodwork and so on'" (*Selected Essays* 13). Such allusions and observations provide a teaching opportunity to distinguish between the analytical and synthetic sides of Stevens, pointing to the seeming paradox of his sense of the universe, simultaneously a breeding ground for epistemological anxieties and a source for discovering poetry.

Both painting and poetry are "acts of the mind," but composed by different means. Language, the teacher should point out or elicit, is the poet's equivalent of paint. To highlight the importance of language in poetry, I have a long-standing practice that each poem is read aloud by a student or students (as an essential part of their training; if the reading is muffled, or fails to bring out essential features of the poem, I will contrive to read it again in the course of the discussion). Pound, in an implied analogy and using a metaphor taken from painting (and arrived at through his reading of Kandinsky), spoke of the image as "the primary pigment" of poetry (*Gaudier-Brzeska* 85–86). Stevens's "primary pigment," as the teacher can demonstrate with a variety of examples, is his "gaudy language."

Surprisingly often, this language is a language of color, as can be shown in such early poems as "Sunday Morning" (*CP* 66), with its fauvist or Matisse-like opening images of "the green freedom of a cockatoo / Upon a rug" and "The pungent oranges and bright, green wings," or in the negative color definitions of houses in the Whistlerian "Disillusionment of Ten O'Clock," or "Banal Sojourn," or "Anecdote of the Prince of Peacocks." Buttel was so impressed by the colorful surface of *Harmonium* that he was almost persuaded that one of Stevens's aims was "to abolish the distinctions between poetry and painting" (148). In the early poems, opening painterly settings often prepare for culminating philosophical reflections or intimations. Most famously, as the teacher can show in an engagement with the poem, this is the case with "Sunday Morning." Equally good for making this point is the three-part structure of "The Poems of Our Climate" (*CP* 193), in which part I is a painterly evocation of a bowl of carnations, part II diminishes the painting into a context for the "evilly compounded, vital I," and part III is taken over by the "never-resting mind" in its imperfect world, which is at once bitter and delightful, the delight resting in the "flawed words and stubborn sounds" of language. In a small compass, one can find together in "Banal Sojourn" (*CP* 62) the delightful and gaudy language, the painterly setting, and the closing intimations:

> Two wooden tubs of blue hydrangeas stand at the foot of the stone steps.
> The sky is a blue gum streaked with rose. The trees are black.
> The grackles crack their throats of bone in the smooth air.
> Moisture and heat have swollen the garden into a slum of bloom.
> Pardie! Summer is like a fat beast, sleepy in mildew,
> Our old bane, green and bloated, serene, who cries,
> "That bliss of stars, that princox of evening heaven!" reminding of
>   seasons,
> When radiance came running down, slim through the bareness.
> And so it is one damns that green shade at the bottom of the land.
> For who can care at the wigs despoiling the Satan ear?
> And who does not seek the sky unfuzzed, soaring to the princox?
> One has a malady, here, a malady. One feels a malady.

Stevens also uses painting not formalistically or analogically, but meta-phorically. A good example for class discussion is "So-And-So Reclining on Her Couch" (*CP* 295), where the (eponymous yet anonymous) subject of the painting is a "mechanism," an "apparition" and, throughout, a "Projection." The painter poses the model in various projections, and that is largely the (teaching) point: she is his project.

At one moment in the painter's project, "The suspending hand" (of the poet) almost reveals itself in the proposition that So-And-So, born "Without lineage or language," has "much to learn." As the teacher can show, this presumption belongs not even to the painter (who is, in fact, Projection D), but only to the poet. In the end, the painter's model walks off the set, so to speak, and is told: "Good-bye, / Mrs. Pappadopoulos, and thanks." In the larger framework of the poem, she is addressed by the painter; in (suppose we call it) Projection D, she is also addressed by the poet. In the mimetic illusion (and, in passing, one might note and, if necessary, deal with the surprising number of times students have difficulties in making distinctions among protagonist, speaker, and writer) Mrs. Pappadopoulos and the painter are more present than "So-And-So," who, after all, is "only" in a painting. Then again, and fruitful teaching points can be made of this, all the protagonists are "only" in a poem.

Before turning finally to the more general questions of Stevens and abstraction, and his affinity with cubist theory, we may bring together in one crucial instance the three lines of approach discussed above. Baird's phrase "the afterimage produced by a poem" is demonstrably acted out in one of Stevens's exemplary poems, "The Idea of Order at Key West" (*CP* 128):

> Ramon Fernandez, tell me, if you know,
> Why, when the singing ended and we turned
> Toward the town, tell why the glassy lights,
> The lights in the fishing boats at anchor there,
> As the night descended, tilting in the air,
> Mastered the night and portioned out the sea,
> Fixing emblazoned zones and fiery poles,
> Arranging, deepening, enchanting night.

In this poem about the making of poetry, the concluding image of a port at nightfall is both part of the scene and illustration. "The order of description suggests the brush of a painter organizing his pictorial space" (Benamou 14). A number of issues central to Stevens may be brought out here by the teacher. Benamou's account furthers an exploration of Stevens's emulative or formalistic use of painting: "The verbs carry the magic of his art: mastering, deepening, enchanting; the nouns and adjectives are fraught with pictorial vividness: fiery poles, glassy lights, emblazoned zones" (14). But on further consideration we, teacher and class together, can locate the analogical thrust of the poem. If its theme is "the victory of art over chaos," then it is a poem about order and, further, a poem exploring poetry as an "idea of order," with the "afterimage" of a painterly perception to provide concrete illustration (14). Further still, both singing (making poetry) and painting are metaphors for creating order although, at last, we are left with one of Stevens's productive epistemological conundrums, which the teacher can use to affirm the essentially dialectical nature of Stevens's art, in that the mastery of the night and portioning out of the sea are (as Benamou fails to note) a consequence of the light, an act of nature. However, though the observer does not will them, the teacher can point out that these phenomena would not exist in the human world if some observer did not experience and record them.

In turning to the question of abstraction, the teacher may note that this central Stevens term is also a key term in twentieth-century painting. Of poetry, "the supreme fiction," his first requirement was that "It Must Be Abstract." He does not suggest by this that the poem dispenses with the concrete and particular, or that a poem may not have a particular occasion, but at least part of his meaning (as the teacher can establish) is that particulars must be experienced without preconceived notions, must be perceived afresh and combined into a new synthesis (an attitude that relates Stevens's practice to that of the cubist painters) and must undergo the "freshness of transformation" (*CP* 397). A relevant instance is Stevens's prose description of a painting by Jacques Villon: "A woman lying in a hammock was transformed into a complex of planes and tones, radiant, vaporous, exact. A teapot or a cup or two took their place in a reality composed wholly of things unreal" (*NA* 166).

The teacher will find two other poems useful here. "The Poems of Our Climate" (referred to briefly above) typically opens with a painterly setting, though it is a representation of conscious reality, which is then proposed as inadequate. Yet, in the meditation that follows, this inadequacy is perceived as a precondition for poetry, for "The imperfect is our paradise," because it affords the paradoxical delight that "Lies in flawed words and stubborn sounds," the poet's medium in the process of transformation.

Sometimes this transformation may be preceded by ground-clearing or definition of a didactic sort, as in "Study of Two Pears" (*CP* 196), the title of which (along with the opening line) reveals the pedagogical intention behind the poem:

> Opusculum paedagogum.
> The pears are not viols,
> Nudes or bottles.
> They resemble nothing else.

They are yellow forms . . .

The teacher can indicate, or elicit through discussion, that the poem alter-
nates between assertive and negative definitions equally balanced, and—in
a sense foreign to, say, Williams—the balancing is dialectical, leading to
the definitive negative exclusion of the last two lines:

> The pears are not seen
> As the observer wills.

These comments digress a little into exegesis, and the point must be kept well
in mind that Stevens here uses painting as a metaphor to explore the distinction between things-as-they-are and any observer's perception of them.

Paradoxically, the pears are discovered "as they are" yet are changed by
being abstracted into the poem. In the fifth stanza, the word "Flowering"
is especially relevant to this aesthetically invisible process:

> The yellow glistens.
> It glistens with various yellows,
> Citrons, oranges and greens
> Flowering over the skin.

The teacher can point out that "Flowering" equals the action Stevens speaks of
in *The Necessary Angel,* in a passage mentioned earlier (*NA* 161–62), where he
writes of Leo Stein's looking at a painting until it ceases to be mimetic and
becomes a *composition,* so the "Flowering" is a paradox in which the will is
abandoned and gives place to (what Stevens and Williams each calls) *ignorance.*
In Stevens's case, "ignorance" ("You must become an ignorant man again") is
a rebeginning from the "muddy centre before we breathed," a decreation of all
previous fictions of "an inventing mind" (*CP* 380, 383).

Thus the teacher may use Stevens's little poem of didactic purpose to
introduce central ideas, such as "abstraction" and "decreation," for later
elaboration. But before we leave these notions entirely, brief attention may
be paid to a painterly passage in "Notes toward a Supreme Fiction" I, canto
VI, part of which is "a description of a landscape as though painted by
Frans Hals." Hals painted portraits, so the passage refers not to a specific
painting but to his "exuberant brush strokes which call as much attention
to their own artificiality as to the 'reality' they depict." This recognition

may be used by the teacher to locate one more instance of Stevens's preoccupation with craft. Stevens once remarked in a letter that "the world has been
painted," and the Hals passage is an instance of his rejoicing in the act of "painting" (Woodland 15–17). His sense that "The imperfect is our paradise" meant,
from one point of view, that he clearly discerned the impossibility of realizing
either the state of "ignorance" (one might say "innocence" were the term not
already tainted by myth) or the "supreme fiction." The joy was in the process,
and the idea of painting as a paradigm of that process appealed to Stevens because of its visual character, notably its use of color, but also because (to his
verbal consciousness) painting as a medium sometimes seemed free of rhetoric,
though he cannot hold this limited view for long, as is shown (for example) in
the opening line of "Add This to Rhetoric" (*CP* 198): "It is posed and it is
posed," where the adverb applies once each to poetry and to painting, both of
which are contrasted to "What in nature merely grows."

Some useful teaching points may also be made through "The Man with
the Blue Guitar" (*CP* 165). As is well known, the poetic sequence, as a
subgenre, was a notable development by the modernist poets, so it is not
unique to Stevens, and "The Man with the Blue Guitar" (1937) is not his
earliest, but it has a relevant interest because a number of exegetes have
seen in its narrative elisions and shifts of focus the influence of cubist
theory. Rajeev Patke, for example, claims, "It was Stevens' first distinc-
tively modern long poem. . . . Painting, and especially Cubist aesthetics,
acted as a catalyst in resolving many of the artistic problems which Stevens
had found himself faced with in his attempts on the form of the long
poem" (70).

The sequence is named after a painting by Picasso, but is usually linked
with a different Picasso painting, "The Old Guitarist," seen by Stevens in a
Hartford Picasso exhibition in the mid-1930s. (To facilitate discussion,
slides of these paintings can be shown, perhaps with other parallel cubist
work.) Of the parts of his poem, Stevens said that "what they really deal
with is the painter's problem of realization: I have been trying to see the
world about me both as I see it and as it is" (*L* 316).

The protagonist is seen as a "shearsman," which in the guise of either
analytical cubist or collagist, can make him a cubist figure. The teacher can
reinforce this point by demonstrating that the poem's thirty-three sections
are not, or not primarily, a sequential argument or a narrative, but a juxta-

position of details, so that the opening of section II—"I cannot bring a world quite round, / Although I patch it as I can"—alludes ironically both to technique and to epistemological limitation. What follows, or in a sense does not follow, is a collocation of verses generated in various ways, through sounds, through metamorphosis of persons, through logical gaps and grammatical lacunae. Detailed commentaries of the sequence abound, but the teacher may usefully look at a segment, say sections XIV and XV: the opening lines of XIV evoke the successive appearance of stars in the night sky and add to these the "tattery hues" of the sea and the "muffling mist" of the shores. In the fourth couplet the teacher can show how Stevens sets up an antithesis between his "candle" (which students may be asked to look for elsewhere, for example in "Valley Candle" and "Final Soliloquy of the Interior Paramour"), which is "enough to light the world," and the showy elaborateness of "a German chandelier." This candle shines always in the "chiaroscuro" of the world and, in the paradox of noon's "essential dark," at the height of the sun of reality, this candle (art) imparts what light there is.

Without some such symbolic reading of the candle, the disjunction between sections XIV and XV is more marked. In XV we are shifted indoors to a consideration of the Picasso painting and to Picasso's seemingly ambiguous remark that any of his paintings is a horde or "hoard of destructions."[1] Influenced presumably by the idea of destruction, some commentators interpret Picasso's words negatively, but it is possible to read them as a thumbnail definition of cubist method. Here the teacher can indicate that Stevens is using Picasso's phrase to raise questions, but (in typical modernist fashion) he does not answer the questions raised, merely promoting them to sustain the poem's momentum and give it forward thrust, reaching the "climax" of his presentation in section XXII in the famous declaration that: "Poetry is the subject of the poem, / From this the poem issues and / To this returns."

Having shown various ways in which painting can be usefully related to Stevens's poetry, the teacher can conclude with one last example, "Landscape with Boat" (*CP* 241), where Stevens presents an oxymoronic antihero, the "floribund ascetic," who attempts to discover origins through an act of unpainting:

> He brushed away the thunder, then the clouds,
> Then the colossal illusion of heaven. Yet still

The sky was blue. He wanted imperceptible air.
He wanted to see. He wanted the eye to see
And not be touched by blue. He wanted to know,
A naked man who regarded himself in the glass
Of air, who looked for the world beneath the blue,
Without blue, without any turquoise tint or phase,
Any azure under-side or after-color. Nabob
Of bones, he rejected, he denied, to arrive
At the neutral centre, the ominous element,
The single-colored, colorless, primitive.

As the teacher can show, this poem considers the difficulty of stripping away suppositions in order to discover "the nothing that is" (*CP* 10), figuratively speaking arriving at a canvas of white-on-white or at Picasso minimalizing his drawing on glass to demonstrate the redundancy of copyists, rejecting the evidence of the senses, or rather preconceptions about such evidence, arriving by abstraction at "the neutral centre."

My purpose above has been to indicate, and where possible demonstrate, ways in which the teacher can show how the art of painting impinges upon Stevens's sister art of poetry, whether as model, analogue, or metaphor, or theoretically, by abstraction, and how Stevens uses painting to wonderful effect in an endeavor to provide both color and objective distance for his energizing dialectic between "things as they are" and "the supreme fiction."

Note

1. Stevens refers to this same phrase of Picasso's in "The Relations between Poetry and Painting," but in that context the phrase is "horde of destructions" (*NA* 161). One other translation has it as "the sum of destructions" (see Ashton). Given that Stevens sometimes wrote as if painting is a medium free of rhetoric, it is interesting that (as Judith Rinde Sheridan has noted) Picasso had a distinctly semiotic sense of the nature of painting:

    "Actually it isn't anything more than a question of signs. It has been agreed upon that a specific sign represents a tree, another a house, a man, a woman; exactly as in a language the word 'man' evokes the image of a man, the word 'house' a house and this in all language although in every language the word varies."
    (Quoted from Ashton [18–19] by Sheridan)

A Stevens Play as Teaching Tool

J. M. FURNISS

The early one-act play *Three Travelers Watch a Sunrise* (*OP* 149) is a useful pedagogical tool for first-time undergraduate students of Wallace Stevens. The play is neither great Stevens nor successful theater, but it does present basic Stevensian themes in a medium initially more accessible than the po-etry. *Three Travelers Watch a Sunrise* is a by-the-numbers, beginner's course in the strangely peopled, seemingly private places of Wallace Stevens.

First-time playwright Stevens provides a clearly defined setting, a dra-matic situation, and the dramatic personae. Although he comments to Harriet Monroe (editor of *Poetry,* which published and awarded *Three Trav-elers*), "A theatre without action or characters ought to be within the range of human interests" (*L* 203), his first venture in the medium retains much that is conventional (certainly more than his next two plays). We watch three Chinese travelers wait to observe sunrise on a wooded hilltop in Au-gust. Setting, situation, and personae may be unusual, but no audience need immediately seek more familiar referents. When the play deals with "seem-ing"—"The difference that we make in what we see," as Stevens writes in "Description without Place" (*CP* 339)—"what we see" is concrete; we are not asked to do "without place." And, as the characters practice "de-scriptions of new day, / Before it comes" with what Stevens later called "a sight indifferent to the eye" that is "A little different from reality" (*CP* 343–44), we are provided with both kinds of "sight" ("indifferent to" and *of* the eye) and can measure that "difference" for ourselves. In short, we can talk about what is fundamental to Stevens in the play and be sure that student and teacher share a concrete frame of reference.

On one level the play is *about* seeming. In fact, Stevens told Harriet Monroe,

The point of the play . . . is . . . in the last sentence of the final speech. . . . The play is simply intended to demonstrate that just as objects in nature offset us . . . so, on the other hand, we affect objects in nature, by projecting our moods, emotions etc. (*L* 195)

Stevens is being reticent or coy with his early editor. The play's "point"—"Sunrise is multiplied, / Like the earth on which it shines, / By the eyes that open on it, / Even dead eyes, / As red is multiplied by the leaves of trees"—cannot be abstracted so "simply." Without overreading we find a number of topics that preoccupy Stevens throughout the later poetry. *Three Travelers Watch a Sunrise* depicts alienated modern people attempting to renew their relationship with their "no man" (*CP* 255) place by seeing the sun "clearly in the idea of it" (*CP* 380) despite the constant, deadening, impoverishing "pressure of reality" (*NA* 13). The title characters represent three distinct sensibilities or, perhaps, a "thrice concentred self" (*CP* 376), engaged in Stevens's version of modern consciousness, a "war between the mind / And sky" (*CP* 407). We not only observe the multiple realities these characters make of the sunrise, but we are encouraged to judge the relative value of those realities.

The play is easily read in thirty minutes. I assign it together with several of the shorter lyrics (the list varies but usually includes "The Snow Man," "Anecdote of the Jar," "Metaphors of a Magnifico," "Gubbinal," "Anecdote of the Prince of Peacocks," "The Latest Freed Man," and "A Rabbit as King of the Ghosts") in preparation for the first class on Stevens. In class we consider basic play elements and reread/perform pieces of the text as discussion requires. I direct and precipitate discussion by integrating selected passages from the poetry (some assigned, some not) and essays. Students will need little direction to recognize connections with certain lines of the assigned lyrics. Consideration of the play requires more than a single class, and additional reading (including medium-length and longer lyrics: "The Man on the Dump," "Asides on the Oboe," "Le Monocle de Mon Oncle," and "Sunday Morning") is assigned for hours two and three.

Setting and exposition are first. Why does Stevens plant Chinese on an eastern Pennsylvania hilltop? They are not "Danes in Denmark" (*CP* 419) or "Adam / In Eden" (*CP* 383). The Chinese, I propose to students, are representatives of Stevens's modern people, who "live in a place / That is not [their] own and, much more, not [them]selves" (*CP* 383). Their alien status is recognizable in the assigned lyrics: the speaker of "The Snow Man" (*CP* 9), who contemplates his world as a chilling "nothing that is"; the consciousness whose ordering jar is "Like nothing else in Tennessee" (*CP* 76). The variety and range of further illustration depend, of course, on what one wants to accomplish with a class; I cite a number of Stevens's personae, early and late, whom students are likely to meet: "Crispin at sea," a "short-shanks in all that brunt" (*CP* 27–28); the "shaken realist," who realizes "How cold the vacancy" when he "First sees reality" (*CP* 320); the pedagogue in "Notes toward a Supreme Fiction," who knows that "heaven /. . . has expelled us and our images" (*CP* 381).

The Chinese have come to the hilltop in order to watch a sunrise. Watching a sunrise, I suggest to the class, is a figurative establishment of a fresh relationship with reality—an activity fundamental to many Stevens personae. This is a convenient time for an introduction of basic Stevensian ontology. The play's sun is Stevens's favorite figure for the absolutely not-us, and the sunrise a frequent model of the process by which the mixture of self and non-self is once again reconstituted, resulting in a "candid kind" that "refreshes life" (*CP* 382). Such language prepares students to talk discerningly about "The Latest Freed Man" (*CP* 204), in which new "being" comes for the title character, "Tired of the old descriptions of the world," as "the sun came shining into his room." I suggest that sunrise is analogous to other moments in Stevens when change or displacement occurs. The speaker of "The Man on the Dump" (*CP* 201)—usually a part of the next assignment—"feels the purifying change" that results as familiar objects are transported to a new environment. The academic persona of "Extracts from Addresses to the Academy of Fine Ideas" (*CP* 252) theorizes that "Ecstatic identities / Between one's self and the weather" (with the sun, a figure for non-self) may occur for one "returning from the moon."

We discuss the play's basic "action": gradual interruption of the travelers' solitude by the "invasion of humanity." The invasion comes insidiously at first—the desire of one traveler for water, then a creaking tree branch, then a story of unhappy lovers—but finally reveals itself as starkly unambiguous external fact: a dead body hanging from the creaking tree and a grieving surviving lover. I explain "invasion of humanity" by introducing Stevens's phrase "pressure of reality" and read from "The Noble Rider and the Sound of Words": "By the pressure of reality," says Stevens, "I mean the pressure of an external event or events on the consciousness to the exclusion of any power of contemplation" (*NA* 20). In *Three Travelers Watch a Sunrise* we watch as that pressure does or does not exclude the power of different sensibilities to experience sunrise (i.e., to refresh and sustain their lives).

The intrusion of death in *Three Travelers Watch a Sunrise* is a concrete, explicit test of a person's imaginative control of his or her own life. Can one see his or her place as anything other than a static, alien presence, a "fatal, dominant X" (*CP* 288) that one is helpless to *know*, let alone affect? The question is quintessential Stevens, and I use the play's unsubtle enactment of it to inform far stranger (and more Stevensian) reenactments in the poetry. *Three Travelers Watch a Sunrise* is plain evidence for video-nurtured twenty-year-olds that Stevens means it when he says poetry "helps us to live our lives" (*NA* 36). A hanging corpse is a pressure of reality more immediately seen as "violence [from] without," that threatens "our self-preservation" (*NA* 36), than Stevens's more typical pressures: the "malady of the quotidian" (*CP* 96); or the "dry catarrhs" of "The Ordinary Women" (*CP* 10); or the "junipers shagged with ice" (*CP* 10); or the "granite monotony" birdsong of "Notes toward a Supreme Fiction" (*CP* 394); or the "lustred nothingness" of an effendi's moon in "Esthétique du Mal" (*CP* 320).

When we turn to the three travelers themselves, generally we are into a second class session and students have a slightly larger experience of Stevens upon which to draw. Joseph Riddel, whose reading of the play is most careful among an understandably limited number of readings, says of the characters,

> the Chinese represent three abstract attitudes one may take vis-à-vis otherness: the First Chinese is a devotee of objective, tangible reality, including necessarily its rude violence; the Third Chinese is purely subjective, speaking only as he feels; while the Second Chinese, the theoretician, is a realist between two extremes. (58)

These observations are useful in the main but they oversimplify the particulars.

Riddel classifies the characters on the basis of what they *say*. The First Chinese is preoccupied with melon and water and local gossip, the Second loves to apply theory (in the form of maxims) to their situation, and the Third longs for the isolation of "windless pavilions." Nothing of what they say creates real disagreement among themselves, nor is anything said proven fallacious by the play's end. The sum of all their remarks could, conceivably, be the contemplations of one man. I encourage students, however, to consider what the characters *do*—especially as their behavior relates to their avowed purpose: watching the sunrise.

When humanity invades in the form of the dead body and devastated lover, only the third traveler is able to bear this pressure of reality and still accomplish his goal. Only he among the Chinese sees the sunrise and, presumably, renews his relationship with "otherness." At the moment of the "invasion," the First is playing raconteur, shaping the local scandal into a "doleful ballad." The Second contemplates potential analogies between their experience and his maxims. They are so stunned by the embodiment of what has been art or theory to them that they drop on the stage what has sustained them so far—an instrument and a book of maxims—and depart before any color is to be seen in the sky (Stevens's stage directions: "*No color is to be seen until the end of the play*," and then, "*A narrow cloud over the valley becomes red*" as the third traveler soliloquizes). The Third is left to recognize that the red of the sunrise is many things, "not only / The color of blood."

Students readily recognize the travelers' individual sensibilities. I encourage them to use their new Stevensian vocabulary. The First Chinese cannot resist the pressure of reality because for him reality is the evidence of his senses. When his companions claim to derive sustenance from porcelain and maxims, he scoffs. Like the persona of "Le Monocle de Mon Oncle" (*CP* 13), the First Chinese is "of middle age," and while the poem's persona is considerably more complex, both characters are implicitly or explicitly preoccupied with the loss of sexuality. Mon oncle's life cycle of death and renewal is no longer mindless, and he questions his ability or desire to continue it: "Shall I uncrumple this much-crumpled thing?" The occasion for his meditations is the arrival of spring, whose powers of rejuvenation are lost for him: "No spring can follow past meridian." When the first traveler twice asks, "Is there no spring?" the urgency of his desire for water is close kin to mon oncle's vernal despair. A related figure is "The Man Whose Pharynx Was Bad" (*CP* 96), for whom "time will not relent," and who can no longer distinguish between "Mildew of summer and the deepening snow."

Mon oncle knows how his malady affects "fops of fancy," less self-aware versions of himself such as the First Chinese, whose singing and storytelling are like the fops' "Memorabilia of the mystic spouts, / Spontaneously watering their gritty soils." Threatened by loss of physicality, the first traveler resorts to what Stevens (following Coleridge) finds a corruption of true imaginative activity, fancy: "an exercise of selection from among objects already supplied by association, a selection made for purposes which are not then and therein being shaped but have been already fixed" (*NA* 10–11). The first traveler's "fixed" purpose is vicarious gratification of his sensual nature; there is nothing new in his present reality to which his song or story is an imaginative response. Because he relies upon fixed association, he is paralyzed by the presence of death. A similar figure is the president in "Notes toward a Supreme Fiction," who "ordains the bee to be / Immortal" but cannot remove "death in memory's dream," causing the persona of "Notes" to ask, "Is spring a sleep?" (*CP* 390–91). The first traveler's response to the corpse is like that of the "round effendi" ("Esthétique du Mal," IX), who feels "Panic in the face of the moon" when he begins "To lose sensibility" and can merely "see what one sees . . . hear only what one hears, one meaning alone."

Students have no difficulty contrasting the First Chinese to the Second; while one succumbs to the pressure of reality due to his preoccupation with the physical, the other succumbs because he is abstracted from the physical. The second traveler encounters the world through the lens of his scholarly maxims, and he is dominated by one in particular that colors all experience for him: "It is the invasion of humanity / That counts." The second traveler informs the final section of "Esthétique du Mal"; his "sight" is obscured by "all the ill it sees," his "ear" by "all the evil sound." Preoccupied with the "mal" of the world, he is blind to "So many selves, so many sensuous worlds" that are potential "Merely in living as and where we live." He illustrates Stevens's "greatest poverty": "not to live / In a physical world" because one feels that "one's desire / Is too difficult to tell from despair."

Like the metaphor-making "Magnifico" the Second Chinese has mental constructions that fail when he is inundated with new sensory input, and "the meaning escapes" (*CP* 19). Or, he is the "doctor of Geneva," whose confined, "Lacustrine" metaphysics are disconcerted by the "Pacific swell" (*CP* 24). He is "X" at his "capitol," whose thought of canna "sleeps not" and remains the same even after "day-break comes" (*CP* 55). In the later, meditational poetry, figures like the Second Chinese sometimes appear after momentary satisfactions. Following the triumphant flight of Canon Aspirin in "Notes toward a Supreme Fiction," we meet one who "builds capitols" and "establishes statues of reasonable men," and we are warned that "to impose is not / To discover" (*CP* 403). In "The Auroras of Autumn" he becomes the "scholar of one candle," who "feels afraid" when his orderly light is engulfed in "An Arctic effulgence" (*CP* 417).

Neither the First nor Second Chinese, preoccupied with fanciful rearrangement or philosophical integration of present experience, sees the colors of the sunrise. Unable to resist the pressure of reality, they fail to realize that "Reality is not what it is. It consists of the many realities which it can be made into" (*OP* 202). I identify the Third Chinese to students as Stevens's figure of the poet. He is distinguished by his desire to bring to the present moment nothing preconceived, an "ever-early candor," an "ignorant eye" that functions by "seeing and unseeing" and "gives a candid kind to everything" (*CP* 380–85). Of course, Stevens's poet no more gets or expects to get what he desires than the Third Chinese gets (or expects) "windless pavilions" in which to experience "the seclusion of sunrise, / Before it shines on any house." In abstraction Stevens's poet may be an impossible transparency, "The impossible possible philosophers' man" who is the "transparence of the place in which / He is" (*CP* 250–51), a no-man "Snow man" who is "nothing himself"; in flesh and blood, however, he "is not the exceptional monster, / But he that of repetition is most master" (*CP* 406)—i.e., alert to the newness of every sunrise.

The Third Chinese is an excellent preparation for a great many of Stevens's personae, several of whom students recognize from the assigned reading. In subordinating the "invasion of humanity" as he beholds sunrise, he is a human variation of the "mind of winter" able "To behold the junipers" and "not to think / Of any misery in the sound of the wind." He is the "Prince of Peacocks," who in resisting red, trap-setting "Berserk" on the "bushy plain," is resisting the trap of single, certain reality "'In the midst of dreams'" (*CP* 58). (Interestingly, the Third Chinese instructs "Take away the bushes" and reveals the play's grieving lover.) Were he an ironist, the third traveler might be the persona of "Gubbinal" (*CP* 85). We could imagine the poem's first lines directed by him to his companions at the play's conclusion,

> That strange flower, the sun,
> Is just what you say.
> Have it your way.
>
> The world is ugly,
> And the people are sad.

He is related to the "Rabbit" who in "peacefullest time" can resist thought of the "Fat cat" and experience "The whole of the wideness of night," reducing the cat to "a bug in the grass" (*CP* 209–10). The Third Chinese's desire for the "seclusion of sunrise" is kin to what the persona of "Martial Cadenza" feels for the evening star that shines over armies "fixed fast in a profound defeat." "What had this star to do with the world it lit," asks the persona, who responds that it is "The present close, the present realized," and his attention to it is renewal, "as if life came back" (*CP* 237–38).

After the class makes initial connections to the individual travelers, I suggest that more complex poetic personae may be seen as composites of the play's types. The woman of "Sunday Morning" (*CP* 66)—assigned for the second or third session—has aspects of all three Chinese. Her "Complacencies"— "late / Coffee" and cockatooed rug and "pungent oranges"—remind us of what sustains the First Chinese, and these too are inadequate resistance to the "dark / Encroachment" of the pressure of Sunday-morning reality: thought of Christ's martyrdom. Like the Second Chinese the woman longs for abstraction, "'some imperishable bliss,'" and comes up with the maximlike "Death is the mother of beauty." She most resembles the third traveler, seeking satisfaction in a "windless pavilion," a "day . . . like wide water, without sound," that makes possible full contemplation of the moment's potential:

. . . "I am content when wakened birds,
Before they fly, test the reality
Of misty fields, by their sweet questionings. . . ."

Finally, she resists thoughts of death and the need for permanence, and, while poem-ending pigeons "sink, / Downward to darkness," she can attend to their "Ambiguous undulations."

With the play as a basic, working vocabulary, I assign an exercise that generates interesting and lively student essays. A number of shorter lyrics are identified (some have been assigned reading already), and students are asked to argue for one of the Chinese as lyric persona. Combinations of the travelers or qualifications of their original sensibilities are encouraged. Excellent poems for the assignment are "The Emperor of Ice-Cream," "Tea at the Palaz of Hoon," "Anecdote of the Jar," "Bantams in Pine-Woods," and "Domination of Black." Alternatively, the exercise can be assigned for oral presentation, a procedure that almost invariably leads to classroom debate. There is value in being able to speak concretely about "which Stevens is talking" in particular poems, and the activity requires close analysis of text. Hoon of the ointmented beard and Chieftain Iffucan of Azcan may not simply be Chinese wearing masks, but the play's characters provide foils that allow critical thinking to begin.

Stevens would endorse none of this. His personae resist categories, and it is certainly true that likenesses are no more than a starting point for the more important work of distinctions—the master of Stevens's repetitions knows that with each going round "My house has changed a little in the sun" (*CP* 385). But Stevens was no teacher. One suspects he wouldn't care to stay long in a room full of twenty-year-olds. A teacher needs a starting point, a frame of reference, from which to venture into Stevens's strangeness, and *Three Travelers Watch a Sunrise* serves that purpose well.

"Sunday Morning" at the Clavier:
A Comparative Approach to Teaching Stevens

DEAN WENTWORTH BETHEA

"Sunday Morning" is certainly Stevens's most frequently anthologized longer poem and probably the one most often taught to undergraduate students. My own experiences as an undergraduate student and later as a professor have shown me the difficulties many students have in contending with this important work. The poem's rigorous argument, the abstract nature of many of its contentions, its complex structure, and its outright rejection of traditional transcendental religions contribute to those difficulties. Ironically, after searching several frustrating semesters for a more accessible entrance into the poem for students, I have found that having them first read and discuss "Peter Quince at the Clavier" (*CP* 89), which some would consider an even more abstract and elusive work, provides a footing for them from which they may scale more easily the imposing edifice of "Sunday Morning" (*CP* 66). The two poems, moreover, allow me the opportunity to emphasize what my students do not readily see—that Stevens's verse constitutes a response to specific historical conditions. Stevens, like Keats, is often considered to be supremely unconcerned with history or society. The works of such poets are taken to offer us "History Without Footnotes," to refer to the title of Cleanth Brooks's formalist manifesto, but I try to show that these poems are clearly the products of particular historical forces.

I familiarize my students with those circumstances and their relationship to "Sunday Morning" and "Peter Quince at the Clavier" by dividing them into small research groups and sending them to the library. If the course does not include Yeats and Eliot, I ask one group to focus on "A Dialogue of Self and Soul" and one on "Ash-Wednesday," since these major modernist works provide a means of distinguishing the thought of three major poets. Both groups produce copies of these poems for the entire class to peruse. Other groups are asked to prepare discussions on issues and works more contemporaneous with the Stevens poems, such as World War I and imagist poetry—issues that may initially appear irrelevant to "Peter Quince" as it is usually read.

"Peter Quince" is, of course, extremely important in its own right, but, as I try to demonstrate to my students, it also compresses the same essential concerns of "Sunday Morning" into a more compact context: the immortality of the flesh as opposed to the impermanence of mental constructs of eternality, the enriching and intensifying powers of death—a "green going" that creates within itself the possibility of rebirth—the celebration of physical pleasure, and the allusion to, and redefinition of, myths are themes central to "Sunday Morning" that are proffered to us more accessibly in "Peter Quince." Moreover, the shorter poem also points outward to "The Idea of Order at Key West," "Notes toward a Supreme Fiction,"and "The Auroras of Autumn," works centering on one of the central if submerged contentions of "Sunday Morning" and Stevens's later philosophical concerns: that individual and collective human minds must construct meaningful, fluid myths more reflective of all that humans find pleasurable than the transcendental theologies that deny what we value most.

By introducing students to the complexities and richness of Stevens's poetry through "Peter Quince," I am able not only to prepare them better for "Sunday Morning" but also to provide a basis for expanded consideration of his entire oeuvre, particularly in its context as "modern" literature and its relationship to a larger historical perspective. Without that basis, I have discovered, most students never quite become comfortable with Stevens's challenging work and thus all too often remain unaware of the great rewards that that work extends to us.

It is relatively easy for students to recognize that both poems take the form of a narrator addressing another person directly and instructing that person by way of anecdote. "Peter Quince" clearly seeks to resituate some aspect of *A Midsummer Night's Dream:* Quince, one of Bottom's accomplices in aesthetic crime, significantly is a "low" figure in contrast to the aristocratic lovers, their parents, and the fairies in the play. In having a decidedly articulate Quince express the complex sensualism of the poem, Stevens elevates the knowledge that such "low" figures have retained through centuries of increasingly abstract philosophies and religions, largely, because, like the peasant Gerasim in "The Death of Ivan Ilyich," they have escaped the distorted ethereality of such systematized thought. I try to indicate to my students that this elevation of Quince is part of a historical debate. Stevens is rejecting elitist notions of the creative mind, siding here with Rousseau and Wordsworth against Locke and Pope, and, of course, against the later Pound and Eliot. Yet Quince reveals himself to be no mere materialist, and this is important for students to realize, since they commonly associate that stance with any work that does not affirm traditional religious views; the beauty of his playing is reflexive and dialectical: "Just as my fingers on these keys / Make music, so the selfsame sounds / On my spirit make a music, too." The physical impress of the clavier's keys creates a patterned spiritual response as well: "Music is feeling then, not sound." Music, viewed superficially, is the most evanescent of art forms, since each note vanishes almost simultaneously with its creation. Yet the passing of each note exemplifies the "green going" of evenings described later in the poem, for the "death" of each note engenders the beauty of its successor, fosters the fulfillment of the entire work, and creates a sequential dynamic of progressive completion. But the poem forces student readers to consider this phenomenon at an even deeper level, for music is not mere sound, but feeling, and thus also what Quince "feel[s], / Here in this room, desiring you." The aesthetic dialectic begins and apparently ends here in the physical, but the physical and spiritual are coalesced, for music *is* what Quince feels in desiring the object of his monologue, in thinking of her "blue-shadowed silk."

The poem suggests that the physicality of the played music does not merely elevate our souls but heightens our sensuality as well. As Edward Kessler has argued in *Images of Wallace Stevens,* "*Real* music becomes neither imaginary nor actual but a composite" (107), but I would extend that perceptive claim much further. For Stevens thus blurs the historical distinction between soul and body, noumenon and phenomenon; in his view spirituality is composite with, not separate from, corporeality, and it is *through* sensuality that we augment the soul. The poem expounds Blake's claim in *The Marriage of Heaven and Hell* that "Man has no body distinct from his soul" (Blake 34). Real *existence* constitutes a composite of the imaginary and the actual, the spiritual and the material, the ideal and the real. I indicate to students here that Stevens moves beyond the polarities of utterly materialist and transcendentalist philosophies, and that his assertions thus represent an important and particular modulation in the history of ideas.

The *extent* of this latter-day Epicurean sensuality—a version informed by the scientific erosion of traditional theology and the aftermath of World War I—typifies it as essentially modern. Stevens felt he had been confirmed by history, that is, by scientific and theological inquiry, by the horrors of war and industrialism, in what Keats and the classical hedonists suspected all along: there is no transcendence; it is not by looking past but by immersing ourselves in mortality and the physical world that we most fully appreciate and realize our existences. "Peter Quince" suggests that the spiritual enlivens, is enlivened by, and dies with, the material and responds to the same cyclical ebb and flow of appetites and satiation as our bodies. I find this juncture to be a profitable one for introducing student responses to the Yeats and Eliot poems in order to set up useful distinctions among versions of modernism. I frame these discussions by indicating that all three poets are reacting implicitly or explicitly to similar general concerns: how do we live meaningfully in the face of the rough beast slouching toward us?

Jerome McGann numbers Yeats and Stevens among "the poets of accommodation," in contrast to those like Gertrude Stein who are poets of opposition and confrontation (199), yet I think Eliot is more properly placed amongst the former, and I find this to be a useful device for students in distinguishing among these three important modernists. Eliot in "Ash-Wednesday" flees the wasteland by accepting that oldest of circus animals, Christianity: he has literally "turned away" from history and does "not hope to know again / The infirm glory of the positive hour" (*Collected Poems* 60). Stevens and Yeats, on the other hand, face the wasteland by celebrating its myriad glories; indeed the "infirm glory of the positive hour" that Eliot laments and flees is the chief blessing of our existence for the older Yeats, and is especially so for Stevens. Stevens's poetry may lack the frequently explicit sociopolitical concerns that Yeats's work evinces, but its celebration of infirm glories, of the eventual process of lived experience creates a profound implicit critique of the status quo. Moreover, "Peter Quince" and "Sunday Morning" envision how we may create a profane comedy from the ruins of our history. These two works anticipate and affirm the rhetorical question of the later "Dialogue of Self and Soul": "What matter if the ditches are impure?" And Stevens, like Yeats, is "content to follow to its source / Every event in action or in thought" (Yeats, *Collected Poems* 231–32). Often these substantial differences are lost in the assertion of some diluting definition of modernism. This is especially unfortunate in the case of Stevens, who still is frequently portrayed as a poet of style, not substance.

Quince likens the physical and spiritual longing awakened in him by his own music to the debased "strain" of physical desire aroused in the elders when they view Susanna at her bath. Stevens manipulates the various ironic possibilities of this apocryphal legend adroitly: in terms of "truth value" for Stevens all scripture is apocryphal, and that is one aspect of its interest for us, for it is clearly not the literality of this incident, whether or not it can be proved, that renders it important, but the "truth" of its critique. Susanna's plight evidences not only the hypocrisy of sexually repressive dogma in her epoch, but also reveals that dogma's vastly unsuitable nature in our own era. The legend indirectly indicates one of the possible criteria by which such works are designated as either sacred or apocryphal: a work that reveals so starkly the antihuman and hypocritical nature of the clergy is not likely to pass muster. Indeed, the content of this narrative is vastly incommensurate with biblical theology, and I find it useful to point out how Stevens's reference to it constitutes an early example of "deconstructionist" reading.

Awakened within the elders are the strained low throbbings and high pizzicati of their corrupt voyeurism. Sexuality for them is an evil, its arousal a failing, and they thus must displace their frustrated desire upon Susanna. Their shrill desire contrasts starkly with the complete physical and spiritual harmony Susanna enjoys in her bath. Here, as the same dialectical interpenetration of the material and the imaginative is recast, Susanna, in the green water, searches for hidden sexual "springs," an overtly masturbatory image, and finds not merely physical pleasure but great "melody" comprised of equal parts "concealed imaginings" and sexual ecstasy. With "spent emotions" she leaves the water and climbs the bank, where the natural world, its dews, grass, and winds, minister to her. The gratifying totality of her state is shattered by the dissonance of the elders' retributive lust. "Susanna and her shame" here clearly reveal that perversion is in the mind of the beholder: shame, prurience reside in the elders. I ask students to consider here that Stevens is manifesting a schematic of the plight of our history in the patriarchal theologies embodied by the elders. I also find it productive at this juncture to discuss from a feminist perspective issues such as the objectification of women, rape, and Susanna's status in relation both to the elders and the speaker. (Mary Nyquist's "Musing on Susanna's Music" raises a number of feminist issues associated with sexism, voyeurism, and the depiction of Susanna in the poem.)

Section IV, as many critics have shown, provides a radicalizing postscript for this digression; Stevens, through Quince, bodies forth his vision of the composite music of existence. Here I ask students to notice how he turns this ostensibly Christian fable to his own purposes, asserting through it an essentially non-Christian concept: the only permanence we experience is in an eternality of transience, in the immortality of the mortal. Our mental constructs of the beautiful change, ebb, and flow as naturally as the configurations of separate waves, but the beautiful is forever manifested anew in the flesh. The individual is not immortal—Susanna is dead—but human beauty is constantly regenerated by, and embodied in, other people, who constitute the ceaseless "wave" of generation and regeneration. Just as "evenings die, in their green going," so we pass away, but our deaths foster the beauty of regeneration. We must experience death as gardens do in scenting the cowl of winter, not as a linear end to discrete existences, but as a glimpse beyond the necessary austerity of winter to the cyclical regeneration of new life. In other words, death, "a green going," not a black cessation, is the mother of all beauty, for all beauty obeys and is defined by this interminable flow. Death is not a static termination but a dynamic of rebirth, one that fulfills and mirrors those things we should value most: the constantly changing natural world and the cyclical nature of our own appetites. I also confront students with a question many of them find provocative: Is Stevens's interpretation of the narrative more or less apt than the Bible's?

But Stevens is not merely reiterating Goethe's "Dauer im Wechsel" or romantic commonplaces here. The implications of his argument look ahead to the critique of transcendental religions in "Sunday Morning," for he implies that Quince's rhapsody of composite existence, in its integration of the physical and the spiritual, will supplant the inappropriately etherealizing dogma of Christianity. Theologies, mental constructs, also burgeon and fade—the fitful and supposititious tracing of the portal to death—as part of the interminable green going of our existential dialectics. The realization that Christianity could be subject to the same process as other now-defunct religions is a disturbing one for many students and a revelatory one for others.

Those reactions are only intensified when I show that, for Stevens, Quince's fabulation is much less hypothetical than that of Christianity, and is grounded much more firmly on the concrete phenomena of our existences: in short, it is a more supreme fiction. This interpretation is underscored in Susanna's music's "escaping" the malevolently salacious response it arouses in the elders, leaving for them only "Death's ironic scraping." Death for them is not the mother of beauty but the "portal" to another "higher" existence. But Death, Quince implies, will show them that they have expended their lives in blindness to the interminable beauty of the waves of mortality. The "immortality" of Susanna's music plays on the viol of her—and our—memory, outlasting the perverting and patriarchal dualism of Christianity.

History was simultaneously confirming Quince's prophecy for Stevens, who composed the poem during the early years of World War I. That war's horrors, perpetrated primarily by "Christian" nations against each other, served as proof of the bankruptcy of Christianity, as it did for the other major writers of Stevens's era, from Yeats to Woolf to Hemingway to Faulkner. Death, or rather the awful deaths we contrive for ourselves, can be the mother of horror when the postulated portal to invisible worlds is "traced" as an entrance into "sweet and fitting" patriotic martyrdom.

This point is proffered more extensively in "Sunday Morning," which forms a symphonic expansion of the rhapsodic prelude of "Peter Quince," exactly doubling that poem's four stanzas. I point out to my students that it retains the same essential structure of "Peter Quince": an explicit dialogue replaces the implicit one of the earlier poem, and there are more extensive allusions to, and indictments of, other religious fabulations, Christianity in particular. Stevens here, I argue, is concerned to expatiate upon the "green going" of existence, to render concrete the eternal moments when the spiritual and the physical interpenetrate completely, as in the beautiful list of epiphanies that ends stanza II of the poem. These moments reveal to us fully that existence *is* a cyclical "going," a meaningfully patterned activity of longing and fulfillment, of becoming. In the same fashion as the radical inversion of the fable of Susanna in "Peter Quince," Stevens appropriates the Sabbath as his title in order to strip it of its reductive religious sanctity by showing that all days are holy. I try to show that the poem's dialogic structure interrogates its own assertions, that its querying dialogue constitutes one means by which more supreme fictions are created. The woman of the poem must learn, lest she meet the fate of the elders, that death is not "that old catastrophe," but the artist of the beautiful, that salvation is a secular matter of mortality, achieved by the individual, not a reward proffered by fate in a hypothetical afterlife.

The poem posits in opposition to such hypotheses the rich pageant of concrete reality. But the female speaker begins by questioning the major assertions of "Peter Quince"; her notions of an afterlife cause her to view the real as "things in some procession of the dead," and thus the vivacity of life is vitiated. For Stevens this vitiation must, of course, be opposed, and by now students generally have little trouble grasping the argument of stanza II, which serves to distinguish further Eliot's values from his, for it is in the transient balms and beauties of this world that we find "Things to be cherished like the thought of heaven." Divinity must live within ourselves and follow the measures assigned our souls, assertions that further indict all phenomenon/noumenon philosophies as falsely separatist. For Stevens, Eliot's faith is misguided escapism, because the divinity postulated by that faith is an abstraction, a shadow, a dream, unreal.

The crucial stanza III is a difficult one for many students, since Stevens indicates how Christianity's origins parallel those of paganism. Christianity for Stevens is a variation on a bad theme: that of all religions that postulate transcendental deities. Regardless of whether they be named Jove or Jehovah, all such deities are inherently inadequate and unsuitable, since "No mother suckled [them], no sweet land gave / Large-mannered motions to [their] mythy minds." I find it productive to ask students to focus on the implications of stanza III's final lines, which assert that the worship of such deities leads us to see ourselves not as a part of, but as apart from, the world we inhabit. I have found it useful here to introduce a few lines from Blake's "The Grey Monk," for there the eponymous monk interrogates his asceticism and worship of an invisible realm:

> When God commanded this hand to write
> In the studious hours of deep midnight
> He told me the writing I wrote should prove
> The Bane of all that on Earth I lovd. . . . (489)

When we dispense with such divisive philosophies, the poem argues, the sky itself will no longer divide us from some postulated telos but rather will appear as what it actually is: one of the benevolent measures destined for our souls.

Stanza IV articulates the meditative fears of the female speaker, which I ask students to formulate in their own words, since we all are products of the same theologies as she, and Stevens has designed a kind of "reader response" dialectic: her fears and doubts are ours. The birdsong of our earthly paradise is rapturous, and the poem's narrator builds on her contentment here by positing, in contrast to stanza II's poignant catalog of epiphanic glory, a litany of the collective delusions, the various dead and current constructs of an afterlife, which only serve to undermine our interconnection with, and appreciation of, this world, of birdsong. At this juncture I ask students to focus on parallels with "Peter Quince," the argument of which is intensified here: beauty felt in the flesh is immortal, unlike our hypothetical sketchings of death's portal; the "green going" of the other poem is here linked to the regeneration of April. The female speaker will die, but her essentially human desire for consummation with June, with evenings, with birdsong, lives on eternally, is remanifested continually in those like her. The eternal dynamic of nature and our desire for it endures in the collective *consciousness* of our race. Students can usually apprehend Stevens's logic here but find it quite provocative, since he completely inverts our traditional notions of the eternal and the transient.

The most famous stanza V usually is easy going conceptually for most students by this point, but the force of the narrator's response to the female speaker's need for "'imperishable bliss'" is stunning: "Death is the mother of beauty" encapsulates all our previous statements to this point. We discuss its extension and intensification of the argument we have been pursuing, and I also find it useful to introduce student findings on the contrast between these works and the World War I poetry I asked them to examine. In an attempt to familiarize them with some current critical perspectives on Stevens, I ask them if they find it reprehensible that Stevens states early in this war (and never revises this statement even after the horrors of the next world war) that death is the mother of beauty: does how and why we die not matter? Is this "accommodationist" poetry then? Or is Stevens drawing a distinction between the discrete manners in which we die and the reality of death itself? These are not questions on which I am entirely resolved myself, and I try to encourage as much meaningful dissent as possible. I do tend to focus on Stevens's reference to the many "paths" that our deaths take. Is the "path sick sorrow took" a reference to the inevitable lamentations that accompany death or an indictment of the kind of horrors we contrive for ourselves? I ask students to focus on what I find to be the immensely significant distinction here between the singular path of sorrow and "the many paths where triumph rang its brassy phrase." I tend to view the former as an improper avenue to death, one constructed for us by our religions.

I invite participation in the discussion of stanza VI by referring to a song most of my students know, one that may in fact have been influenced by a reading of this poem: the group Talking Heads's "Heaven" ("Heaven is a place where nothing ever happens"). Even vaguely religious students are somewhat startled by the clarity of the narrator's argument in this stanza, which asserts not only the impropriety of any abstract afterlife, but particularly the absurdity of a static paradise, one thus wholly incommensurate with "all that on Earth [we] lovd," in Blake's phrase. I ask students to see the close echoes of "Peter Quince" in lines such as "The silken weavings of our afternoons, / And . . . the strings of our insipid lutes." Mornings, afternoons, evenings constitute the rich tapestries, the green going and becoming, the composite music of our existences: music here as in "Peter Quince" is the mellifluous manipulation of time and thus metaphor for the proper "path" to our mortalities.

These references to music are expanded in stanza VII, where we exorcise our "inhuman" gods by chanting holy music to the sun itself. I ask students a fairly elementary question: to what object are most "chants of paradise" as we define it directed? The poem implies that only when we dispense with those chimerical notions will we sing truly paradisal songs, for the true paradise is constituted for Stevens by a "heavenly fellowship / Of men that perish," of people who grasp fully the holiness of the secular and the transient. Nature's constant reminders to us of our eternal transience—the dew on our feet—when properly apprehended lead us to completely different insights, to an orgy of exhilaration, not lamentation or sick sorrow. Perhaps this stanza also qualifies stanza V, for to perceive our mortal kinship properly allows us to establish a "heavenly fellowship" in the midst of the wasteland of the Western world in 1915.

I begin discussion of the wonders of stanza VIII by asking students to focus on the introduction of a voice whose source we do not know, only that it is neither speakers': is this for Stevens the voice of reality or that of truly humanized insight, an insight omnipresent but marginalized by transcendental theologies? In any event, its strong assertion enters into the dialogue confirming and consolidating the narrator. Jesus' tomb is not "the porch of spirits lingering" but only another supposititious tracing of the portal to death. I point out how the narrator's litany of "either/or" constructions in the ensuing lines is historically grounded: however we live we are "free" of the limiting theology centered in Palestine. The narrator's reference to our "island solitude" contains profound historical resonance, invoking and disagreeing with both Donne in the famous "Meditation 17" and Arnold in "Dover Beach." All people are akin to islands for Stevens, but this is not a reason for Christian faith as it is for Donne, nor the source of deep angst as it is for Arnold, for the receding "Sea of Faith" must be replaced by the "heavenly fellowship" of people who conceive of paradise properly.

The beautiful catalog that ends the poem I ask students to focus on intensely. What we note in these lines is not only their final delineation of the dynamism, the spontaneity, the glory of the transient, but the evening descent into darkness—a green going—of the pigeons. Obviously, this is an important development in the history of poetic subject matter, as many scholars have already pointed out: why not, I ask, nightingales, or birds of paradise, or cardinals? This "elevation" of the common pigeon, I suggest, parallels that of "Peter Quince": in the deceptively mundane resides the holy.

In response to the woman's wistful and lingering need for the consolation of an afterlife, the narrator iterates a modified version of Keats's exhortation in "Ode on Melancholy": "Then glut thy sorrow on a morning rose, / Or on the rainbow of the salt sand wave / Or on the wealth of globed peonies" (*Poems* 349). The speaker here has grasped the realization expounded in Keats's "Ode to a Nightingale" that to be half in love with easeful death is to deaden ourselves to the pains and joys of life, to what Stevens terms the "measures destined for [our] soul[s]," and the concrete "Things to be cherished like the thought of heaven." To turn away from the phenomena of this world in pursuit of some ideal, transcendental essence is to ignore "the silken weavings of our afternoons," and to accept an inferior fiction instead of the supreme fiction of "the chant of paradise" uttered by "the heavenly fellowship of men that perish" in stanza VII. And this supreme fiction delineating the "green going" of life is uttered most beautifully in the famous echo of Keats's "To Autumn" in stanza VII, which is a chronicle of the poignantly beautiful dynamism of our world. "Sunday Morning" and "Peter Quince" help students to see that poetry produces supreme fictions, and that these fictions are not merely exquisite entertainments. In changing constantly how we view and use art, we change as well the manner in which we view and exist in the world. Such fictions lead us to embrace, like descending birds, the ultimate fate, the beauty and pain, the green going of our existence.

Wallace Stevens, Computers,

and Creative Writing

JANET McCANN

The monotony

Is like your port which conceals

All your characters

And their desires. . . .

Clasp me,

Delicatest machine.

"Romance for a Demoiselle Lying in the Grass" (*OP* 44)

Wallace Stevens hovers on the edges of poetry-writing classes in any case. So we invite him in. We sit at our computer monitors in the lab, the shiny new machines we are using to talk to each other, even though the sixteen of us are almost within touching distance in this tiny room. Using *Discourse,* each student will tap out his or her thoughts on the keyboard, and then they will be sent to a central pool where everyone in the class can read them. Why, one might wonder, should we not simply discuss the subjects for the day and the poems brought by students? Because this method allows each student a persona, an individual that he or she creates to speak for him or her. Each student has a chosen pseudonym. This will allow Joe Bob, the Blunt Person, to say things like "Your last line is thumpingly bad. What a disappointment after the intricate buildup of imagery in the third stanza!" And few will realize that behind Joe Bob stands Priscilla, a tiny fragile child who never said a single word in class until we got these monitors.

So, about Wallace Stevens: he is always there, with Eliot and Pound and a few others, hanging around in the hall. Eliot slipped in without invitation, and

I'm sorry: I have recently had too many lusty sophomores writing about old bones and dry sticks rattling. Some of them even slip in a few words now and then from French II. I have had to give Eliot the bum's rush, and now there seems to be no one here but us, and we are really tired of ourselves and our projects. I will try to entice Stevens. Tonight I have graduate students, so I can take risks. I tap out on my keyboard:

> The poem must resist the intelligence
> Almost successfully.
> > Wallace Stevens, "Man Carrying Thing"
> > RESPOND IN POETRY.

There is perhaps a full minute of total silence, then I hear answering taps here and there in the room. Someone who calls himself High Flyer doesn't like the proposition[1]:

> Just as Mother Delight began to tantalize my thoughts,
> Mental storms of reason and interpretation stormed my embattlements
> And in the ensuing fury,
> I lost all pleasure
> And became a skeptic scholar.

Brunhilde and others support the position, more or less. The argument in verse continues; Snevets Ecallaw seems to find poetry a substitute for sex, or perhaps he finds sex and intelligence incompatible and poetry irrelevant:

> My intelligence
> must resist
> this thing
> that man
> must carry
> for this thing
> resists
> my intelligence
> quite successfully

His argument, which goes on for several screens, engages some of the silent members of the class. Anthill Mob wants to argue that the Thing Carried is asexual, and that understanding lies "not in gender / nor in thought / but in resisting it." Others disagree, and the tone of the discussion plummets downward, where I will not follow it. But then it ascends, as someone who calls him/herself Monster Mash makes a determined effort to raise it:

> I'd as lief be embraced by a bellhop
> > as to engage this cumbersome trollop
> that rides atop my atlases
> > when frolicking across unpronounceably exotic landscapes . . .
>
> The point is that now the anatomy of angels must be annotated,
> > must be inscribed however circumspectly
> onto those onion skins. Shred them as the tears come.

Snevets reappears, boisterously restating his position. In a limerick, Anne Hathaway accuses Snevets of frivolity; we are arriving at the end of the hour. In fact, I see with alarm that we've passed it. I tell them to finish up what they are doing and "send" it to the main pool, and my voice, the first audible speech in quite a while, startles us all. Monster Mash is putting the final touch on "Thirteen Ways of Violating a Dachshund." It begins, "Small wiggly wienie with legs / wags tail in glass carriage. / I stare back at myself." Mash has finished the first three violations; we are promised that "Ten sordid verses here follow, contiguous but robust." Anne Hathaway then concludes with a quatrain that pretty well wraps it all up for us:

> Thoughts, the threads of cranial streams
> with interwoven hopes and dreams
> what resistance comes to mind
> when traveling with cargo of different kinds?

We all leave, to ply our blue trades elsewhere. However, the following week I receive poems that have tiny and subtle Stevens traces on them in title, in imagery, in tone, and in subject. The poems are clearly the distinctive voices of their creators, and only someone who had been present for the computer session would see the indications that Wallace Stevens had been present.

This session illustrates only one of the Stevenses I invite into the creative writing class. This Stevens I think of as the Aphorist, the purveyor of descriptive statements about poetry that have the ring of finality to them and that force their recipients to think about what they believe poetry to be. I may throw out to the class:

> Natives of poverty, children of malheur,
> The gaiety of language is our seigneur.

Students may be asked to take on the end of "Of Modern Poetry," or even respond to a pair of lines like

> The moon follows the sun like a French
> Translation of a Russian poet.

(That offering provoked a hostile sonnet.) Stevens the Aphorist is a presence to be reckoned with—by graduate students in verse, and by undergraduates in prose.

The other Stevenses may be approached in the creative writing classes with and without hardware. One is simply the model poet whose techniques can make student poets more aware of what they are doing and what they can do with language. In the undergraduate classes we scan Stevens, using on the computer (or on paper) a simplified system containing only an acute accent for each stressed syllable, a breve for each unstressed syllable, and a macron for a syllable with partial stress. Undergraduates who have just got the hang of blank verse tend to go for it with a hammer, turning out line after line of metronomelike verse such as these two lines (taken from a three-page blank-verse narrative):

> Alas, he said, I really did not know
> That I could be a cause of so much pain. . . .

Therefore, on the class meeting after they have turned in a poem in blank verse, we look at what Stevens does with blank verse in "Sunday Morning," especially at the end. I ask the students to scan the poem, and they end up with something like this:

Ăt évenĭng, cásŭăl flócks ŏf pígeŏns máke
Ămbíguŏŭs úndŭlátiŏns ăs thĕy sínk,
Dównwărd tŏ dárknĕss, ōn ĕxténdĕd wíngs.

The half-stresses, they decide, could be read as full stresses, as this reading underscores the iambic pentameter of the poem, but the poem reads more naturally with muted stresses on these syllables. I then ask them to respond to the question on the screen: WHAT IS STEVENS DOING WITH THIS RHYTHM? They answer variously:

1. He doesn't want the rhythm to get boring, so he changes it.
2. He is trying to catch the downward motion of the pigeons by the falling off of the syllables in the last line.
3. He wants his rhythm to be "casual" like the flocks of pigeons.
4. His language is too complicated for strict blank verse.

I then ask them to select the response exclusive of theirs that says most to them; they choose 2 and 3. We discuss these responses for a while, until everyone is aware that one can purposefully manipulate blank verse to achieve desired effects. Then I return their poems to them, with comments and suggestions for revision; I ask them to turn their poems in again the following week. Before doing so, however, they are requested to mark ten lines in their revisions, scan these lines, and explain in a brief paragraph what they are doing with the basic pattern in these lines and why.

Stevens, of course, is not the only model I invoke. But he is the most frequent. After a discussion of imagery, imagism, and the image, I ask the undergraduate class to examine "Thirteen Ways of Looking at a Blackbird." (The graduates get "Someone Puts a Pineapple Together" as a chaser.) With "Man Carrying Thing" still in mind, I then assign them a Thing to focus on as an in-class exercise, an actual physical object: a cockroach, old boot, fishhook, banana, magnifying glass, paper clip, hamster, scissors. I direct them to focus on the object for a full five minutes, saying and writing nothing. (This is eternity for the undergraduate class, unless, of course, the Thing escapes somehow, causing a gleeful chaos and many merry metaphors.) Then I ask: how many ways can you find to look at this Thing? If they are graduates, I restrict them to some form: haiku and senryu, perhaps. For undergraduates, anything goes. They write out their ways of looking, initial them, send them to the central pool. A poem grows, created by the class. The initialed segments can be reclaimed by their authors for their own projects. After class they will choose their own focus of attention for a sustained effort at variations-on-an-image.

A third Stevens is occasionally invited whenever things get too heavy in the class, and everyone seems to be talking doomsday absolutes and writing suicide poems. This is Stevens the Juggler, experimenter with forms, the playful poet who juggles words and sounds to produce delight, alarm, and a number of other sensations. We read "The Comedian as the Letter C," and look at the puns, word games, and sound effects that help produce the ironic tone in which Stevens presents Crispin's discoveries. I read to them the passage from his letter to Hi Simons in which he points out the humor of the poem, which he seems to fear will be lost in too-heavy interpretation. He wants his readers to be aware that the letter C dominates the poem, appearing throughout in all its possible variations, and he adds: "The natural effect of the variety of sounds of the letter C is a comic effect. I should like to know whether your ear agrees" (L 352).

I question the class: Is this repeated "whistling and mocking and stressing and, in a minor way, orchestrating, going on in the background" (L 352) funny? What kind of funny? What effect does repetition of other sounds have—the l sound, for instance? What about l and s together? We look at a poem like Archibald MacLeish's "You, Andrew Marvell," with its sequences of l's and s's. Then I wake them all up with a rousing passage of Vachel Lindsay, and we discuss the sounds in that. We return to their poems, as a conclusion, and discuss what they are doing or trying to do with the sound repetitions in them.

Other Stevens the Juggler selections I use, and the kinds of questions they evoke, are:

1. "Disillusionment of Ten O'Clock": What is he doing with repetition? What about the odd sounds of odd combinations, "baboons and periwinkles," for instance? How does a change in sound signal a change in tone for the last four lines?

2. "The Plot against the Giant": What effect do the words "yokel" and "hacker" in the first two lines have? (What's a "hacker," anyway?) What would be a "world of gutterals"? Why are labials "heavenly"?

3. "The Search for Sound Free from Motion": Why does Stevens create the word "gramophoon" from "gramophone" and the implied "typhoon" ("West-Indian hurricane")? What does this new word have to do with his claim for "The world as word"?

4. "The Ordinary Women": How are sounds used for purposes of play? It's unusual for Stevens to use stanzas this rigid and to incorporate internal rhyme: why does he do these things in this poem? What can be said about the rhyme *guitars/catarrhs*?

Any number of other poems will serve to illustrate Stevens's playfulness and irony. As for computer-game exercises to accompany this kind of discussion, there are several, mostly for undergraduates, although graduate students can use them as well. My most successful exercises include:

1. Write a poem based on a letter of the alphabet: the sound of it, the shape of it, the associations that seem to accompany it. Represent the letter in various sizes and typefaces on the screen as part of the poem or as inspiration.

2. Try to translate another art form into poetry. For instance, create a poem that suggests country and western music, or hard rock, or impressionist painting, or pop art. Choose an art form you know and try to use its terms and its sounds in your poem. (This assignment is always presented as an option, to avoid screams and/or Q-drops.)

3. Collaborate on the computer with a classmate to produce a poem which represents two distinct voices. Each of you will invent a self which you will define partly through the sounds of the words you use.

4. Collaborate on a poem of a particular form, e.g., rhymed iambic pentameter couplets. Bat lines back and forth: see how neatly you can corner your classmates with difficult rhymes and impossible situations.

We use the computer in these classes for a number of reasons. It provides a sense of excitement to be communicating across the room in this high-tech way, like children shouting messages through tin-can telephones across a twenty-foot space. When the class works on a project like a cooperative poem, they find it exhilarating to watch the thing take shape before their eyes, each contribution falling into place. This method does, as mentioned, allow people to speak more freely, because even when the students have a good idea of who is behind the pseudonyms, the speakers feel that they can take on the characteristics of their persona, and let this imaginary person take some of the blame for the bluntness. It also allows students a chance to see what they say before they "send" it, making last-minute changes in tone if desired. It allows us to keep a record of the conference, and print any part of it should someone wish to review the comments about his or her work or to look at the remarks he or she has made. However, using Stevens and these exercises does not require the hardware. An overhead projector or even a blackboard will serve, with students taking turns at the board or writing on transparencies. The alternative methods don't provide the privacy of thought of the individual machines, but they work.

However, the evocation of these shades of Stevens does depend on other classes in which Stevens has been read and studied in the usual ways. Undergraduates have usually had the American literature survey and are familiar with "Sunday Morning," "The Emperor of Ice-Cream," "Of Modern Poetry," "The Idea of Order at Key West," and perhaps a half dozen others. The graduate students have often had a course in modernist/ postmodernist poetry, and know Stevens fairly well. It was these earlier encounters and the delighted recognition that came with them that brought Stevens to haunt these halls in the first place.

Note

1. I am grateful to Joy Castro (Monster Mash), Larry Clark (Snevets Ecallaw), Dipika Mukherjee (Anne Hathaway), Glen Holt (High Flyer), Jim Gillespie (Anthill Mob), and other members of English 689 and English 236 for permitting me to use their in-class work. I also wish to thank Larry Clark, doctoral student at Texas A & M, for introducing *Discourse* to the class and showing me how to use it.

Part IV. Contexts

"Compass and Curriculum":
Teaching Stevens among the Moderns

A. WALTON LITZ

When amorists grow bald, then amours shrink
Into the compass and curriculum
Of introspective exiles, lecturing.

"Le Monocle de Mon Oncle," VI

For some years I have taught the poetry of Wallace Stevens in an upper-level course on modern American poetry, gradually adjusting the assignments and his position in the syllabus as I searched for a coherent way to present his unique achievements and his special place in the modern tradition. The course as now conceived—and it changes from year to year—opens with Robert Frost. The rationale is that his poetry is, on the surface, most accessible to the student, but that its hidden intricacies gradually emerge in the process of rereading. One of the major themes of the course is the "difficulty" of modern poetry, and how it varies from writer to writer; unlike the poets of a more unified period, we have to learn to read the moderns one by one, gradually habituating ourselves to the unique difficulties of each poet.

Other binding themes in the course are the American sense of place; the search for a usable past; the differences between international modernism (Pound and Eliot) and a native American modernism (Stevens and Williams); and the project of writing a long poem under the conditions of modern poetry. All these themes are raised by Frost's poems, especially "Directive," which (with its use of the Grail legend) is both an ironical riposte to Eliot's *The Waste Land* and a moving exploration of the price one pays in recapturing the past; but they take on greater urgency with the next two poets, Pound and Eliot. Here I concentrate on the long poems—*Hugh Selwyn Mauberley, The Waste Land, Four Quartets*—and the virtual collaboration between the two poets in the years 1915–22, when they were engaged in the joint enterprise of forging a new poetic. Pound's recasting of *The Waste Land* shows this new poetic in action. Then, with Hart Crane, the course veers toward Stevens and Williams. Although little more than a decade younger than Eliot, Crane went through his formative stage in a literary world far different from that which confronted Eliot, Pound, Stevens, and Williams earlier in the century. Remembering this earlier scene in his 1936 Dublin lecture "Tradition and the Practice of Poetry," Eliot declared that "there were no American poets at all" when he began to write (878). Eliot was not just thinking of his weak contemporaries, mired in the diction of academic romanticism. In 1909 nineteenth-century American literature had yet to be processed into literary history; even the place of Whitman was obscure. A decade later, when Crane began to write, the "tradition" was much clearer. Melville and Dickinson had been rediscovered, and what was soon to be called the "American Renaissance" was taking shape. Even more important, the early works of Pound and Eliot and Stevens and Williams provided him with a rich store of contemporary models. All these resources are on full display in *The Bridge,* where the native materials already explored by Williams are expressed through techniques that owe a great deal to Pound and Eliot.

Stevens follows Crane in my sequence, and the course then closes with Williams and Marianne Moore. Williams's poems of 1917–23 are compared with those of Stevens, to uncover the strong similarities and the origins of their later divergence. Moore provides a fitting close, since she was there at the beginning of modernism and lived to see its end. Her responses to her contemporaries, both in her criticism and her poetry, make her an authoritative witness to the entire movement.

At the outset in my teaching of Stevens I try to distinguish the difficulties of his poetry—especially that of the later "philosophic" poems—from the difficulties already encountered in Pound and Eliot and Crane. I stress that his writing is philosophic poetry, not poetic philosophy, combining the pleasures of abstract argument with the solaces that only poetry can provide. It is my experience that one can put *Mauberley* or *The Waste Land* aside for months or even years and return to the poems at exactly the point where one left off. The allusions have already been identified; the themes encountered earlier are still in force. With Stevens my experience has been quite the opposite. Returning to Stevens after a lapse of time, one must begin again and become familiar with a special way of thinking and feeling—a way that is embodied in the language. In "The Figure of the Youth as Virile Poet" Stevens remarks, "Anyone who has read a long poem day after day as, for example, *The Faerie Queene,* knows how the poem comes to possess the reader and how it naturalizes him in its own imagination and liberates him there" (*NA* 50). I emphasize to the students that with Stevens—in contrast to Pound and Eliot—there are no seminal allusions, no essential glosses. One must read and reread the poetry until the way of thinking and saying becomes familiar and "liberates" us.

I begin with the poems of *Harmonium,* trying to give a sense of the volume's tones and frontiers. After some talk about Stevens's early development, and the remarkable—and always mysterious—transformation of 1914–15, I focus on two poems, "The Snow Man" (*CP* 9) and "Tea at the Palaz of Hoon" (*CP* 65): they were first printed side by side in 1921, and, although separated in *Harmonium* and the *Collected Poems,* they are reunited in *The Palm at the End of the Mind.* Taken together, they map out the dimensions of *Harmonium,* winter and summer, the impersonal and the personal, the meditative and the gaudy. With its single flowing sentence and impersonal pronouns, "The Snow Man" is the ultimate early poem of "finding," in which the mind lays back and discovers "Nothing that is not there and the nothing that is." By contrast, "Tea at the Palaz of Hoon" is the ultimate poem of "making," in which the mind creates out of itself a new reality: "I was the world in which I walked, and what I saw / Or heard or felt came not but from myself." Later in the course, to emphasize the continuity of Stevens's poetic, I examine the "rewriting" in old age of these two poems, using as my examples "The Course of a Particular" (*OP* 123) and "Of Mere Being" (*OP* 141). With its firm rejection of the pathetic fallacy, reflected in the long, leaden lines, "The Course of a Particular" reduces all autumnal experience to a single cry of physical reality heard "in the final finding of the ear," while "Of Mere Being" presents an image equally strong, but one made out of pure mind. Throughout the section on Stevens I try to balance this sense of a basic unity ("The Whole of Harmonium") against a sense of Stevens as a poet of one time and one place who must be read in the context of social and intellectual change.

The centerpieces in my presentation of early Stevens are "Sunday Morning" and "Le Monocle de Mon Oncle." I approach "Sunday Morning" through "Peter Quince at the Clavier" (*CP* 89) to establish the theme of permanence within cyclical change ("The body dies; the body's beauty lives"), and then treat "Sunday Morning" as a radical departure from the great nineteenth-century poems of doubt and religious anxiety. Here I find the shortened version that Stevens authorized for publication in *Poetry* magazine a useful foil. Stevens referred to this ordering (stanzas I, VIII, IV, V, VII) as "necessary to the idea" (*L* 183) of the poem, and in comparing the shorter and full versions one can make the essential point that the poem lives not in its "idea," but in the ambiguous subtleties of language and argument.

Although "Sunday Morning" is a great poem, it is not, in its stately blank verse and measured argument, a typical Stevens poem: for that I turn to "Le Monocle de Mon Oncle" (*CP* 13), where I stress that the variation in tone and diction—the war between high and low styles—is the poem, and that love and language are complementary parts of one great theme. In "Le Monocle" one can give the student a sense of that endless dialogue between fact and fiction that is the bedrock of Stevens's poetic. In this poem there is a "voice" found in no other modern writer, a voice that in its fluctuations defines the ambiguous nature of language and traces the scholar/poet's difficult search for the meanings of love. Embedded in the poem is a definition of scholarship that Pound and Eliot would have applauded: "An ancient aspect touching a new mind."

After discussing the silence of 1924–30, and its many possible origins—including the sterile preciosity of some of the later poems in *Harmonium*—I move into the 1930s, a world where the forms of "mountain-minded Hoon . . . have vanished" (*CP* 121). I try to give the essential social background for Stevens's uneasy progress through the 1930s, using "Mr. Burnshaw and the Statue" (and Stanley Burnshaw's review of *Ideas of Order*) as a central text. Stevens's failure of nerve and subsequent recovery can be encapsulated in the program pieces for the first and second printings of *Ideas of*

Order, "Sailing after Lunch" and "Farewell to Florida," which reflect his hesitant claims for poetry and his brave (if too oratorical) recovery. By giving attention to a group of shorter poems, I attempt to trace several themes that prepare the student for the long poems of the 1940s: the impact of the Great Depression ("Mozart, 1935"), the search for an American Sublime ("Autumn Refrain," "Lions in Sweden"), poetry as a source of order ("The Idea of Order at Key West"), and the quest for a credible modern hero (selections from "The Man with the Blue Guitar").

At this point in the course, and before entering the 1940s, I usually give a lecture on Stevens and the visual arts, taking my text from "The Relations between Poetry and Painting."

> There is a universal poetry that is reflected in everything. This remark approaches the idea of Baudelaire that there exists an unascertained and fundamental aesthetic, or order, of which poetry and painting are manifestations, but of which, for that matter, sculpture or music or any other aesthetic realization would equally be a manifestation. Generalizations as expansive as these: that there is a universal poetry that is reflected in everything or that there may be a fundamental aesthetic of which poetry and painting are related but dissimilar manifestations, are speculative. (*NA* 160)

The aim of this lecture (which uses slides) is to cleanse the course of a too-theoretical or abstract approach to Stevens, and to confront him at the most basic and important level: the redemption of physical reality. In the midst of explaining Stevens's creation of believable fictions that one must live by while acknowledging that they are fictions, it is important to remind the student that all Stevens's fictions must ultimately be tested by an appeal to physical reality. I begin with "A Postcard from the Volcano," where Stevens—like the art historian Ernst Gombrich—sees the artist as a creator of *schema* for apprehending the physical, and then I show through quotations from the letters how a Tal Coat painting was transformed into "Angel Surrounded by Paysans." Other headings are Stevens as Collector and Connoisseur; Stevens in the Museum (allusions from the visual tradition, such as the use of Botticelli's *The Birth of Venus* in "Le Monocle"); Stevens as Colorist; Stevens and Imagism ("Six Significant Landscapes" and "Thirteen Ways of Looking at a Blackbird"); Studio Poems ("Study of Two Pears" and "So-And-So Reclining on Her Couch"); Still Lifes ("A Dish of

Peaches in Russia"); and Impressionism: Master Soleil ("Of Hartford in a Purple Light"). This appeal to the visual arts provides a welcome change of pace, and a grounding for the more speculative projects of the later poetry.

Entering the 1940s, I concentrate on "Notes toward a Supreme Fiction" because it is the most organized and symmetrical of Stevens's long poems, and because it repeats and transforms so many of the earlier themes. Also, the temporal/spatial pattern of the poem follows neatly from *Four Quartets;* I stress that both poems must be read sequentially and as a single image, with the parallel sections superimposed on each other in the reader's imagination. In exploring "Notes" we discover that many of the assumptions underlying "Sunday Morning" are called into question, with Stevens emphasizing the fortuitous and even irrational qualities of experience. The only way to grasp "Notes" is to read and reread it patiently, as Stevens lived with *The Faerie Queene,* until "the poem comes to possess the reader and . . . naturalizes him in its own imagination." The greatest lesson of "Notes" is that the reader must discover, not impose, finding the proper tropes that will make her the master of stale repetition. One hopes that the student will finally understand that there is no reason why poetry "should not give up to the keenest minds and the most searching spirits something of what philosophy gives up and, *in addition,* the peculiar things that only poetry can give" (*L* 292; emphasis added).

Although the teaching of modern poetry is often, of necessity, an impersonal activity, I feel that at least once in the course (and perhaps only once) the teacher should reveal his or her deepest conviction—should declare which poems speak to him or her with greatest emotional authority. For me, "Notes toward a Supreme Fiction" provides the occasion for such a declaration. If you think as I do that all we have is physical reality and the reach of our own minds, then Stevens becomes the ultimate poet of belief for a skeptical age. His provisional fictions give us models that help us to conduct our lives. In presenting the later Stevens I do not shirk "theory," since in many ways Stevens—more than any other modern poet of his generation—anticipated the assumptions about language and reality that have governed so much recent speculative criticism. But I also try to present him as a poet of his time and place, and in selecting the final readings I try to balance the often-quoted passages (which can give the student an impression that Stevens was most entranced by "poetry about poems") with poems that confront such themes as heroism ("To an Old Philosopher in Rome"), love ("The Rock"), the serenity of childhood ("A Child Asleep in Its Own Life"), and the desolations of old age ("A Clear Day and No Memories"). Seen in the light of these poems, the later Stevens seems less a poet obsessed with theories of language and perception, and the later canon begins to resemble that of William Butler Yeats. To the young reader of today, the claims by J. Hillis Miller and Helen Vendler that Stevens's authentic voice is unaffected by historical and biographical factors seem almost irrelevant.

In "Effects of Analogy" Stevens says that the "adherents of the imagination are mystics to begin with and pass from one mysticism to another. The adherents of the central are also mystics to begin with. But all their desire and all their ambition is to press away from mysticism toward that ultimate good sense that we term civilization [the phrase is borrowed from Alfred North Whitehead]" (NA 116). More than any other modern poet, Stevens knew that the pure good of theory (to which he was immensely attracted) is a form of mysticism or theology, but in his greatest poetry he always returns to "that ultimate good sense which we term civilization." If a student understands this, then Hartford is indeed seen in a new light.

Teaching Stevens as a Late Romantic Poet

JOSEPH CARROLL

I teach Stevens in relation to romanticism not as one of several possible such contextualizations in literary history but as the one single most important context for his work. I argue that for him romanticism defines the very essence of poetry, that the romantics establish the boundaries of imaginative possibility for him, and that the central motive of his own poetic career is to fashion a vital modern continuation of the romantic sublime. As he says in his essay "Two or Three Ideas," "The whole effort of the imagination is toward the production of the romantic" (*OP* 266). I situate Stevens within the Victorian effort to find a substitute for traditional religion, and I argue that it is within the romantic sublime that he is able to create an imaginative spiritual equivalent for Christianity. In "The Man with the Blue Guitar" (1937), Stevens's projective interlocutors declare that "Poetry / Exceeding music must take the place / Of empty heaven and its hymns" (*CP* 167). My central interpretive hypothesis is that Stevens responds to this challenge by using the concepts and motifs of romantic poetry to construct a modern mythology. To substantiate large initial claims of this sort, I find it helpful to present a collect of passages from the prose in which Stevens himself explicitly identifies the spiritual and mythic character of his poetic enterprise. (For example, see *NA* 42, 44–45, 50–51; *OP* 201–2, 259–61, 264, 267, 274, 279; *L* 348, 369–70, 378, 435.)

Students readily understand straightforward propositions about spiritual motives for writing poetry, and their understanding helps to allay their fear that the fabled difficulty of Stevens's work must render him unintelligible to them. Even if they ultimately disagree with my interpretive hypotheses, they can use these hypotheses as a point of departure from which to formulate alternatives of their own. This pedagogical situation seems preferable to that in which students are left to feel that the supposedly ineffable character of Stevens's poetry must excite a correlative indeterminacy of critical response.

The corpus of Stevens's writing is small enough so that in graduate seminars devoted exclusively to Stevens it is possible to assign all of his primary texts, including *The Necessary Angel, Opus Posthumous,* and the letters. For undergraduate surveys of modern poetry, I order the *Collected Poems,* assign substantial selections from it, and photocopy selections from the other texts. In both formats, I incorporate readings of central texts in the romantic visionary tradition, a category that I expand to include Tennyson, Whitman, and Emerson. Among the romantic poets proper, I concentrate on Wordsworth, Keats, and Shelley. Stevens seems to give only marginal attention to Blake and Coleridge, and Byron seems outside of his ken altogether. Since I make specific reference largely to a few major poems or essays by each of the romantic writers, text selection can be limited to an anthology, a few paperbacks, or photocopies.

To provide a main point of reference for my argument about Stevens's relation to romanticism, I discuss the letter to Hi Simons in which he explains the conceptual structure of "The Comedian as the Letter C." In this letter, Stevens suggests that "the way of all mind is from romanticism to realism, to fatalism and then to indifferentism, unless the cycle re-commences and the thing goes from indifferentism back to romanticism all over again" (*L* 350). He maintains that "[a]t the moment, the world in general is passing from the fatalism stage to an indifferent stage," but he nonetheless feels that "what the world looks forward to is a new romanticism, a new belief." I argue that Stevens himself assumes responsibility for creating this new romanticism. The old romanticism provides him with figurations of a transcendental spirit that manifests itself in the images of nature and that mingles itself indistinguishably with the creative imagination of the individual poet. The crucial modern twist to Stevens's poetic spiritualism— what makes it "new"—is that for Stevens poetry itself takes the place of God. Poetry becomes the supreme manifestation of the transcendental spirit. The "supreme fiction," which I treat as the ultimate goal of Stevens's work, is simultaneously the source of poetry and the object of representation. The ultimate figure in Stevens's poetic mythology is thus "The essential poem at the centre of things" (*CP* 440). In "A Primitive like an Orb," Stevens depicts this essential poem as an originative force that creates all phenomenal images, including those of poetry. Within this religion of poetry, then, the highest possible function of poetry—the function of "cosmic poetry"—is to create images of this originative force (*OP* 271). I conclude that by writing allusively and synthetically within the romantic tradition Stevens not only mines the work of his predecessors to obtain material for his own poetry but also identifies this tradition as itself the living medium of the transcendental spirit. As he says of one of his mythic figures in "The Owl in the Sarcophagus" (*CP* 431), his poetry has "the whole spirit sparkling in its cloth, / Generations of the imagination piled / In the manner of its stitchings."

I teach Stevens's poetry not as continuous and consistent within itself but rather as a struggle and a dramatic progression. Using the categories he himself provides in letters, essays, and poems, I argue that Stevens gradually comes to envision his poetry as operating within two distinct modes: the poetry of normal life and "pure poetry." These modes associate themselves with contrasting philosophical constructs. The poetry of normal life, which I shall refer to as "normal poetry," operates within a dualistic conceptual range. This is the mode in which Stevens divides the world into two qualitatively distinct elements—the individual imagination and concrete, material reality—and seeks only momentary points of contact between the two. In his early thinking, Stevens treats of "pure poetry" in an aestheticist fashion as a poetry without concepts, consisting only of "images and the music of verse" (*L* 288). I argue that beginning with *Ideas of Order,* and gaining definitive formulation in *Parts of a World,* he comes to identify pure poetry with the romantic sublime and that this mode becomes the chief vehicle for the idea of "a supreme fiction." Pure poetry in its later form operates within the philosophical range of transcendental spiritualism. Within this range, both material reality and the individual imagination are contained within a "mind of minds" (*CP* 254), that is, a supreme mind that is essentially the mind of God. It is, for example, to this basic transcendental concept that Stevens refers when he asserts that "[t]he extreme poet will produce a poem equivalent to the idea of God" (*L* 369–70) and when he proclaims, in "Final Soliloquy of the Interior Paramour" (*CP* 524), "We say God and the imagination are one."

I explain to my students that in my understanding Stevens's whole poetic career works itself out as a dialectical interaction between pure and normal poetry. Since I think this dichotomy is of fundamental importance for the shape of Stevens's poetic development, I introduce it at the very beginning of the course, as part of my introductory lectures. As in introducing the theme of romanticism, I present a collect of passages in which Stevens himself formulates the concepts I am presenting. (For example, see *L* 352; *OP* 227–28, 232–33, 253.) I have found that merely to mention or even to describe a highly abstract concept on any subject makes only a shallow and transient impression on the imagination of my students. By reading and discussing some of Stevens's own formulations, I can bring the students to focus on the concept. As they consider the passages from Stevens's prose, students also register that the dichotomy between pure and normal poetry is not just another arbitrary theoretical construct generated by the fertile fancy of an English teacher; it is Stevens's own construct. Having registered this point, some students, believing either in the irrelevance of authorial intent or in the wholly noncognitive character of poetry, might still doubt that Stevens's own theoretical constructs have any significant bearing on his poetic practice. In order to respond to such doubts, and at the same time to give more imaginative definition to the dichotomy, I have the students look at a small sampling of illustrative passages from the poetry. For example, "Domination of Black" conveniently illustrates Stevens's early concept of pure poetry. I cite the letter in which Stevens says, "I am sorry that a poem of this sort has to contain any ideas at all, because its sole purpose is to fill the mind with the images & sounds that it contains" (*L* 251). Students quickly grasp that there is a significant difference between poems of this sort and poems with titles like "The Ultimate Poem Is Abstract."

I associate normal poetry with philosophical materialism and pure poetry with philosophical idealism. Such concepts are not likely to have much meaning for students at first; and indeed reading Stevens is likely to provide the strongest imaginative impression of the concepts most students will ever get. To orient them, I cite Emerson's declaration, from "The Transcendentalist," that "as thinkers, mankind have ever divided into two sects, Materialists and Idealists; the first class founding on experience, the second on consciousness; the first class beginning to think from the data of the senses, the second class perceive that the senses are not final" (I, 329). In support of Emerson's contention that these concepts are of the most comprehensive significance, I offer a sweeping sketch of the role the concepts have played in the history of Western philosophy, particularly in respect to literary theory, from Plato and Aristotle, through Locke and Kant, Hume and Coleridge, and on into the most recent versions of Darwinian and Marxist materialism on the one side and semiotic transcendentalism on the other. Such a broad brush can do little more than establish that there is a large historical and theoretical background for these concepts, but to have established even that much helps convince the students that the concepts are not marginal or trivial. If students grasp the idea that Stevens's poetry will educate them in the imaginative dynamics that have governed and still govern the thought of Western culture, they are likely to settle in to reading him with more serious, studious attention.

While trying to define the relevant philosophical concepts as clearly as I can, I also emphasize that pure and normal poetry are not merely abstract propositions for Stevens; they are modes of poetic experience. They are part of Stevens's personal sense of the world. I maintain that as specifically poetic concepts their emotional and aesthetic qualities must ultimately take priority over their propositional content. I argue that poetic logic is a logic of tone, image, and rhythm, and I specify that each of Stevens's two modes has its own characteristic range of emotional and aesthetic qualities. Normal poetry is robust, concrete, skeptical, and human. It affiliates itself with the sun, day, and rational thought. Pure poetry is meditative, mythical, and visionary. It emerges at night and associates itself with sleep, dreams, and the unconscious.

In initial lectures, I offer a few specific illustrations of the imagery characteristic of the two modes, and I argue that through the dialectical interaction of these two modes each mode becomes richer, stronger, and more complex. Each mode assimilates the resources of the other and also builds on itself. I argue that Stevens ultimately attributes primacy—the highest synthetic power—to pure poetry, but that the interactive alternation between the two modes never ceases. In teaching Stevens, I have found that this idea of a perpetual internal struggle offers a valuable surrogate for the paucity of actual dramatic relations in the poetry. Struggle is a precondition for dramatic interest, and there is a crucial dramatic difference between the mental image of a poet sitting in serene cerebral solitude working variations on set themes and the image of two poetic personas strenuously and sometimes violently seeking to dominate one another.

However necessary for the purposes of conceptual orientation, the kind of initial overview I have been describing is likely to give students a rather giddy feeling of being suddenly transported into a sphere of cosmic abstractions. While Stevens himself declares that "It Must Be Abstract," the abstraction should be presented with as much circumstantial particularity as the teacher can muster. In order to give a more specific sense of Stevens's historical position as a successor to Victorian post-Christian thinking, I offer a few synoptic comments on his relation to Santayana at Harvard and later, and I explain how Santayana's religious ideas echo those of Matthew Arnold in works such as *Literature and Dogma*. Arnold's views on the relations of religion and poetry are easy to summarize because he intentionally reduced his theories to a few simple formulas—essentially that the active element in traditional religion is its unconscious poetry, and that poetry must be the main medium for modern spiritual experience. Whether or not students agree with Arnold's doctrines about religion and poetry, they understand his formulas, and by seeing the linkages among Arnold, Santayana, and Stevens, they gain a more definite feel for Stevens's position within a continuous cultural tradition.

This contextualization in cultural history leads directly into a reading of "Sunday Morning" (*CP* 66). In my experience, this poem provides the best place to start focusing on Stevens's own poetry. Unlike much of his poetry, "Sunday Morning" has actual characters situated in a highly localized setting and engaged in dialogue. It thus has the kind of accessibility as a dramatic enactment that for my students has always made Browning one of the easiest poets to read. Moreover, "Sunday Morning" is Stevens's most famous poem, his first major poem, and still often regarded as his greatest poem. Consequently, students who feel that they understand the basic motives and structure of this poem have gained a crucial measure of confidence—in Stevens and in themselves—that helps them to attend patiently to other poems that seem more cryptic, abstract, or obscure.

In presenting "Sunday Morning," I have students themselves identify the situation of the opening stanza. I ask very simple questions about the title in relation to the setting, and I always find this orientation worthwhile, for many students will not have focused clearly on the literal, concrete character of the imagery. Whatever symbolic values might be imputed to them, the oranges, coffee, and parrot are in the first place "real" items in the setting, and when this point registers, I usually hear a quiet "Ah!" from those who have prematurely flung themselves into the realm of occult symbolistic signification. Working out from the title and the setting—it is Sunday morning and the couple is not in church—I lead the students (or let them lead me) into the main dramatic situation. The woman—I unabashedly identify the couple as Stevens and his wife—expresses a yearning for the imaginative satisfactions of Christian belief: the bliss of paradise and the passion of "the blood and sepulchre." As an alternative to these forms of Christian poetry, Stevens offers her two forms of romantic lyricism: a tender intimacy with nature and a dark elegiac mysticism. To illustrate how these types of imaginative experience—the religious and the poetic—come close together in Stevens's mind, I cite the early journal entry in which he meditates on having first taken a long walk and then "spent an hour in the dark transept of St. Patrick's Cathedral" (*L* 58). He reflects, "Two different deities presented themselves. . . . The priest in me worshipped one God at one shrine; the poet another God at another shrine. The priest worshipped Mercy and Love; the poet, Beauty and Might. . . . As I sat dreaming with the Congregation [cf. "Stilled for the passing of her dreaming feet"] I felt how the glittering altar worked on my senses stimulating and consoling them; and as I went tramping through the fields and woods I beheld every leaf and blade of grass revealing or rather betokening the Invisible" (*L* 59). (The associations here with *Leaves of Grass* and with Wordsworth's "splendour in the grass" are worth pointing out.)

In order to substantiate my claims for the romantic character of the poetic rhetoric Stevens offers as a response to his companion's religious yearnings, I cite specific parallel passages—close correlatives in diction and imagery—from Wordsworth and Keats. (For more specific references, see my reading of this poem in *Wallace Stevens' Supreme Fiction: A New Romanticism*.) I argue that, for Stevens, Wordsworth and Keats are the fountainheads of, respectively, lyric naturalism and the elegiac sublime, and I discuss the close kinship in these modes that Wordsworth has with Whitman and Emerson, and that Keats has with Whitman and Tennyson. While taking "Sunday Morning" as a matrix for Stevens's poetic development, I also argue that there is one crucial element of the romantic sublime that does not yet present itself in "Sunday Morning": the high, clear transcendentalism that he derives in a primary way from a synthesis of Shelley and Emerson. This element emerges most distinctly in "The Greenest Continent" from "Owl's Clover," and through it Stevens gains greater access to the transcendental dimension of his other romantic sources.

While not preempting more detailed discussion further on in the course, I take the opportunity offered by "Sunday Morning" to outline the later development of some of the images and tonal qualities established in the poem, especially the Keatsian mode of the elegiac sublime and its association with a mythic feminine figure ("Death is the mother of beauty, mystical"). I suggest that this mythic feminine figure will be comprised of various sources: Stevens's impressions of his own mother and his wife, Wordsworth's maternal thematics, Whitman's maternal symbolism, Tennyson's mythic figurations in "Demeter and Persephone," as well as Keats's Melancholy and the figure of Moneta from "The Fall of Hyperion: A Dream." At this point, I merely glance at the main poems in which Stevens's mythic feminine figure will appear, but I draw special attention to her culminating significance in "The Owl in the Sarcophagus" and "The Auroras of Autumn" (CP 411). In "The Owl in the Sarcophagus," death as the mother of beauty becomes "The earthly mother and the mother of / The dead," and in "Auroras" she becomes "the innocent mother" who "sang in the dark" and "Created the time and place in which we breathed." She thus becomes the central mythic embodiment of "The essential poem at the centre of things." It is worth alerting students to these later developments so that they will attend to the ways in which a figure like this gains substance and complexity in the course of Stevens's work. Moreover, this sort of focal point provides a means for comparing the various modes and phases of Stevens's poetic experience. Other motifs to which I direct students' attention when the images first present themselves include paradise and the sun (both in "Sunday Morning"), the moon and stars, the comedian, the father, the giant, the circle and center, the shadow, the crown, transparence, and the color green. I explain that these motifs are crucial topographical features within Stevens's "landscape of the mind" (CP 305) and that we shall devote a good deal of attention to mapping the relations among these features.

Depending on the format and pacing of the course, discussion of "Sunday Morning" can provide an appropriate occasion for isolating and at least beginning to discuss a few major romantic poems that can serve as constant points of reference. I shall offer here a list of those works that have seemed most important to me either because Stevens alludes directly to them or because they exemplify crucial elements of his romantic style: from Wordsworth, "Tintern Abbey," "Intimations of Immortality," selections from *The Prelude* and *The Recluse,* and "Westminster Bridge" (which Stevens cites in his essay "The Noble Rider and the Sound of Words"); from Keats, "Ode on a Grecian Urn," "Ode on Melancholy," "To Autumn," "When I Have Fears," "Ode to a Nightingale," and segments of "The Fall of Hyperion: A Dream"; and from Whitman, "Out of the Cradle Endlessly Rocking," "Song of the Universal," "Chanting the Square Deific," and "When Lilacs Last in the Dooryard Bloom'd." Later, when Shelley becomes important, I would recommend reading "Mont Blanc," "To a Skylark," "Hymn to Intellectual Beauty," and "Hymn of Apollo." The main poems of Tennyson that seem to have penetrated Stevens's poetic memory are "The Ancient Sage," "Demeter and Persephone," and sections of *In Memoriam.* Tennyson seems most important for the visionary poems of *The Auroras of Autumn,* but I also make use of "The Ancient Sage" in discussing "Le Monocle de Mon Oncle." At some point early on, the students should begin reading Emerson and should ultimately read "Fate," "The Over-Soul," "Nature," "The Transcendentalist," and "Circles." (In my reading, Emerson's prose provides the single most important theoretical source for Stevens's poetic thought.) Any individual teacher will no doubt wish to modify this list according to his or her own perceptions of Stevens's affinities and responses. Moreover, good students will probably identify sources and parallels that have escaped the teacher's own attention. They will certainly find ways of interpreting all this material in ways not directly dependent on the teacher's formulations.

Students are likely to have widely varying degrees of familiarity with the romantic writers, and even among the initiated little can be safely assumed about ready recall. Obviously, not all the items on the list I have given can be discussed in any detail, even in a course devoted exclusively to Stevens. One workable solution is to read a few poems with the whole class and to reserve others for specific citation at those points where allusion renders them specially relevant. For example, "Tintern Abbey" should probably be read along with "Sunday Morning" or before, but the "Hymn of Apollo" can be reserved for citation as a direct source for segments of "The Greenest Continent"; the "Ode on Melancholy" can be read in conjunction with "Waving Adieu, Adieu, Adieu"; and "Demeter and Persephone" can be read as a source for the mythic configuration in "The Owl in the Sarcophagus."

As Stevens's career progresses, his poetry becomes increasingly self-allusive. Later poems reflect on earlier poems and take achieved poetic realizations as points of departure for new meditations. In selecting poems for an undergraduate survey, it is important to identify and preserve this structure of references for the sake of understanding both individual poems and the whole autobiographical poetic narrative Stevens constructs. Once students have grasped this concept of internal allusion, they take keen pleasure in turning literary detectives and seeking out parallels in motifs, repeated phrases, and particular tonal qualities. They learn quickly that to identify parallels is not the end of interpretation. The question must always be posed: What function does this allusion have in Stevens's poetic memory? How is it changed by being incorporated within a new poetic structure? Is it being combined with yet other motifs or assimilated to more complex compositional patterns? Is it part of "the whole, / The complicate, the amassing harmony" (CP 403), or is it one of those despairing repetitions that betray stasis or even degeneration? Posing questions like these makes it possible for students to see each poem as a singular dramatic occasion even while regarding all of the poems as part of a total structure—the "total building" and the "total dream" (CP 335).

Whether teaching the whole corpus or a skeletal selection, I identify a distinct dramatic shape in the progression of Stevens's career, and I take his relation to romanticism as a key to the phases of his imagination. In the poems of *Harmonium*, Stevens rejects conventional religion and poses as an alternative to it a lyric naturalism suffused with romantic affect but skeptically holding back from the crucial visionary element of transcendental spiritualism. As a result, in "The Comedian as the Letter C," the imagination is absorbed into concrete, material reality and poetry becomes superfluous. Crispin, Stevens's protagonist, ends in silence, and Stevens's own poetic career very nearly comes to an end. When he returns to poetry seven years later, with the poems of *Ideas of Order*, he begins to reconstruct the romantic sublime, though still struggling to resist any spiritualist illusion.

This struggle manifests itself most dramatically in "Evening without Angels," a poem that responds directly, polemically, to Shelley's "Mont Blanc." In "Owl's Clover," he introduces the idea of the subconscious as a source of archetypal mythic images, and henceforth the dialectic between pure and normal poetry complicates itself through the dialectic between the unconscious and the speculative reason. In *Parts of a World,* the conceptual structure of the poetry gains new definition—as the opposition between materialism and idealism combines itself with an opposition between pluralism and monism—and at the same time Stevens begins to focus much more clearly and purposefully on the most important figure in his poetic mythology: the feminine figure who appears variously as an interior paramour, a queen, and an "ancient mother" (*NA* 28). *Transport to Summer* provides a phase for the expansive elaboration of all Stevens's figures and poetic modes. I argue that the culminating phase of his visionary enterprise occurs in *The Auroras of Autumn,* especially in three long visionary poems of 1947 and 1948: "The Owl in the Sarcophagus," "The Auroras of Autumn," and "A Primitive like an Orb." His final phase consists of retrospective reflection on his whole career.

In presenting this outline of Stevens's trajectory, I emphasize that these are my own critical hypotheses, and I explain that many of Stevens's critics would not agree with them. I suggest that the students themselves might well formulate very different views on the nature of Stevens's work and the shape of his career, and I encourage them to pursue whatever line of thought seems most fruitful to them. Again, a student who offers a distinct alternative to a distinct proposition is thinking critically, and definite propositions seem preferable to vague impressions.

In elaborating my contention that the major visionary poems of *The Auroras of Autumn* represent the culmination of Stevens's effort to create a supreme fiction, I argue that in these poems Stevens achieves both the most complete synthesis of all his own main themes and motifs and also the most complete integration of all his main romantic sources. I do not have sufficient space here for an extensive illustration of these claims, but I shall present one final example of the way in which I seek to substantiate such claims for my students. (For this example, I shall assume the context of a graduate seminar on Stevens. For undergraduate surveys, some of the material would not already have been discussed earlier in the course and would have to be introduced here.)

In canto IX of "The Auroras of Autumn," Stevens abruptly asks, "Shall we be found hanging in the trees next spring?" Students recognize that this is an image of death and that it evokes the foreboding of an aging man. Having established this point, I then ask the students to consider the tonal relation between this passage and the passage that immediately follows:

> The stars are putting on their glittering belts.
> They throw around their shoulders cloaks that flash
> Like a great shadow's last embellishment.

Even students who are not deeply versed in romantic poetry tend to recognize the sublime character of this passage. Building on this recognition, I argue that the images of stars, belts, and shadow provide an allusive genealogy of Stevens's romantic heritage. I contend that the theme and the dramatic movement of the stanza draw most directly from passages in Emerson's "Nature" and Tennyson's "Ancient Sage," and I argue that through the association of images the stanza assimilates passages in Shelley and Keats. I outline this general argument, and then lead the students through the sequence of allusions that define the imaginative structure of this stanza.

First, I quote Emerson's declaration that nature "always speaks of Spirit. It suggests the absolute. It is a perpetual effect. It is a great shadow pointing always to the sun behind us" (I, 61). The sun has served Stevens primarily as the central image of normal poetry. In Emerson's formulation, the sun is a metaphor for the transcendental spirit of which "nature," that is, material reality, is but a "shadow," or effect. I claim that by alluding to Emerson's statement Stevens invokes the whole doctrinal force of Emerson's transcendental vision; he thus tacitly subordinates the materialist side of his own poetic persona to the transcendental side. (Students are perfectly free to disagree about these interpretive judgments, but I request enough latitude to present the argument whole, initially, rather than negotiating each detail as I go.) I argue that in passages like this Emerson helps Stevens to imagine the kind of poetry he describes in the essay "A Collect of Philosophy": "a poetry of ideas in which the particulars of reality would be shadows among the poem's disclosures" (*OP* 270).

At this point in the course, I have already made close connections between Emerson and Shelley in Stevens's poetic thinking. Developing these
connections, I argue that by associating the "great shadow" with the image
of belted stars Stevens tacitly situates Shelley within the Emersonian doctrinal range. The "glittering belts" of the stars allude to Apollo's declaration that "the pure stars in their eternal bowers / Are cinctured with my
power as with a robe." The most alert students may well recall that the use
of the word "glittering" evokes other important moments in Stevens's relations to Shelley. In "Mont Blanc" Shelley describes "The everlasting universe of things" as "Now dark—now glittering," and in "Evening without
Angels" (*CP* 136) Stevens counters Shelley's transcendental vision by de-
claring that "Air is air, / Its vacancy glitters round us everywhere." I have
argued that at the end of "Evening without Angels" Stevens reverses his
antiromantic stance, and the students know that in "Owl's Clover" Stevens
has invoked "all celestial paramours" to come and "suddenly with lights, /
Astral and Shelleyan, diffuse new day" (*OP* 79). Again, the most alert students might also recall that in "Owl's Clover" Stevens also describes the
stars as "dark-belted sorcerers" (*OP* 77). I bring these references to bear in
support of my contention that the illumination provided by these Shelleyan
astral lights is that of a transcendental spirit. Extending the circumstantial
particularity of my argument, I point out that in the "Hymn to Intellectual
Beauty" Shelley himself provides a pattern for associating the stars with a
transcendental power, and he uses the metaphor of a "shadow" in a way
that would forge a close link between these images and Emerson's declaration that nature is a "great shadow." Shelley describes Intellectual Beauty
as "The awful shadow of some unseen Power" that appears "Like clouds
in starlight widely spread."

In the earlier cantos of "Auroras," Stevens's preoccupation with the pathos of human mortality and his forays into the visionary sublime might
have seemed disjunctive. I have argued that the contrasting tonal qualities
actually constitute a dynamic tension, and I can now identify this tension
as a dramatic interplay of allusions. The students are already familiar with
the way in which for Stevens mortal pathos articulates itself within the
Keatsian tradition of the elegiac sublime, and they might recall that in
"When I Have Fears" Keats uses a complex of images similar to Shelley's.

Keats's images do not focus on transcendent power; they suggest what he will lose through his own death.

> When I behold, upon the night's starr'd face,
> Huge cloudy symbols of a high romance,
> And think that I may never live to trace
> Their shadows, with the magic hand of chance. . . . (462)

Keats's poem ends in stoic renunciation, but not before leaving behind an indelible association between stars, shadows, and "high romance." I argue that in evoking this visionary romance Stevens now situates it within a consolatory tonal range. Tennyson's "The Ancient Sage" provides the model for this strategic move. The dramatic progression between the two stanzas in "Auroras"—from the fear of death to visionary elevation—seems to have been inspired by the following lines from Tennyson's poem:

> If utter darkness closed the day, my son—
> But earth's dark forehead flings athwart the heavens
> Her shadow crowned with stars—. (1355)

The first thing for students to grasp is the parallel in emotional rhythm between this passage and Stevens's stanza. In order to clarify this parallelism, the teacher can draw attention to the similarity of Tennyson's verb "flings" and Stevens's verb "throw." I contend that in this passage Tennyson has himself assimilated the imagery of Keats and Shelley. Having already considered how Stevens synthesizes Emerson and Shelley, the next step is to work out in detail how Stevens here synthesizes Tennyson and Emerson. The crucial linkage is the image of the shadow. In Tennyson's lines the shadow is that of earth as a feminine figure, and within Stevens's poetic mythology Emerson's "Spirit" is embodied at important moments in "The earthly mother and the mother of / The dead." Both Emerson's Spirit and the earthly mother are images of a vital creative force. It is only a few lines before the passage I have cited from "Auroras" that the earthly mother appears as "the innocent mother" who "Created the time and place in which we breathed."

Having delved this far into the intricate logic of allusive association in Stevens, it is worth reiterating the thesis that all such associations are part of the total meaning of Stevens's imagery. I explain that I would myself identify this total meaning in terms of tonal modulation, and I suggest further that through this tonal modulation Stevens integrates and gives expressive aesthetic form to two basic elements of his poetic experience: his power of transcendent spiritual reflection, and his sense of mortal pathos. Through the great shadow's last embellishment, Stevens both expresses reverential awe before the awful shadow of some unseen power and also invests this power with the tenderness of a maternal mythic figure. Transcendent spiritual reflection and mortal pathos are clearly qualities not specific to romanticism; they are universal. My largest interpretive claim, then, is that romanticism provides a rich symbolic heritage through which Stevens can articulate universal qualities of human experience.

What I hope to have suggested here is that by paying attention to Stevens's relation to romanticism the teacher can provide students with a crucial guide to the symbolic value of his images and the tonal dynamics within his poetic sequences. Particular associations like those in the stanza from "Auroras" can provide points of reference for hypotheses about the structure of whole poems and of Stevens's whole poetic career, and these hypotheses in turn can help to reveal the meaning of other particular associations. It is not self-evident that any of Stevens's poems or that his whole poetic career constitutes coherent structures of themes, images, and tonal modulations; and because it is not self-evident, the hypothesis is substantive. Whether or not students ultimately agree about the details of a structure, or even about its existence, in responding to the hypothesis that there is such a structure, they necessarily enter the range of determinate critical reflection. The best evidence I have for the pedagogical value of this process is that by the end of the semester the students themselves have substantive things to say, and reasons for saying them.

Conceptualizing the Postmodern Enigma: *"The Poems of Our Climate"*

JANET ELLERBY

One of the lamentations I hear most often from my upper-division and graduate students is how difficult they find it to grasp the assumptions of deconstruction. As a teacher of both twentieth-century literature and contemporary theory, I have discovered that rather than assigning more Derrida, the reading of fiction and poetry can better help students find a solution to their predicament. Stevens's "The Poems of Our Climate" (*CP* 193) is a particularly helpful poem in illustrating the limitations of language, a concern central to postmodern deconstructionist theory.

In the current postmodern skepticism prevalent in the academy, we are quick to dismiss the phenomenological possibility of joining our consciousness with the author's or of arriving at the ineffable presence of the signified by way of the reading process. This has not always been the case and for many of my more ingenuous students, it still sounds like a real possibility. Like the imagists, many of my students find it easier to believe that a poet's impression of reality is accessible to them than to try to understand why the signified remains ultimately inaccessible. It is therefore important to develop a pedagogy that gradually leads them to experience—not just intellectually understand—the postmodern suspicion of representation. Through a combination of large group discussion, small group work, dialectical journals, and lecture, I find students can both cognitively and affectively situate themselves in the postmodern conversation about language and reality. In class, I use primarily "The Poems of Our Climate" as the vehicle for creating this situation. In addition, I use other Stevens poems whose pedagogical underpinnings support and encourage students to move to various kinds of insights about the complexities of postmodernism.

In "The Poems of Our Climate," students can see not only tracings of the imagists' belief in the transcendental potential of the image, but also echoes of the despairing anguish of Eliot's Prufrock exclaiming, "It is impossible to say just what I mean!" Stevens's poem is in many ways a palimpsest of modernity. I invite my students to read like medieval clerics, looking through an ancient parchment to find remnants of earlier, imperfectly erased writing. By looking through the language of Stevens's poem, they come to see the remnants of the imagists' attempts to communicate the vivid image through precise accuracy. As an imagistic poet, Stevens struggles to capture the exact image that he sees, yet he also reveals the frustrating inability of his language to capture fully the signified behind his chain of signifiers.

Thus Stevens serves as an important link for students in the movement from Plato to postmodernism. They find in the poetry neoplatonic ideas that seem incongruous to the postmodern temper, but they also come to recognize how he anticipates the postmodern hopelessness in representing the thing itself. At first it is difficult for them to see why postmodernists conceive of representation as a situated concept—an interpretation. But as Stevens enacts his struggle between the ideal, the real, and the representation that is possible in language, students come to experience the postmodernist debate and to understand the premise that language cannot recapture and represent the thing itself, the signified.

Stevens begins "The Poems of Our Climate" with the carefully delineated image—"Clear water in a brilliant bowl, / Pink and white carnations." For the imagists, it was possible that this fixed model could be so precisely accurate that the vividness of the image would be intuitively accessible for the ordinary person. In small groups, it is illuminating to have students recreate the "original" bowl of carnations. It becomes quickly apparent as we compare drawings that the signifiers are suggesting quite different bowls and flower arrangements to different people. Although the image may have intuitive impact, students see firsthand that language will not suffice. Stevens repeats, "Pink and white carnations," but he continues, "one desires / So much more than that." This compelling note of dissatisfaction and the accompanying desire for that which could remain infallibly explicit through the medium of language echoes throughout

Stevens's poetry. In "The Well Dressed Man with a Beard" (*CP* 247), Stevens concludes, "It can never be satisfied, the mind, never."

What Stevens knows and what students learn from his poems is that no matter how fresh the image or how exact the language that represents it, both will finally fail to capture the thing itself. Students admit that they surely find pleasure in the representation of the image, but they also ultimately see that representation as nothing more than a chain of carefully organized associations that suggest an infinite series of personal and cultural possibilities to them. However explicit the language of representation might be, their desire for presence is not to be satisfied.

Still, by reading closely, students note that in the second stanza of "The Poems of Our Climate" Stevens postulates an image of such "complete simplicity" that it would suffice. His wish is for an image that "Stripped one of all one's torments, concealed / The evilly compounded, vital I / And made it fresh in a world of white." This longing is for a signifier so perfected that it might restore the singularity and clarity of the image—"a world of white and snowy scents" rather than the compounded murkiness of our existence. The words "a bowl of white, / Cold, a cold porcelain, low and round, / With nothing more than the carnations there" attempt to serve as signifiers of the definite, but like a still-life painting, they are separated from the living. Students begin to grasp how signifiers can temporarily conceal the discomposed "vital I" (or signified), but also the enigmatic notion that the word can never be the thing itself because it is mediated through a human consciousness that is always other.

In the third stanza, Stevens opposes two desires: one is the desire "to escape, come back / To what had been so long composed," that we might escape the torment of the vital mind that won't let us rest in contemplation of a perfectly rendered image. But against this desire for stasis is the knowledge that we would not long be content with that composition. He writes, "There would still remain the never-resting mind." Despite the desire for fixed, definitive poetic images, we cannot find in them a lasting repose; hence, our desire is inextricably woven into language, though it cannot be satisfied through language, however clear our words might be.

It is helpful for students to read "The Noble Rider and the Sound of

Words" with the poetry. In the essay Stevens explains the dichotomy he has established between the actual physical thing (i.e., the bowl of carnations) and the seemingly inevitable insufficiency of its poetic image. Maintaining that we are under "the pressure of reality," he measures the poet by his ability "to abstract himself and also to abstract reality, which he does by placing it in his imagination" (*NA* 23). He posits a dialectic between the real and the abstract, between reality and the imagination, and between the word and the idea. The poet as the noble rider encompasses both realms of the dialectic. The realm of the abstract is available only to the imagination in which resides the myth of the ideal.

I find it is easiest for students to grasp the oppositions of "real" and "abstract" by keeping a dialectical journal in which they oppose the two realms on the two sides of their notebook paper as they come across their different representations in Stevens's work. With this journal in hand, they can better understand the task of the poet according to Stevens: compelled to idealize, to create pure forms imaginatively, and then to attempt rigorously to achieve these forms. However, it is not just the poet who desires the perfection of pure forms. In "Notes toward a Supreme Fiction," he writes, "[T]he priest desires. The philosopher desires" (*CP* 382).

Students may become confused when they realize that for Stevens the ideal is a myth. Its pure forms can be pursued, but they can only be named metaphorically by language. Still, in the section "It Must Be Abstract" of "Notes," Stevens writes, we desire the ideal—"the sun when seen in its idea, / Washed in the remotest cleanliness of a heaven / That has expelled us and our images" (*CP* 381). Always the ideal "is an imagined thing" (*CP* 387). The cold white bowl of carnations is "An abstraction blooded" (*CP* 385), expelled from the ideal as soon as it is expressed in language. Even in the face of inevitable disappointment, the imagination for Stevens is still of vital importance; it is "the power of the mind over the possibilities of things" (*NA* 136). It is the struggle, then, that we can recognize as crucial, since this neoplatonic quest for the ideal is chimerical.

Together we discuss Stevens's notion that the idea behind the image must be imaginatively pursued. He writes in "Notes," the "major abstraction" is "More fecund as principle than particle" (*CP* 388). Behind MacCullough is "*the* MacCullough." He is the potential for abstraction—the fictional idea of man, the "major man," the one whom Harold Bloom describes as "the giant of imagination concealed within each ephebe" (*Ringers in the Tower* 240). With "the MacCullough" the modern poet must confect MacCullough, the "blooded" man, "not to console / Nor sanctify, but plainly to propound" (*CP* 389). Unlike romanticism, which attempts to sanctify the ordinary, Stevens's task as a modern poet is to set forth the confection of imagination and reality. For Stevens, the poem represents not only a vision of the world (the real) but also its possibilities (the imagined).

By recognizing and recording in their journals the dialectic between what has been called the real (i.e., reality, change, language, and signifier) against the abstract (i.e., idea, ideal, center, and signified), students begin to understand why a Platonic center where permanence is a given is suspect. Stevens deconstructs such a center by writing in "Notes," "The first idea is an imagined thing" (*CP* 387). Thus, one side of the dialectic, the abstract, although it must be pursued, is at the same time fictional and exists only because of an immanent desire for such a fiction. Stevens provides us with an origin or logos and at the same time denies it. To underscore this I turn my students to "Adagia," where he writes:

> The final belief is to believe in a fiction, which you know to be a fiction, there being nothing else. The exquisite truth is to know that it is a fiction and that you believe in it willingly. (*OP* 189)

What Stevens knows is that "true" is a fiction. This is difficult for students to conceptualize, but Stevens provides several examples. For instance, in canto IV of "Esthétique du Mal" (*CP* 313), the Spaniard believes in "*the* rose" that he pursues (emphasis added). Stevens is probably referring to Picasso, but it is anyone driven toward the supreme fiction—the ideal. This is the "genius of misfortune" who cannot be contented with "All sorts of flowers": "And then that Spaniard of the rose, itself / Hot-hooded and dark-blooded, rescued the rose / From nature, each time he saw it, making it, / As he saw it, exist in his own especial eye." The genius of misfortune relentlessly pursues the abstract, filled with the feeling of the imperfect, which, Stevens says in "The Poems of Our Climate," "is so hot in us." He is "that evil in the self, from which / In desperate hallow, rugged gesture" attempts finally to capture the signifier that will reveal the signified as he sees it "in his own especial eye." What is his misfortune? Though his gesture is hallowed, it is forever "wrong and wrong" as "fault / Falls out on everything." Even the genius in attempting to rescue "the nakedest passion" is "Spent in the false engagements of the mind." The abstraction of *the* rose is a fiction, and he is doomed to fail in its retrieval. Students begin to see a connection between the tragic quest of the genius's desire and Sisyphus; both are relentless but wrong and wrong again.

In "The Poems of Our Climate," the clear water and carnations cannot suffice. These carefully chosen words are one attempt to create an image of perfection, but they fail. Always "one would want more, one would need more," yet it would be an oversight if students did not find that it is in the pursuit of what is ineluctably unattainable that Stevens locates our paradoxical paradise. Having been denied an accessible perfection, Stevens still recognizes, as he writes in "Sunday Morning" (*CP* 66), our "'need of some imperishable bliss.'" However, rather than the imperishable, it is the gesture toward the imperishable that becomes our passion. In "The Poems of Our Climate," he writes, "The imperfect is our paradise. / Note that, in this bitterness, delight, / Since the imperfect is so hot in us, / Lies in flawed words and stubborn sounds." "The evilly compounded, vital I" can only delight in the "flawed words and stubborn sounds"—there will be no transcendental signifier. However, because the perfect abstraction is what we pursue, we engage relentlessly in a search for that which we forever misname, forever hope for even though we simultaneously understand its elusiveness. It is in this dialectic between the flawed word and the perfect abstraction that students locate the tension that goads the poet to create. Finally, however, the perfect remains unattainable; if it were achieved, it would be stale like the paradise of "Sunday Morning," where ripe fruit never falls and "boughs / Hang always heavy in that perfect sky, / Unchanging." The stasis of such imperishable perfection smothers the creative anima with boredom.

But how, a student may ask, is this relevant to anyone other than a poet? Possibility resides in the gesture toward the perfect not just for the poet, but for the very self. Stevens perceives this self as compounded with evil, and, most important, with an imagination that is restorative; the self can find its vitality in its desire for the inaccessible. In one of his notebooks Stevens writes, "Imagination is the only genius" (*OP* 204), but he also warns, "Eventually an imaginary world is entirely without interest" (*OP* 200). "The imagination loses vitality as it ceases to adhere to what is real" (*NA* 6). The genius of misfortune imaginatively pursues *the* rose, but can give us only the imperfect signifier, which, adhering to a changing reality, joins in an endless link of tropes. Stevens seems to grasp proleptically the Derridean concept of *differance,* for he realizes that language cannot bring about the condition of self-present meaning. The signifiers that the poet will use in the attempt to bring forth the full presence of the signified, *the* rose, will only be a trace of that rose. Language cannot ever offer a total and immediate access to the thought the poet had about the rose, nor of course to the actual, specific flower that the signifier only imperfectly represents. Meaning is always mediated through language, always partial, always flawed.

With direction, students will find that it is in the insufficiency of the signifier to name the abstract that we can locate desire. Stevens suggests in the poem "The Motive for Metaphor" (*CP* 288) that it is our desire for "the exhilarations of changes" that provokes the poet to create the tropes that language will allow. Furthermore, despite the insufficiency of the signifier, there is comfort to be found in metaphor for the very reason that it is also incapable of naming the real. In the same poem, he writes that it is in "half colors of quarter-things" that we find protection from "The weight of primary noon, / The A B C of being." Thus, metaphor allows for change and at the same time mitigation from what Stevens sees as the raw-edged rudiments of being. To represent his notion of "being" (which again seems to be an enigma that students always pursue with verve), he moves away from images like the carnations in the snow-white air. Instead he writes of "The ruddy temper, the hammer / Of red and blue, the hard sound— / Steel against intimation—the sharp flash, / The vital, arrogant, fatal, dominant X." There is something menacing, even deadly, about the "X." It is important for students to question if they are not more pleased by intimations of "The obscure moon lighting an obscure world / Of things that would never be quite expressed" than by the "sharp flash" of the "X."

By opposing "The Emperor of Ice-Cream" (*CP* 64) with "Notes toward a Supreme Fiction," observant students will point out how Stevens contradicts himself, and this provides the opportunity for investigating yet another postmodern characteristic. In "The Emperor," the poet asks that there be no confluence of the real and the abstract, writing "Let be be finale of seem." If the corpse's "horny feet protrude," let them do so "To show how cold she is, and dumb." Here, students argue that Stevens wants his language to reveal the immediate reality of the corpse rather than temper it with an attenuating metaphor. In "Notes" he writes that without the commingling of the real (what is) with the abstract (what can be imagined), the real will be like "a beast disgorged" (*CP* 404). In this poem "to find the real" would mean the collapse of the dialectic of the real and the abstract and would deny us "the fiction of an absolute," which for Stevens is the only angel we have left. The real would obviate the need for the imagination, our desire would disappear, our art would no longer be possible.

Students who continue to trace in their journals the dialectic between the imagined and the real find it a fertile opposition. Stevens writes in the "It Must Change" section of "Notes" that the two are "sun and rain a plural, like two lovers / That walk away as one in the greenest body" (*CP* 392). It is in the conjunction of the real and the imagined that Stevens locates "the origin of change." It is the contrariety between the imagination and the real that allows for the creative, and we take pleasure in the metaphors that issue from their confluence. For an example, we can turn to the poet, who with unprovoked sensation names the "terrestrial" object of his love flatly—"Fat girl." Yet he revises his initial description by using the abstracting capacity of his imagination. Thus he can write:

Even so when I think of you as strong or tired,

Bent over work, anxious, content, alone,
You remain the more than natural figure. You
Become the soft-footed phantom, the irrational

> Distortion, however fragrant, however dear.
> That's it: the more than rational distortion,
> The fiction that results from feeling. Yes, that. (*CP* 406)

The new image, which replaces "Fat girl," is the irrational distortion that qualifies the initial impulse of the realist to "waste no words, / Check [her] evasions, hold [her] to [her]self" (*CP* 406). "Notes" thus concludes with the acknowledgment that the poet's image of his world is both rational *and* irrational. As rational, it is the never-satisfied mind's attempt once more to name the ideal. As irrational, it is the never-satisfied mind's attempt once more to name the ideal that will be forever a supreme fiction, and consciously *only* a fiction.

How does this contradictory stance illuminate modernism for students? The modernists not only had to face the philosophical death of the gods, but also to give up the long-held humanistic belief in a centered, knowable self. World War I caused many to lose faith in an inherent goodness of humanity. As a result, modernists were faced with the removal of a consensual centering myth. Stevens wrote in a letter to Henry Church,

> One of the visible movements of the modern imagination is the movement away
> from the idea of God. The poetry that created the idea of God will either adapt it to
> our different intelligence, or create a substitute for it. (*L* 378)

And indeed, it is helpful to point out that Yeats did create a new myth to replace the old, just as Eliot embraced the old by means of a cryptic intellectualized poetics. Stevens not only interrogates the origins of myth and god, but also looks carefully at the ideal forms that have haunted the artistic temper for millennia. Alternately, he privileges the quest for truth (as in "Let be be finale of seem") and admits the hopelessness of such hubris. However, recognizing the potency of the flawed language that attempts to represent reality, Stevens celebrates not only the physical world of pink and white carnations, the green corn that gleams, and the deer that walk upon our mountains, but also what "can never be satisfied, the mind." Perhaps he destabilizes the modernist center by affirming a dissatisfaction with that which is aesthetically or formally perfect. Always, he writes, "one would want more, one would need more," but that too is part of the modernist project: the never-to-be-satisfied desire that is the creative anima of the poet who will always seek "the exhilarations of change."

When instructors create an atmosphere in the classroom in which the ineffable somehow permeates the site of instruction, students can combine both intellectual and emotional responses in a way that seems appropriate for Stevens's enigmatic poetics. They learn that the ideal is a useful fiction, a catalytic trope, a spur for the imagination. They come to recognize the limitations of language and the desire for the ideal with an equipoise that helps them face the inexorable failure of creativity. Finally, as postmodern critics, they learn that they are not prevented from delighting in the imperfect pursuit of the "flawed words and stubborn sounds" that are "so hot in us."

Penelope's Experience:
Teaching the Ethical Lessons of Wallace Stevens

MICHAEL BEEHLER

> Proust's most profound lesson, if poetry can contain lessons, consists in situating reality in a relation with something which for ever remains other, with the Other as absence and mystery, in rediscovering this relation in the very intimacy of the "I."
>
> —Emmanuel Levinas

Does Wallace Stevens have anything to teach us about ethics, and can we teach his poetry in such a way that it begins to resonate with ethical questions that concern our relations with the "other," and with others? Does his poetry demand of us a teaching that can provoke our students to think differently about terms like *witness, passivity, exposure, nonviolence,* and *love*? Is this a teaching whose profound lesson, like the one Emmanuel Levinas finds in Proust, makes possible the rediscovery of an ethical experience in human being, an experience that situates reality in "a relation with something which for ever remains other"? Such a teaching would not only present a particular theme or content—something it knows—but, more importantly, it would witness to the reality of this relation with the "Other as absence and mystery": as, that is, an excess *in* teaching that withdraws from *what* teaching teaches (*Levinas Reader* 165). Exposing itself to this excessive other that never ceases coming but that also never finally arrives or presents itself as such, this teaching would bear a phatic surplus that announces what Stevens, in "The Region November" (*OP* 140), describes as "the way things say / On the level of that which is not yet knowledge." To hear in what we know and teach the "not yet" that witnesses to what precedes and is always yet to come to knowledge is to find ourselves responsible for—and irrecusably indebted to—this radical otherness of the other, and to emphasize the priority and importance of this relation. To bring students to an awareness of a "*relation* prior to knowing" (Handelman 281), and to alert them to the conditions of this relation with an other not reducible to *what* is known, is to respond to the impractically paradoxical—and provocatively *ethical*—challenge of teaching Wallace Stevens.

Stevens's poetry may seem an unlikely subject for a teaching concerned with ethical relations, since the poet observes in his "Adagia," for example, that "[e]thics are no more a part of poetry than they are of painting" (*OP* 190). And yet this statement, like many others throughout his writings, suggests his rejection of a classically metaphysical discourse of ethics as a set of general prescriptions governing in advance our relations to others. As Stevens warns us here, we should not seek to find the question of ethics emerging within his poetry as a thematizable and teachable content: as, that is, a matter of what this poetry can *know* and *say*. Quite literally, Stevens's poetry *has nothing to say* about ethics, and teaching Stevens from an ethical perspective must begin with the question of this silence and with this refusal to *account* for the other in an ethical philosophy. Students may hear this silence as simply negative: as, that is, a carelessness about ethics and an indifference to relations with others. And yet it can also be heard as other than negative: as a silence resonating with an alert responsibility to the other *as* other, as that which withdraws from every philosophical reckoning of it. A philosophical teaching seeks to *account* for the other and has something to say about it, thus making the other disappear *as* other by reducing it to what philosophy can practically speak *about*. But Stevens's poetry will not be this kind of philosophical accounting, for as he puts it, again in the "Adagia," "The poet must not adapt his experience to that of the philosopher" (*OP* 196).

An ethical teaching of Stevens gets under way when students are asked to consider seriously this distinction between the experience of the poet and the experience of the philosopher, and thus between what poetry and philosophy can say. To teach the question of ethics in Stevens means that we must explore with our students how his poetry approaches the point of having *nothing* to say (*about* ethics or *about* the other), a point that is neither a falling silent nor the negative of the philosopher's experience of saying *something,* but rather a speaking *as witness to the otherness of the other* and, therefore, the annunciation of a certain irrecusable obligation: a having-to-say that announces the radical insufficiency of *what* it says. "To have nothing to say," Stevens writes, "and to say it in a tragic manner is not the same thing as to have something to say" (*OP* 192). The saying that says "nothing in a tragic manner" does not say a "nothing" that yields a practical return by presenting itself as a "something" one can know and teach as a theme or content. Such saying is not, that is, a philosopher's experience or a matter for philosophical teaching. Rather, it is a gesture addressed to an unthematizable excess in saying itself and to a surplus that takes place beyond *what* is said. The return of this excess marks saying's "tragic" point of insufficiency. The poet's experience, for Stevens, is of the inevitable coming back of this withdrawal, and thus his poetry, *before* it says any *thing, before* it is a matter of themes and content—of the *what* that it says—witnesses to its relation with an other that remains other. The priority of this relation is what an ethical teaching must seek to make resonate in Stevens's poetry by soliciting its prethematic, aphilosophical experience of the other.

What good is there to a teaching of Stevens that raises in the poetry the question of ethics, that evokes the ethical not as a matter of knowledge, but as a certain relation with an other? A discussion of the ethical in Stevens can be brought into focus for students by a look at the kind of thinking this sense of ethics contests: the philosophical thinking that has privileged being and identified it with knowing. In order to provide this context, a turn to Levinas is particularly helpful. According to Levinas and other contemporary ethical thinkers, the Western philosophical tradition has habitually denied the importance of any experience of the other *as* other, for by framing its discussions of the other in terms of being and knowing, it has guaranteed that "the other, in manifesting itself as a being, loses its alterity." Levinas's interpretation of this tradition provides for students a lucid analysis of how philosophy's denial of the other's alterity is symptomatic of an "insurmountable allergy" to which it has been subject "from its infancy," and of how this allergy has marked philosophy's violent "horror of the other that remains other" ("Trace" 346). His reading of the history of Western philosophy is the story of its "refutation of transcendence" and of the inevitable *"reduction of the other to the same,"* a story culminating in a "modernity" that privileges "the identification of being *and* knowing" (*Otherwise Than Being* 169; *Philosophical Papers* 48; *Levinas Reader* 77–78). In this philosophical modernity, "Being excludes all alterity," and thus "nothing . . .

is absolutely other in the Being served by knowing" (*Philosophical Papers* 70; *Levinas Reader* 245).

It has been Levinas's project, however, to contest "the philosophical privilege of being" and to inquire after "what is beyond or on its hither side" (*Otherwise Than Being* 18). This project has led him to another sort of questioning, one that begins not with the "what is . . . ?" of ontology or epistemology, but with the question of the good and of the other to whom one finds oneself always already indebted and for whom one bears an infinite responsibility. It is this questioning that provides students with a starting point for a consideration of the ethical in Stevens's poetry, and enables them to see Stevens in the Levinasian light of an ethical challenge to the violent reductiveness of philosophical modernity. For Levinas—and, as I suggest to my students, for Stevens as well—"transcendence itself [is] the proximity of the other as other" (*Philosophical Papers* 70), and it is this proximity that evokes what Levinas calls the "first fact of existence." On the hither side of my knowing or my being—and of my subjectivity and freedom—this "fact" is "neither being in-itself (*en soi*) nor being for-itself (*pour soi*)," but a relation with an other: a "being *for the other* (*pour l'autre*)" (*Levinas Reader* 149). Being-for-the-other is the ethical relation.

Speaking toward the "radical challenge to thought posed by the philosophy of Levinas," an ethical challenge "based on peace for the other," one of Levinas's commentators suggests that "in the age of Auschwitz, Levinas shows that to be or not to be is not the ultimate question: it is but a commentary on the better than being, the infinite demand of the ethical relation" (Hand, *Levinas Reader* 7–8). It is this original relation with the other as other that opens the ethical in human experience by wrenching that experience "out of its aesthetic self-sufficiency" and awakening the ego "from [the] imperialist dream" in which Western philosophy, as a history of the destruction of transcendence, has shut it up (*Levinas Reader* 148; *Otherwise Than Being* 164). For Levinas, "there is more to being than being," and this "surplus of the Other's nonencompassable alterity is the way ethics intrudes, disturbs, commands being," thereby putting "the Same" into question "by the Other" (Cohen 10; "Philosophy and Awakening" 215). In the age of Auschwitz—or, for that matter, in the age of Rodney King and the Los Angeles riots—our challenge is to teach Stevens as addressing a human experience that, against the denials of philosophical modernity, demands to be seen as profoundly and disturbingly ethical. Providing our students with a Levinasian framework with which to think about this first fact of existence—the original fact of one's relation with an other he or she can never finally determine—constitutes an initial step in response to this challenge.

Many Stevens poems can be used to turn students' attention toward the intrusive disturbance of the ethical. "A Discovery of Thought" (*OP* 122), "The Course of a Particular" (*OP* 123), and "Not Ideas about the Thing but the Thing Itself" (*CP* 534) are particularly helpful as evocations of this relation with an other before and beyond determination, an other that exceeds and puts into question the self-sufficiency of the poems' speakers. Starting with these poems, students can begin to explore how Stevens addresses what Levinas has described as the "nostalgia for totality [observable] everywhere in Western philosophy, where the spiritual and the reasonable always reside in knowledge" (*Ethics and Infinity* 76). "A Discovery of Thought," for example, invites a critique of this nostalgia in its fascination with "The accent of deviation in the living thing / That is its life preserved": with, that is, a certain excessiveness of living that survives or lives on beyond the horizon of life itself, what the poem calls "being born" or the "event of life." The poem lays out the philosopher's refutation of such a transcendence and his reduction of the other to the order of the same. "At the antipodes of poetry," Stevens writes, one thinks of the "first word spoken," and thinks that it "would be of the susceptible being arrived, / The immaculate disclosure of the secret no more obscured." This word of arrival, this thought of the de-secreting of the secret—of the secret's susceptibility to disclosure, to its presenting itself as that which arrives in being, as an "event of life"—discovers, however, life's excess, the deviation that does not give itself to being or that is not susceptible to "being born": "the effort to be born / Surviving being born, the event of life." In this excessiveness Stevens evokes the liveliness of life that disturbs the self-sufficient "event" of being and of the "life" that it both precedes and makes possible, and beckons toward the "accent of deviation" that interrupts the totalizing dream of the "first word" by never arriving as such and by never taking place or being born as an "event." Here, the livingness of life is not a matter of a coming to being, but of a withdrawal—the nonevent of a not-taking-place—of which being and the "event of life" are the trace. Within the poem's discovery of thought something essential has passed without ever having been present—either *in* being or *in* words—and this poem gets students thinking about the strangeness of this passage to which "life" itself silently bears witness.

Equally provocative for students is "The Course of a Particular," which can be seen as addressing a similar withdrawal in its meditation on the "cry." In looking at this poem, students can be asked to focus on the experience of the speaker who, passively hearing the "busy cry" of the leaves, finds himself situated in a relation to that which "concerns no one at all," least of all himself as receptive, hearing subject. Stevens is careful to evoke the otherness of the cry by rejecting a hearing that incorporates it into an order of meaning or reduces it to an element of the hearer's knowledge. "It is not," he writes, "a cry of divine attention, / Nor the smoke-drift of puffed-out heroes, nor human cry." "[C]oncerning someone else," the cry is not addressed *to the one who hears it,* and it is this situation of not-being-addressed by what one nevertheless hears—the nonrelation of this relation—that most concerns the poem's speaker. The experience here is of a profound disinterestedness the speaker can neither decline to hear—in this poem he cannot *not* hear the cry—nor reduce to a matter of *his* interest. This disinterestedness situates the speaker in a nonreciprocal, one-way relationship with an other that is never *for him*—"the cry concerns no one at all"—but one in which he, as the hearer of a lack of concern he cannot fail to hear, nevertheless finds himself to be *for the other.* The speaker cannot address the other's disinterestedness: he can only experience or suffer this situation of nonaddress in a profound passivity or non-in-difference that marks his exposure to the other, an exposure that awakens the subject from its dream of self-sufficiency, priority, and egological privilege. This disturbing awakening to the proximity of the other as other and to its nonencompassable alterity puts the subject in question and brings back the question of ethics.

Such a careful consideration of the speaker's relation to the other—an essential relation that is not a matter of knowledge—makes it possible for students to hear the radical alterity of the other's cry: to hear this cry, that is, as an excessive event, or as the advent of an excess that disturbs the totality of *their* (and the speaker's) knowledge and can never be experienced as belonging to *their* (or his) history. To hear the cry is to be disturbed by an other('s) time that breaks into *my* time—the time of the subject—and that cannot be synchronized with it, and to experience the withdrawal of this time (of the other) from my time, in which it has never taken place. Students can see, then, that for this poem time is never simply *my own,* for the cry evokes a temporality that shows itself to be irreducibly multiple or diachronic, a plural time both of the subject *and* of an other to which it is originally related. With this radical diachrony in mind, the lines "He knew that he heard it, / . . . at daylight or before," from "Not Ideas about the Thing but the Thing Itself," take on a particular resonance for students, for they evoke the passage of this time of the other. From the very beginning, the hearing of this poem's "scrawny cry from outside," the cry that "would have been outside," is already the experience of an unrecollectable "before": of a lapse that has always already come . . . to pass, and of a future that is yet to arrive (the sun is "Still far away").

Moving from the cry in "The Course of a Particular" to a consideration of the cry's disturbing effects in this poem, students become alert to how this cry awakens the poet from the "vast ventriloquism / Of sleep's faded papier-mâché," in which every "other" is only the return of the same or the coming back to itself of the poet's own voice, to an experience of transcendence and non-self-sufficiency in which the other or "outside" remains other by withdrawing from the time of the poet's awakened consciousness. Sleep and its ventriloquism suggest an experience closed to the alterity of the other (what Levinas, if he were to quote Stevens, might call the "philosopher's experience"), but the poet's hearing marks the way in which the other intrudes on that shut-up totality as though it were of an "outside" or an other time, a time "outside, beyond or above, the time recuperable by reminiscence in which being and entities show themselves in experience" (*Otherwise Than Being* 85). The intrusive cry awakens the speaker to the reality of his relation with an other that from the beginning overflows the totality of his thought and does not harmonize into the ventriloquism of his voice. The speaker rediscovers himself to be in a relation characterized by this incessant receptivity to the other with which he can never coincide, an awakening Levinas describes as "the first rational teaching [and] the condition of all teaching" (*Totality and Infinity* 203). By following the course of the cry in "The Course of a Particular" and "Not Ideas about the Thing," and by relating it to the "accent of deviation" in "A Discovery of Thought," we begin to see how the question of the speakers' relation with "something which for ever remains other"—the question of ethics that emerges with the critique of the self-sufficiency of the subject—becomes central to teaching Stevens.

When students read more of Stevens, however, it becomes clear to them that not all the poems witness so affirmatively to the essential alterity of the other or face so passively (or nonviolently) its disruptive nonappearance—its appearance *as* nonappearance—within what they know and say. Many of these poems, in fact, describe the event of meeting with the other in classically philosophical terms, as a matter of contact or communication: a matter, that is, of being, or of being-together in a common time or a mutual present in which the other, by manifesting itself, loses its alterity. To envision the relation to the other as such a being-together is to succumb to philosophy's allergy and to the ventriloquizing sleep in which the transcendence figured by the cry of the other is refuted. It is provocative to explore with students the ways in which these poems sketch out the consolations of this sleep's dream of egological self-sufficiency and address its inadequacies. For instance, "Final Soliloquy of the Interior Paramour" (*CP* 524) is a particularly helpful poem to contrast with the poems discussed above, for in it students can find a classic example of the philosopher's dream of contact and the story of an "intensest rendezvous" in a "Here, now" in which, "Out of all the indifferences," we "collect ourselves . . . into *one* thing" (my emphasis). Lit by a single candle, shut up in a "single shawl," the refutation of transcendence and alterity is reenacted in an imagined ritual in which "We feel the obscurity of an order, a whole, / A knowledge, that which arranged the rendezvous." This is the totalizing order of being and of the same, the egological "dwelling" in which the disturbing otherness of the other can be denied by saying "God and the imagination are one": by, that is, arranging a space and time ("Here, now") in which the other manifests itself as a being with which one can fuse and be "together," and thus "In which being there together is enough." This reductive, restful scene of being-together—an insightful depiction of Western philosophy's assumption that the other can (and should) be reduced to the experience and knowledge of philosophy itself—

appropriates to itself the status of "the ultimate good," but with the question of the ethical in mind and the cry of the other in their ears, students are quick to point out the insufficiency of this dream and to call attention to Stevens's caution that it is "for small reason" that this philosophical scene of contact can claim such an ethical privilege.

The insufficiency of this "small reason" can be brought into even sharper focus for students by juxtaposing the ultimate (re)solution of the "good" of "Final Soliloquy" to the acknowledgment by other poems that this reductive scene of contact and knowledge may be neither final nor good enough, and to their evocations of a relation with the other that would be better than philosophy's dream of being-together: of, that is, a nonreductive relation based on the (non)"contact" to which an awakened sense of the other's alterity witnesses. Here, it is particularly helpful for students to read the classical staging of the scene of contact of "Final Soliloquy" against a different scene: the meeting-as-non-meeting of Penelope and Ulysses in "The World as Meditation" (*CP* 520). A productive discussion of this poem can be launched by observing that, contrary to "Final Soliloquy," being-together is here out of the question: Ulysses approaches only by withdrawing into the enigma and mystery announced by the contradictory statement "It was Ulysses and it was not." What is the significance, we can then ask, of this strange (non)coming of an other who keeps "coming constantly so near," yet never arrives, whose approach is at once an infinite coming-into-nearness and an infinite withdrawal-into-distance? Through Penelope's experience of the incessant coming of Ulysses' nonarrival, we can explore with students Stevens's evocation of a relationship in which the otherness of the other is not reduced to a question of being-together—not reduced, that is, to the order of being and the same—but is maintained as the fundamental condition of this (non)"meeting."

At this point in the discussion, a return to Levinas and to his thoughts on the "pathos of love" can clarify this relation:

> The pathos of love . . . consists in an insurmountable duality of beings. It is a
> relationship with what always slips away. The relationship does not *ipso facto*
> neutralize alterity but preserves it. The pathos of voluptuousness lies in the fact of
> being two. The other as other is not here an object that becomes ours or becomes us;
> to the contrary, it withdraws into its mystery. (*Levinas Reader* 49)

"The World as Meditation," as I suggest to my students, sketches out a relation better than the being-together philosophy sees as the "ultimate good": a "pathos of love" that, in its preservation of the alterity of the other and the "insurmountable duality of beings," goes beyond the egological dream of identification and fusion. For Levinas, this preservation is what characterizes the "ethical relation" and its basis in a "nonviolence . . . [that] maintains the plurality of the same and the other" (*Totality and Infinity* 203). Through the lens of this Levinasian perspective, the class can explore how the meeting of Penelope and Ulysses takes place not as contact, but as caress, and thus how it evokes a relation that is "like a game with something slipping away . . . not with what can become ours or us, but with something other, always other, always inaccessible, and always still to come" (*Levinas Reader* 51). Ulysses' "coming constantly so near" marks the coming of what does not come— the nonarrival of his infinite approach is his arrival *as* other—and thus of what remains, essentially and irreducibly, "always still to come." Penelope's "patient syllables" do not determine or command the presentation of Ulysses in the here and now of *her* presence. Rather, beyond their content and in a patience that is an extreme passivity, they are an invocation to the other as *other,* and thus her "Repeating his name" is an act of remembrance ("Never forgetting him that kept coming constantly so near") testifying to the other's essential alterity. In the indefinite patience of Penelope's syllables, students are faced with a saying distinctly different from sleep's reductive ventriloquism: with, that is, a saying-as-caress that, by preserving "the fact of being two," gestures toward a mode of being that is radically nonviolent and essentially non-self-sufficient, and to the "being *for the other*"—the ethical relation—that constitutes this first fact of existence (*Levinas Reader* 149).

Penelope's saying, then, bears witness to the insurmountable reality of the other's *nonencompassableness* and to the experience in which the other's withdrawal or nonarrival constitutes the trace of his approach or proximity as *other.* It is toward this experience that an ethical teaching of Stevens's poetry must be addressed. Encouraging students to hear the phatic witness of Penelope's words means asking them to come to terms with speaking as the way subjectivity is exposed to an other who remains other and therefore unassimilable (as some content or theme) to its own speech. It means asking them to hear those words with a certain ethical or aphilosophical ear: to hear them, that is to say, as a kind of offering or prayer that, as Levinas might explain it, says "'Here I am!'" to the other as other and, in so saying, testifies to the radical indebtedness of the speaking subject to an other who incessantly exceeds the subject's own intentionality, perception, and thematization (*Ethics and Infinity* 106). The ethical importance of this testimony is not *what* the subject says, not what the speech is *about* as a matter of content, but rather the very event of *saying itself* as the invoking call that lays the subject open to an other it cannot incorporate into itself and that thereby breaks up the reductive dream of egological self-sufficiency. Here is Levinas's elaboration of this ethical importance: "The act of expression makes it impossible to remain within oneself (*en soi*) or keep one's thought for oneself (*pour soi*) and so reveals the inadequacy of the subject's position in which the ego has a given world at its disposal. To speak is to interrupt my existence as a subject and a master. . . . By offering a word, the subject putting himself forward lays himself open and, in a sense, prays" (*Levinas Reader* 149). The phatic witness of Penelope's words is thus, like Levinas's sense of prayer, a "revelation which is not a knowledge," and as such constitutes saying as the "ethical testimony" that this approach to teaching Stevens invites students to reflect upon (*Ethics and Infinity* 108).

To teach the ethical lessons of Wallace Stevens demands, then, that we help students see Penelope's experience as fundamental to what it means to be human. Having students read Stevens *in conjunction with* Levinas is a way of bringing into relief the first fact of existence—our relation with and being-for an other we do not determine—and, hopefully, of disturbing our students' thinking with a question sometimes overlooked in their quest for knowledge: the question of ethics. One final poem can clarify for students the way Stevens situates the ethical relation "in the very intimacy of the 'I'" (*Levinas Reader* 165). The first section of "The Pure Good of Theory" (*CP* 329) lets the essential reality of this relation be heard in the temporal heartbeat it associates with the rhythm of breathing. Here, time appears as an enemy to the closed self-sufficiency of "the mind, silent and proud," and to its knowledge:

> It is time that beats in the breast and it is time
> That batters against the mind, silent and proud,
> The mind that knows it is destroyed by time.

In this section of the poem, it is the very beating of the subject's heart that keeps the time of an other time, a time that the subject cannot finally make its own, that it cannot assimilate to its own intentionality, and that it thereby associates with destruction: an unsettling time to which the subject's proud mind is irrecusably exposed, and to which, in a profound passivity, it "sits listening and hears . . . pass." This experience of time is thus of a transcendence or otherness lodged in the most intimate heart of the subject, the experience of an alterity *in what should be most the subject's own:* a rediscovery that shatters its pretentious dreams of total self-sufficiency. For this poem, respiration itself is similarly the mark of the subject's involuntary exposure to a nonencompassable exteriority (to, that is, the "atmosphere to which the subject gives himself and exposes himself in his lungs, without intentions and aims" [Levinas, *Otherwise Than Being* 180]) to which it has always already been laid open or exposed as the initial condition of its existence. This passive exposure of the subject to what lies beyond it, and the opening of a space *within* the subject to an exteriority that it does not determine but that gives it life, suggests the way in which the subject, from the beginning and *even before its own intentional initiative,* is cored out by the other, for "Even breathing," writes Stevens, "is the beating of time." The poem's eventual proposal of the "platonic person, free from time," is an allergic, traditionally philosophical reaction to this original being-as-exposure-to-the-other of the subject, and a defensive overlooking of the alterity of the breath (of life) that, like an indefinite prelude, precedes and sustains the subject and its speech. The rhythm of breathing that Stevens makes audible in this poem confronts students with the reality of an irrecusable relation or sociality *prior to and more fundamental than* the knowledge of the "silent and proud" mind, for inspiration and expiration—the sustaining, diachronic rhythm of life itself—involuntarily witnesses to "transcendence in the form of opening up" and to the ethical situation that is this "openness of the self to the other" (Levinas, *Otherwise Than Being* 181).

The rationale for teaching Stevens from this ethical perspective extends beyond the desire to acquaint our students with his poetry and to make them better readers of it. For this teaching to be successful, it must provoke our students to a rethinking of the basis of their own humanness by providing them with a different envisioning of that humanness, one in which the first fact of existence is not a matter of being or knowing, but of relations and *ethics*. The poems I have discussed here, and the Levinasian context that enables this discussion, make it possible for our teaching to be the enactment of this provocation, whose consequences can lie beyond the literature classroom. For if, by reading Stevens, our students can be awakened from the violent reductiveness—the vast ventriloquism—of the Western dream of total knowledge and egological self-sufficiency, and awakened to an extreme humanism based on the experience of a prevoluntary relation—to, that is, a non-self-sufficiency in which being human *means* being-for-the-other—then they can begin to address a certain crisis of our contemporary age. Levinas has argued that this is a "crisis of humanism which began with the inhuman events of recent history," a "crisis of the human ideal" that is "in its essence hatred for a man who is other than oneself—that is to say, hatred for the other man" (*Difficult Freedom* 281). Taught from an ethical perspective, Stevens's poetry can suggest to students a way to think through the impasse of this crisis, for it evokes a humanism beyond humanism, one in which, as Levinas has it, "the humanity of man" is no longer understood "on the basis of transcendental subjectivity," but rather on the basis of each subject's radically essential relation with and "passivity of exposure" to an other who "bears alterity as an essence" (*Otherwise Than Being* 139; *Levinas Reader* 50). This extreme humanism emerges from the pathos of love and obligates us to a nonviolence capable of maintaining the plurality of the same and the other, a radical nonviolence in which "the other is the end" (*Levinas Reader* 117).

Teaching the New Stevens

MARGARET DICKIE

Teaching Wallace Stevens today in light of the new scholarship and criticism on the poet must start with the question: which Stevens? Is he the poet aloof from his world, interested only in the abstractions that he names "imagination" and "reality"? the man who lived through world wars and depressions and responded to them in his work? the lawyer who felt poetry was a feminized occupation and yet wanted to write it anyway? And, within these choices, which poems best represent him? Newly published archival materials (the revised edition of *Opus Posthumous* (1989), *Sur Plusieurs Beaux Sujets: Wallace Stevens' Commonplace Book* (1989), and biographical studies by Peter Brazeau (1983) and Joan Richardson (1986, 1988) as well as Alan Filreis's *Wallace Stevens and the Actual World* (1991) and James Longenbach's *Wallace Stevens: The Plain Sense of Things* (1991) have combined to revise the idea of the canonical poet writing poetry about poetry in favor of the poet intimately tied to his time and place. At this critical juncture, the basic question for the teaching of Stevens is: which poems are now central to an understanding of the poet?

There is, as yet, no consensus on which poems can best represent the newly conceived Stevens. "Owl's Clover" and "The Irrational Element in Poetry" indicate a poet engaged in the social issues of the depression. "Extracts from Addresses to the Academy of Fine Ideas" or "Description without Place" provides evidence of Stevens's involvement with World War II. "A Postcard from the Volcano" will alert students to the debate between Frank Lentricchia and Sandra Gilbert and Susan Gubar on the question of Stevens's relationship to the patriarchy: is it occasioned by a double desire for literary and economic substance, as Lentricchia argues, or by a wistful backward look at the treasures of Western culture, the patrimony of male writers, as Gilbert and Gubar suggest? Again, looking at Stevens's treatment of women in his poetry, students can consider a Kristevan reading of "The Auroras of Autumn," concentrating on his treatment of the nurturing and pre-Oedipal mother and examining the poem in terms of what Kristeva calls the semiotic and the symbolic. Interest in placing the poet in the context of his legal profession will lead students to "Insurance and Social Change" or "Surety and Fidelity Claims," essays newly available in the revised *Opus Posthumous,* and to consider the interest that lawyers, such as Thomas Grey, take in Stevens (*The Wallace Stevens Case: Law and the Practice of Poetry* [1991]). Yet, each of these approaches will provide entry into only a specialized corner of Stevens's career, and few of them can claim to be concentrating on his major works. What is more, frequently anthologized poems such as "Peter Quince at the Clavier," "The Snow Man," "Bantams in Pine-Woods," "The Idea of Order at Key West," for example, need never be considered in any of these contexts.

If the long-familiar poems are not sufficient and the newly selected works are too limited in appeal, which poems can now be chosen to represent Stevens's major achievement? How can the poet, so long identified with a "world of words" remote from history, be reconciled with the poet now imagined to be intimately responsive to the depression and two world wars? This last question can be posed, in some form, directly to the students as central to any understanding of Stevens, in particular, and of American modernist poetry, in general. It can also lead into a discussion of how critical emphases can shape a poet's career: how the New Critics read not only different poems but in different ways from the Marxists. Which is the best poetry and who decides? These are questions that should send students back to the poems to make some discoveries themselves, and they might be asked to make some value judgments, choosing five poems that they consider best represent Stevens's imaginative achievement.

Stevens's own statements can be surveyed as a starting point of discussion. For example, two adjoining comments in "Adagia" pose the problem succinctly:

> Poetry is not the same thing as the imagination taken alone. Nothing is itself taken alone. Things are because of interrelations or interactions.

> The final belief is to believe in a fiction, which you know to be a fiction, there being nothing else. The exquisite truth is to know that it is a fiction and that you believe in it willingly. (*OP* 189)

Students might be asked if the "interactions" in the first excerpt change in the context of the next excerpt where the "final belief" in a fiction cannot be read as belief in a fiction created from the imagination alone, but rather from the imagination in relation to something else. They then might consider what that something else is. What kinds of interactions engage this poet's imagination? Is he interested only in interactions of art, as, for example, those witnessed in the still life of "Study of Two Pears," or is he willing to consider a more complicated range of interactions, as in "Human Arrangement"?

Directed to Stevens's own comments in his letters and essays, students will discover that he offers plenty of evidence to suggest that he had no interest in any relations with the social or political events of his time. And students can consider, for example, the response to Oscar Williams's request for a statement about war, which he made on 4 December 1944:

> A prose commentary on War and Poetry is out of the question. I wonder if the war has not ceased to affect us except as a part of necessity, as something that must be carried on and finished, with no end to the sacrifice involved. But I think that even the men in the Army etc. feel that it is no longer anything except an overwhelming grind. (*L* 479)

Can this apparently unequivocal statement be reconciled to the sentence that follows immediately: "The big thing in the world today, the thing that really involves the future, is not the war, but the leftist movement." He goes on to write that he considers the labor movement "as great as the force of war, which will survive the war, so that, in that sense, it is definitely the great thing in the world today" (*L* 480). But since we know that Stevens had tried and, to his own satisfaction, failed in "Owl's Clover" to write about the left and the labor movement, even this comment can tell us little about how Stevens the poet would react to what he considered the great thing in his world.

Critics have presented arguments for and against Stevens's involvement in the social and political events of his time (see Vendler, Perloff, Lentricchia, Filreis, Longenbach, and the special issue on Stevens and politics in the *Wallace Stevens Journal* [Fall 1989]). In part, the argument follows the development of criticism itself from the formalism of the New Criticism through poststructuralism to the social and political interests of the cultural critics. Helen Vendler has never relinquished the New Critical interest in Stevens's form which she initiated; Joseph Riddel moves from his early New Critical reading (*The Clairvoyant Eye* [1965]) to a deconstructive one ("Metaphoric Staging" [1980]), but still keeps the poetry outside history; Marjorie Perloff has argued against Stevens's politics even as she presents his poetry as remote from the political events surrounding its composition; Lentricchia in a long crusade against aestheticism has argued first for Stevens's "radical poetics" and then for his "conservative fictionalism" (see Schaum for a history of Stevens and his changing critical fate). Quite apart from his critics, Stevens himself offers evidence for being, as Jacqueline Vaught Brogan argues, both in and not in history.

If neither the criticism nor Stevens's own prose commentary, much of it written by the later Stevens and not entirely applicable to the developing poet, is conclusive evidence of his involvement or removal from his times, it is perhaps because the poetry itself offers conflicting evidence. Looking at it in the context of its composition, students might ask what evidence it presents.

Although Stevens always argued that he wrote only for himself, claiming that "poetry is one of the sanctions of life and I write it because it helps me to accept and validate my experience" (*OP* 309–10), like other modernist poets, he turned again and again in his poems to consider the value of poetry and the importance of the poet. Approaching Stevens through these poems, students can start to place Stevens in the literary, if not the social and political, history of his time. Harold Bloom cites three poems as central to Stevens's poetic anxieties—"The Man Whose Pharynx Was Bad," "The Snow Man," and "Tea at the Palaz of Hoon" (*The Poems of Our Climate* 50–67). In these poems, Stevens presents the need for language, if not poetry, to confront the "malady of the quotidian," and shifts between two possible styles and sources for such language: the reductiveness of "The Snow Man," faithful to reality, and the expansiveness of Hoon, responsive to the imagination.

Students reading these poems can be asked to place them in the context of poems such as Eliot's *The Waste Land*, Pound's *Hell Cantos*, and Williams's "By the road to the contagious hospital" in order to estimate the strange contrast of reticence and exuberance in Stevens's concept of the imagination, a contrast

that underlies his treatment of the world and distinguishes him from his contemporaries. Stevens did not share Eliot's interest in tradition, Pound's devotion to history, and Williams's concern for the American idiom and soil;
but he, alone among the modernists, had a theory of the imagination. Students can be directed to see that, if such a theory had its roots in a literary
tradition, was tied to a particular history, language, and place, it was nonetheless devoted primarily to the generative possibilities of the imagination
even in a poetry concerned with social and political issues.

Still, the "malady of the quotidian" did not remain stagnant in Stevens's
imagination nor in the history he witnessed. As his world deepened into
the depression, Stevens's attitude toward it quickened. While the "malady
of the quotidian" in "The Man Whose Pharynx Was Bad" could be considered a rather abstract, if personal, ennui, it becomes something different
when experienced by "these sudden mobs of men" whom Stevens imagined as "Requiring order beyond their speech" in "Sad Strains of a Gay
Waltz" (*CP* 121). A discussion of his dismissal of the "mountain-minded
Hoon," who created the world in which he lived, can lead into a consideration of his new interest in men who are victims of their circumstances
without the power to shape or control them, "crying without knowing for
what." In such a situation, Stevens began to understand that the poet will
be "Some harmonious skeptic" who "Will unite these figures of men and
their shapes." This poem, along with excerpts from "Owl's Clover," can
serve as a brief link between the poems that Stevens wrote in the period
right after World War I where he was intent on asserting the primacy of
the imagination and the work Stevens began to write at the outbreak of
World War II. In contrast to his earlier abstract statements about poetry,
Stevens was now willing to specify his interest in war, a subject to which
he refers pointedly in "Man and Bottle" (*CP* 238) and "Of Modern Poetry" (*CP* 239), where he claims that poetry "has to content the reason
concerning war" or "It has to think about war / And it has to find what
will suffice."

Some of the problems that such a subject entailed for Stevens may be
explored by a reading of "Extracts from Addresses to the Academy of Fine
Ideas" (*CP* 252) or "Examination of the Hero in a Time of War" (*CP*
273). Students may be helped by considering these poems as part of what

Filreis calls "The War-Poem Business" (130–47) and by comparing them to treatments of the war in the poetry of H.D. or Eliot or Marianne Moore, for example. In this context, students will notice that Stevens's deepening interest in the social and communal has complicated rather than simplified his experiments in language. Discussing the difficulty of the poems, their experimentations with varied tones and vocabularies, their combination of mutually exclusive poles of expression, students can begin to see the way in which Stevens strained to be responsive to the world of reality without relinquishing his trust in the "world of words."

These poems are usually considered among Stevens's less successful work, and the question to be posed here is why? Is it because they are flawed formally or because their subject is not adequately treated, or is it because their subjects and their forms do not fit into any established view of Stevens's interests? In discussing the problems of assessing these poems, students can begin to understand the imaginative problems that Stevens faced in writing them.

The titles of the poems—"Extracts from Addresses to the Academy of Fine Ideas" and "Examination of the Hero in a Time of War"—can lead into a discussion of the conflicting roles of lecturer, preceptor, and inquirer that Stevens assumes alternately now in approaching the subject of war, death, and heroism. Moreover, the titles' simplicity and seriousness can be contrasted to the fantastic titles of his earlier poems as an indication of a new tentativeness, even reticence, in his work. They will also serve to call attention to Stevens's formal retreat from the whole to parts as he moved toward the political events of his time. The variations in the form among the sections of "Extracts" and the variations of voice in the sections of "Examination" may be compared to the formal experiments of earlier long poems in order to estimate Stevens's uneasiness with the artifice of poetry in this period of his life.

In "Extracts," particularly baffling sections may be considered not only to question the adequacy of Stevens's treatment of death and evil but also to indicate the seriousness with which he approached these subjects and the difficulties he had with them. He himself admitted that this poem grew out of "the Lightness with which ideas are asserted, held, abandoned, etc." (L 380), and it may at first appear that it is itself an expression of such

"Lightness," as it moves from one idea about death to another. But students should be alerted to Stevens's antithetical method, his expression of poetic attitudes that he acknowledges only to oppose as, for example, the easy aestheticizing of evil in the passage from section II, where he warns a Keatsian "Secretary for Porcelain" of the hazards of converting deaths into metaphors. Students will want to consider the preposterous language of equating "ten thousand deaths / With a single well-tempered apricot" as a judgment against the equation. Another approach that Stevens rejects by including is that of the Eliotic poet, one of "The lean cats of the arches of the churches," who veers toward an excess of a different kind: "They bear brightly the little beyond / Themselves, the slightly unjust drawing that is / Their genius." The poem moves then through some of Stevens's own poetic excesses to conclude that even the "brooder seeking the acutest end / Of speech" must "Behold the men in helmets borne on steel, / Discolored, how they are going to defeat" and, in this act, recognize his own poetic defeat.

Stevens wrote this poem in a season marked by personal loss in the death of his only surviving brother and by public notices of impending war, as he acknowledges in a letter to Henry Church, claiming, "the climate is changing, and it seems pretty clearly to be becoming less and less a climate of literature" (*L* 365). In such a situation, feelings of defeat were more hazardous than they had been in the earlier poetry where defeat was imagined as internal, a psychological and artistic phenomenon; now defeat could easily come from without and be completed in the silencing of poetry. Against this background, Stevens's entire volume *Parts of a World* must be judged as a powerful, if conflicted, counterstatement. Like the romantic poets before him, he made poetry out of dejection, his fear of defeat and of a climate inhospitable to poetry driving him to write.

In the sparer language and tropes of "Examination," Stevens inquires into his own imaginative resources "In the presence of the violent reality of war" when "consciousness takes the place of the imagination," as he said in his prose statement on the poetry of war (*OP* 241). He never gave up the idea, fostered in the depression, that society needs poets, and, in the time of war, this need was intensified by the tendency to falsify the hero. Against the popular notions of the hero as "Creature of / Ten times ten times dynamite," the speaker here enjoins the poet to create his own more accurate hero: "Devise. Make him of mud, / For every day." But, as Stevens realizes, the problem with the hero is that he nourishes an imagination that falsifies the consciousness of war, "Leafed out in adjectives as private / And peculiar and appropriate glory." The poet's task is to counter the popular aggrandizement of the hero with a more useful hero so that the poet's hero and his season, summer, "May truly bear its heroic fortunes / For the large, the solitary figure."

As the war continued, Stevens turned from what the poet could or should do to consider what the war had done to the imagination. In two experimental long poems, "Esthétique du Mal" (1944) and "Description without Place" (1945), Stevens again writes in the two quite different styles of extravagance and restraint that have characterized his writing almost from the beginning. Once again, the strain in the language and the experiments with style reveal Stevens's efforts to come to terms with new ranges of experience: the *mal,* or pain, of the war and antiwar sentiment. Here, in these experimental works, students may best examine the extent to which the poet, even at the peak of his imaginative achievement, kept open the issue of how the imagination could interact with the world. It was the problem that had plagued him from the beginning and with which he still sought some accommodation.

Something of the contexts in which these two poems were written can serve as a useful introduction here. John Crowe Ransom, editor of the *Kenyon Review,* had received a letter from a young soldier lamenting the fact that the poetry in the review was cut off from pain, and, dismissing it in an editorial, Ransom drew this comment from Stevens:

> What particularly interested me was the letter from one of your correspondents about the relation between poetry and what he called pain. Whatever he may mean, it might be interesting to try to do an esthetique du mal. (*L* 468; see Filreis 130–37)

Students will want to consider whether Stevens's opening commentary on writing in "Esthétique du Mal" (*CP* 313) is an advance over his earlier statements about poetry, whether the consideration of pain brought him to a new awareness of the possibility of imaginative literature. Writing letters home from Naples as Vesuvius groans, the poem's speaker finds himself implicated in catastrophe. This link between writing and catastrophe, by now familiar in Stevens's poetry, is formed here by naming the genres and poetic forms that have served to mark death, pain, and loss. Nonetheless, the poet of the first three sections of the poem can never write a work that will satisfy Ransom's correspondent. He is too controlled, too controlling, and too hopeful, "As if pain, no longer satanic mimicry, / Could be borne, as if we were sure to find our way." It is not until section IV that Stevens finds the "genius of misfortune," "that evil in the self," "the genius of / The mind, which is our being, wrong and wrong" who will confront pain directly.

This genius will find the soldier's "wound is good because life was." He is the realist, but not the defeatist. Stevens writes of "the yes of the realist spoken because he must / Say yes, spoken because under every no / Lay a passion for yes that had never been broken." The final third of the poem is an elaboration of the realist's acceptance of pain as part of reality: "It accepts whatever is as true, / Including pain, which, otherwise, is false." In the end, Stevens asks, "One might have thought of sight, but who could think / Of what it sees, for all the ill it sees?"

Following Stevens's developing awareness of how the poet can confront the political events of the world, students may go on to consider the poem that Stevens wrote the next year when he was asked to deliver the Phi Beta Kappa Poem at the Harvard commencement. "Description without Place" (*CP* 339) is a commentary on what it means to be merely "living as and where we live," that forces us back to a consideration of how much we make the world in which we live. Students will want to consider the context in which the poem was delivered in June 1945. The Phi Beta Kappa Oration accompanying the poem that year was given by Sumner Welles, former undersecretary of state and a "vociferous proponent of the nascent United Nations organization" (Filreis 151). Against this political choice, Stevens appeared to deliberately break with the tradition of this public occasion by refusing to comment on events of the day, insisting rather that "It is a world of words to the end of it, / In which nothing solid is its solid self."

Whatever its audience made of a poem that was, for the occasion, both long and difficult, Stevens himself appears to have written it with some awareness of the divergence of his interests from the world around him, even from those of his friends in wartime Europe. Writing to Henry Church, he commented, "People in Germany must be in an incredible predicament, in which even correctness is incorrect. This makes it difficult to chatter about the things that interest me" (*L* 494; see Filreis 151–60). He went on to say that he had taken as his subject for the Phi Beta Kappa poem he was writing "DESCRIPTION WITHOUT PLACE" (*L* 494).

Students confronting this poem might be interested to consider that poets and critics alike have reacted to the poem with extremes of responses. William Carlos Williams was affronted by what he took to be a caricature of himself and countered with "A Place (Any Place) to Transcend All Places" in which he comments on Stevens among his contemporaries:

> while perspectived
>
> behind them following
>
> the crisis (at home)
>
> peasant loyalties inspire
>
> the avant-garde. Abstractly? (*CPWCW* II, 165)

Critical estimates of "Description without Place" have varied from Vendler's sense that it is an "ode to the Adjective," and parts of the poem, if not "unspotted imbecile revery," are not far from it (*On Extended Wings* 218–19) to Brogan's estimate that it may well be "his finest anti-war poem" ("Stevens in History" 174). It has evoked deconstructive and historicist readings (Beehler, Filreis) that disagree about the meaning of the poem's resistance to referentiality. These different responses to the poem may alert students to both its difficulties and its significance.

Although the poem opens with the jaunty statement "It is possible that to seem—it is to be," Stevens appears to be interested only in descriptions of the future. He concludes, the "theory of description" matters "because everything we say / Of the past is description without place, a cast / Of the imagination, made in sound; / And because what we say of the future must portend, / Be alive with its own seemings." Placed in the context in which these lines were delivered, they assume an added interest. The Orator, sharing the platform with Stevens, could conclude, commenting on America's place in the postwar world in the platitudes encouraged by the occasion, "'Even though the immediate present be darkened, we can look forward with confidence to the future'" (Filreis 160). Here, Stevens's own sense that "The future is description without place" was not without a certain power to describe the historical moment.

The poems that I have discussed here are not part of the canonical Stevens nor, I should imagine, are they taught frequently. Alone, they would not give a very complete understanding of Stevens's achievements or interests. And yet to omit consideration of them or poems like them is to leave a wide gap in our understanding of the poet's development. They might be added to even an undergraduate syllabus not only for their own interest but for the way in which they would allow students to appreciate Stevens's imaginative involvement with the political events of his time. They should also be helpful as an important context in which to consider canonical poems such as "The Man with the Blue Guitar" or "Notes toward a Supreme Fiction," which may not appear to have any political content and yet which must be read now as part of Stevens's anguished effort to write the poetry of his time.

Works Cited

Works of Wallace Stevens

The Collected Poems of Wallace Stevens. New York: Alfred A. Knopf, 1954.

Letters of Wallace Stevens. Ed. Holly Stevens. New York: Alfred A. Knopf, 1966.

"Letters to Ferdinand Reyher." Ed. Holly Stevens. *The Hudson Review* 44 (1991): 381–409.

The Necessary Angel: Essays on Reality and the Imagination. New York: Alfred A. Knopf, 1951.

Opus Posthumous. Revised, enlarged, and corrected edition. Ed. Milton J. Bates. New York: Alfred A. Knopf, 1989.

The Palm at the End of the Mind: Selected Poems and a Play. Ed. Holly Stevens. New York: Alfred A. Knopf, 1971.

Secretaries of the Moon: The Letters of Wallace Stevens and José Rodríguez Feo. Ed. Beverly Coyle and Alan Filreis. Durham, N.C.: Duke Univ. Press, 1986.

"Sur Ma Guzzla Gracile." *Poetry* 19 (October 1921): 1–9.

Sur Plusieurs Beaux Sujects: Wallace Stevens' Commonplace Book. Ed. Milton J. Bates. Stanford, Calif.: Stanford Univ. Press and the Huntington Library, 1989.

"Thirteen Ways of Looking at a Blackbird." *Others: An Anthology of the New Verse*. Ed. Alfred Kreymborg, 109–11. New York: Alfred A. Knopf, 1917.

Books and Articles

Ashton, Dore. *Picasso on Art: A Selection of Views*. New York: Viking Press, 1972.

Axelrod, Steven Gould, and Helen Deese. *Critical Essays on Wallace Stevens*. Boston: G. K. Hall & Co., 1988.

Baird, James. *The Dome and the Rock: Structure in the Poetry of Wallace Stevens*. Baltimore: Johns Hopkins Univ. Press, 1968.

Barth, John. *Chimera*. New York: Random House, 1972.

Barthes, Roland. *The Pleasure of the Text*. Trans. Richard Miller. New York: Hill, 1975.

Bates, Milton J. *Wallace Stevens: A Mythology of Self*. Berkeley: Univ. of California Press, 1985.

Beckett, Lucy. *Wallace Stevens*. London: Cambridge Univ. Press, 1974.

Beehler, Michael. *T. S. Eliot, Wallace Stevens, and the Discourse of Difference*. Baton Rouge: Louisiana State Univ. Press, 1987.

Benamou, Michel. *Wallace Stevens and the Symbolist Imagination*. Princeton, N.J.: Princeton Univ. Press, 1972.

Berger, Charles. *Forms of Farewell: The Late Poetry of Wallace Stevens*. Madison: Univ. of Wisconsin Press, 1985.

Blackmur, R. P. "Examples of Wallace Stevens." *Form and Value in Modern Poetry*, 183–212. New York: Doubleday, 1957.

Blake, William. *The Complete Poetry and Prose of William Blake*. Ed. David V. Erdman. Berkeley: Univ. of California Press, 1982.

Bloom, Harold. *The Ringers in the Tower*. Chicago: Univ. of Chicago Press, 1971.

———. *Wallace Stevens: The Poems of Our Climate*. Ithaca, N.Y.: Cornell Univ. Press, 1977.

———, ed. *Wallace Stevens*. Modern Critical Views Series. New York: Chelsea House, 1985.

Borroff, Marie. *Language and the Poet: Verbal Artistry in Frost, Stevens, and Moore*. Chicago: Univ. of Chicago Press, 1979.

———. "Sound Symbolism as Drama in the Poetry of Wallace Stevens." *ELH* 41 (1981): 914–34.

———. "Wallace Stevens's World of Words." *Modern Philology* 74 (1976): 42–66, 171–93.

———, ed. *Wallace Stevens: A Collection of Critical Essays*. Twentieth Century Views. Englewood Cliffs, N.J.: Prentice-Hall, Inc., 1963.

Brazeau, Peter. *Parts of a World: Wallace Stevens Remembered, An Oral Biography*. New York: Random House, 1983.

Brogan, Jacqueline Vaught. *Part of the Climate: American Cubist Poetry*. Berkeley: Univ. of California Press, 1991.

———. *Stevens and Simile: A Theory of Language*. Princeton, N.J.: Princeton Univ. Press, 1986.

———. "Stevens in History and Not in History: The Poet and the Second World War." *Wallace Stevens Journal* 13.2 (1989): 168–90.

Brown, Ashley, and Robert S. Haller, eds. *The Achievement of Wallace Stevens*. Philadelphia and New York: J. B. Lippincott Co., 1962; rpt. New York: Gordian Press, 1973.

Burney, William. *Wallace Stevens*. Twayne's United States Authors Series, 127. New York: Twayne Publishers, Inc., 1968.

Burnshaw, Stanley. "Turmoil in the Middle Ground." *New Masses* 17 (1 October 1935): 41–42.

Buttel, Robert. *Wallace Stevens: The Making of Harmonium*. Princeton, N.J.: Princeton Univ. Press, 1967.

Bynner, Witter, trans., and Kiang Kang-Hu, ed. *The Jade Mountain: A Chinese Anthology, Being Three Hundred Poems of the T'ang Dynasty, 618–906*. New York: Alfred A. Knopf, 1929.

Carroll, Joseph. *Wallace Stevens' Supreme Fiction: A New Romanticism*. Baton Rouge: Louisiana State Univ. Press, 1987.

Cavell, Stanley. *Conditions Handsome and Unhandsome: The Constitution of Emersonian Perfectionism*. Chicago: Univ. of Chicago Press, 1990.

————. *In Quest of the Ordinary: Lines of Scepticism and Romanticism*. Chicago: Univ. of Chicago Press, 1988.

————. *The Senses of Walden: An Expanded Edition*. San Francisco: North Point Press, 1981.

————. *This New Yet Unapproachable America: Lectures after Emerson after Wittgenstein*. Albuquerque, N. M.: Living Batch Press, 1989.

Cohen, Richard A. "Translator's Introduction." *Ethics and Infinity*. Emmanuel Levinas. Pittsburgh: Duquesne Univ. Press, 1985.

Coleridge, Samuel Taylor. *The Collected Works of Samuel Taylor Coleridge*. Ed. James Engell and W. Jackson Bate. Vol. 7. Princeton, N.J.: Princeton Univ. Press, 1983.

Cook, Eleanor. *Poetry, Word-Play, and Word-War in Wallace Stevens*. Princeton, N.J.: Princeton Univ. Press, 1988.

Costello, Bonnie. "The Effects of Analogy: Wallace Stevens and Painting." *Wallace Stevens: The Poetics of Modernism*. Ed. Albert Gelpi, 65–85. New York: Cambridge Univ. Press, 1985.

Culbertson, Signe. "An Interview with Wallace Stevens: One Angry Day-Son." *In Context* 3 (1955): 11–12.

Culler, Jonathan. *Structuralist Poetics: Structuralism, Linguistics and the Study of Literature*. Ithaca, N.Y.: Cornell Univ. Press, 1975.

de Man, Paul. *Blindness and Insight: Essays in the Rhetoric of Contemporary Criticism*. 2d ed. Minneapolis: Univ. of Minnesota Press, 1983.

Dewey, John. "Americanism and Localism." *Dial* 68 (June 1920): 684–88.

Dickinson, Emily. *The Complete Poems of Emily Dickinson*. Ed. Thomas H. Johnson. Boston: Little, Brown and Company, 1960.

Doggett, Frank. *Stevens' Poetry of Thought*. Baltimore: Johns Hopkins Univ. Press, 1966.

Doggett, Frank, and Robert Buttel. *Wallace Stevens: A Celebration*. Princeton, N.J.: Princeton Univ. Press, 1980.

Edelstein, J. M. *Wallace Stevens: A Descriptive Bibliography*. Pittsburgh: Univ. of Pittsburgh Press, 1973.

Eliot, T. S. *The Complete Poems and Plays, 1909–1950*. New York: Harcourt, Brace, & World, Inc., 1963.

————. "In Memory." *Little Review* 5 (August 1918): 44–47.

————. "Tradition and the Practice of Poetry." *Southern Review* 21 (October 1985): 873–88.

Emerson, Ralph Waldo. *The Complete Works of Ralph Waldo Emerson*. 12 vols. Concord Edition. Boston: Houghton, Mifflin, 1904.

"An Enquiry." *New Verse*. No. 11 (October 1934): 15–16.

Filreis, Alan. *Wallace Stevens and the Actual World*. Princeton, N.J.: Princeton Univ. Press, 1991.

Frost, Robert. *Selected Letters of Robert Frost*. Ed. Lawrance Thompson. New York: Holt, 1964.

Frye, Northrop. "Expanding Eyes." *Spiritus Mundi: Essays on Literature, Myth, and Society*, 99–122. Bloomington: Indiana Univ. Press, 1976.

Gelpi, Albert, ed. *Wallace Stevens: The Poetics of Modernism.* Cambridge: Cambridge Univ. Press, 1985.

Gilbert, Sandra M., and Susan Gubar. *The Madwoman in the Attic: The Woman Writer and the Nineteenth-Century Literary Imagination.* New Haven, Conn.: Yale Univ. Press, 1979.

———. "The Man on the Dump versus the United Dames of America; or, What Does Frank Lentricchia Want?" *Critical Inquiry* 14 (1988): 386–406.

Gombrich, Ernst H. *Art and Illusion.* Princeton, N.J.: Princeton Univ. Press, 1969.

Grey, Thomas C. *The Wallace Stevens Case: Law and the Practice of Poetry.* Cambridge, Mass.: Harvard Univ. Press, 1991.

Gross, Harvey. "Hart Crane and Wallace Stevens." *Sound and Form in Modern Poetry,* 225–46. Ann Arbor: Univ. of Michigan Press, 1964.

Halliday, Mark. *Stevens and the Interpersonal.* Princeton, N.J.: Princeton Univ. Press, 1991.

Hand, Seán. "Introduction." *The Levinas Reader.* Emmanuel Levinas. Cambridge, Mass.: Basil Blackwell, 1989.

Handelman, Susan A. *Fragments of Redemption: Jewish Thought and Literary Theory in Benjamin, Scholem, and Levinas.* Bloomington: Indiana Univ. Press, 1991.

Heaney, Seamus. "Sounding Auden." *The Government of Tongues: Selected Prose: 1978–1987,* 109–28. New York: Noonday Press, 1988.

Heinzelman, Kurt. "Williams and Stevens: The Vanishing-Point of Resemblance." *WCW & Others: Essays on William Carlos Williams and His Association with Ezra Pound, Hilda Doolittle, Marcel Duchamp, Marianne Moore, Emanuel Romano, Wallace Stevens, and Louis Zukofsky.* Ed. Dave Oliphant and Thomas Zigal. Austin: The Harry Ransom Humanities Research Center, Univ. of Texas at Austin, 1985.

Hines, Thomas J. *The Later Poetry of Wallace Stevens: Phenomenological Parallels with Husserl and Heidegger.* Lewisburg, Pa.: Bucknell Univ. Press, 1976.

Hollander, John. *Rhyme's Reason: A Guide to English Verse.* Rev. ed. New Haven, Conn.: Yale Univ. Press, 1989.

Honig, Edwin. "Meeting Wallace Stevens." *Wallace Stevens Newsletter* 1 (1970): 11–12.

James, Henry. *Literary Criticism: Essays on Literature, American Writers, English Writers.* New York: Library of America, 1984.

James, William. *The Principles of Psychology.* Cambridge, Mass.: Harvard Univ. Press, 1983.

Justice, Donald. "The Free-Verse Line in Stevens." *Antaeus* 53 (1984): 51–76.

Keats, John. *Poetical Works.* 2d ed. Ed. H. W. Garrod. Oxford: Clarendon Press, 1958.

Kermode, Frank. *Wallace Stevens.* Edinburgh: Oliver and Boyd, 1960; rpt. with new preface and bibliography. London: Faber and Faber, 1989.

Kessler, Edward. *Images of Wallace Stevens.* New Brunswick, N.J.: Rutgers Univ. Press, 1972.

Leggett, B. J. *Early Stevens: The Nietzschean Intertext.* Durham, N.C.: Duke Univ. Press, 1992.

———. *Wallace Stevens and Poetic Theory: Conceiving the Supreme Fiction.* Chapel Hill: Univ. of North Carolina Press, 1987.

Lensing, George. *Wallace Stevens: A Poet's Growth*. Baton Rouge: Louisiana State Univ. Press, 1986.

———. "Wallace Stevens and Stevens T. Mason: An Epistolary Exchange on Poetic Meaning." *Wallace Stevens Journal* 4 (1980): 34–36.

Lentricchia, Frank. *After the New Criticism*. Chicago: Univ. of Chicago Press, 1980.

———. "Andiamo!" *Critical Inquiry* 14.2 (1988): 407–13.

———. *Ariel and the Police: Michel Foucault, William James, Wallace Stevens*. Madison: Univ. of Wisconsin Press, 1988.

———. *The Gaiety of Language: An Essay on the Radical Poetics of W. B. Yeats and Wallace Stevens*. Berkeley: Univ. of California Press, 1968.

Leonard, James S., and Christine E. Wharton. *The Fluent Mundo: Wallace Stevens and the Structure of Reality*. Athens: Univ. of Georgia Press, 1988.

Levin, Harry. *Grounds for Comparison*. Cambridge, Mass.: Harvard Univ. Press, 1972.

Levinas, Emmanuel. *Collected Philosophical Papers*. Trans. Alphonso Lingis. The Hague: Martinus Nijhoff, 1987.

———. *Difficult Freedom: Essays on Judaism*. Trans. Seán Hand. Baltimore: Johns Hopkins Univ. Press, 1990.

———. *Ethics and Infinity*. Trans. Richard A. Cohen. Pittsburgh: Duquesne Univ. Press, 1985.

———. *The Levinas Reader*. Ed. Seán Hand. Cambridge, Mass.: Basil Blackwell, 1989.

———. *Otherwise Than Being or Beyond Essence*. Trans. Alphonso Lingis. The Hague: Martinus Nijhoff, 1981.

———. "Philosophy and Awakening." *Who Comes After the Subject?* Ed. Eduardo Cadava, Peter Connor, Jean-Luc Nancy. New York: Routledge, 1991.

———. "The Trace of the Other." *Deconstruction in Context: Literature and Philosophy*. Ed. Mark C. Taylor. Chicago: Univ. of Chicago Press, 1986.

Litz, A. Walton. *Introspective Voyager: The Poetic Development of Wallace Stevens*. New York: Oxford Univ. Press, 1972.

———. "Wallace Stevens' Defense of Poetry: *La poésie pure*, the New Romantic, and the Pressure of Reality." *Romantic and Modern: Revaluations of Literary Tradition*. Ed. George Bornstein, 111–32. Pittsburgh: Univ. of Pittsburgh Press, 1977.

Longenbach, James. *Wallace Stevens: The Plain Sense of Things*. New York: Oxford Univ. Press, 1991.

Macaulay, Thomas Babington. "Horatius." *The Complete Works of Lord Macaulay*. Vol. 12. London: Longmans, Green and Company, 1898.

McGann, Jerome J. *Social Values and Poetic Acts: The Historical Judgment of Literature*. Princeton, N.J.: Princeton Univ. Press, 1987.

MacLeod, Glen G. *Wallace Stevens and Company: The Harmonium Years, 1913–1923*. Ann Arbor, Mich.: UMI Research Press, 1983.

Martz, Louis L. "Wallace Stevens: The World as Meditation." *The Poem of the Mind: Essays on Poetry English and American*, 200–223. New York: Oxford Univ. Press, 1966.

Mauron, Charles. *Aesthetics and Psychology.* Trans. Roger Fry and Katherine John. London: Hogarth Press, 1935.

Merrill, James. *Recitative: Prose by James Merrill.* San Francisco: North Point Press, 1986.

Miller, J. Hillis. "Wallace Stevens." *Poets of Reality: Six Twentieth-Century Writers,* 217–84. Cambridge, Mass.: Harvard Univ. Press, 1965.

———. "William Carlos Williams and Wallace Stevens." *Columbia Literary History of the United States.* Ed. Emory Elliott et al., 972–92. New York: Columbia Univ. Press, 1988.

Moore, Marianne. "Two Poems: 'Diligence Is to Magic as Progress Is to Flight,' 'To a Steam Roller.'" *The Egoist* 2 (1 October 1915): 158.

Morse, Samuel F. *Wallace Stevens: Poetry as Life.* New York: Pegasus, 1970.

Nyquist, Mary. "Musing on Susanna's Music." *Lyric Poetry: Beyond New Criticism.* Ed. Chaviva Hošek and Patricia Parker, 310–27. Ithaca, N.Y.: Cornell Univ. Press, 1985.

O'Connor, William Van. *The Shaping Spirit: A Study of Wallace Stevens.* Chicago: Henry Regnery Co., 1950; rpt. New York: Russell and Russell, 1964.

Pack, Robert. *Wallace Stevens: An Approach to His Poetry and Thought.* New Brunswick, N.J.: Rutgers Univ. Press, 1958.

Patke, Rajeev S. *The Long Poems of Wallace Stevens.* Cambridge: Cambridge Univ. Press, 1985.

Pearce, Roy Harvey. "'Anecdote of the Jar': An Iconological Note." *Wallace Stevens Journal* 1 (1977): 64–65.

———. *The Continuity of American Poetry.* Princeton, N.J.: Princeton Univ. Press, 1961.

Perloff, Marjorie. "Revolving in Crystal: The Supreme Fiction and the Impasse of Modernist Lyric." *Wallace Stevens: The Poetics of Modernism.* Ed. Albert Gelpi, 41–64. Cambridge: Cambridge Univ. Press, 1985.

Poirier, Richard. *Poetry and Pragmatism.* Cambridge, Mass.: Harvard Univ. Press, 1992.

Pound, Ezra. *Gaudier-Brzeska: A Memoir.* New York: New Directions, 1970.

———. *Literary Essays of Ezra Pound.* Ed. T. S. Eliot. 1954. New York: New Directions, 1968.

Proust, Marcel. Preface to *Green Shoots,* by Paul Morand. Trans. H. I. Woolf. London: Chapman, 1923.

Quinn, Arthur. *Figures of Speech: 60 Ways to Turn a Phrase.* Salt Lake City: G. M. Smith, 1982.

Ransom, John Crowe. *The World's Body.* Baton Rouge: Louisiana State Univ. Press, 1968.

Rehder, Robert. *The Poetry of Wallace Stevens.* New York: St. Martin's Press, 1988.

Richards, I. A. *Practical Criticism: A Study of Literary Judgment.* New York: Harcourt, Brace, 1929.

Richardson, Joan. *Wallace Stevens: The Early Years, 1879–1923.* New York: William Morrow, 1986.

———. *Wallace Stevens: The Later Years, 1923–1955.* New York: William Morrow, 1988.

Ricks, Christopher. *T. S. Eliot and Prejudice.* Berkeley: Univ. of California Press, 1988.

Riddel, Joseph N. *The Clairvoyant Eye: The Poetry and Poetics of Wallace Stevens.* Baton Rouge: Louisiana State Univ. Press, 1965; rpt. with "Postscript '90," 1991.

———. "Metaphoric Staging: Stevens' Beginning Again of the 'End of the Book.'" *Wallace Stevens: A Celebration.* Ed. Frank Doggett and Robert Buttel, 308–38. Princeton, N.J.: Princeton Univ. Press, 1980.

———. "Wallace Stevens." *Sixteen Modern American Authors: A Survey of Research and Criticism.* Ed. Jackson R. Bryer, 529–71. New York: Norton, 1973.

———. "Wallace Stevens." *Sixteen Modern American Authors, Volume 2: A Survey of Research and Criticism Since 1972.* Ed. Jackson R. Bryer, 623–74. Durham, N.C.: Duke Univ. Press, 1990.

Riffaterre, Michael. *Semiotics of Poetry.* Bloomington: Indiana Univ. Press, 1978.

Schaum, Melita. *Wallace Stevens and the Critical Schools.* Tuscaloosa: Univ. of Alabama Press, 1988.

Serio, John N. *Wallace Stevens: An Annotated Secondary Bibliography.* Pittsburgh: Pittsburgh Univ. Press, 1994.

Shelley, Percy Bysshe. *Complete Poetical Works of Percy Bysshe Shelley.* Ed. Thomas Hutchinson. New York: Oxford Univ. Press, 1951.

Sheridan, Judith Rinde. "The Picasso Connection: Wallace Stevens's 'The Man with the Blue Guitar.'" *Arizona Quarterly* 35 (1979): 77–89.

Smith, Barbara Herrnstein. *Poetic Closure: A Study of How Poems End.* Chicago: Univ. of Chicago Press, 1968.

Stearns, Harold E., ed. *Civilization in the United States: An Inquiry by Thirty Americans.* New York: Harcourt, Brace and Company, 1922.

Stevens, Holly Bright. *Souvenirs and Prophecies: The Young Wallace Stevens.* New York: Alfred A. Knopf, 1977.

Strom, Martha. "Wallace Stevens' Revisions of Crispin's Journal: A Reaction Against the 'Local.'" *American Literature* 54 (May 1982): 258–76.

Sukenick, Ronald. *Wallace Stevens: Musing the Obscure.* New York: New York Univ. Press, 1967.

Taylor, Dennis. "The Apparitional Meters of Wallace Stevens." *Wallace Stevens Journal* 15 (1991): 209–28.

Tennyson, Alfred. *The Poems of Tennyson.* Ed. Christopher Ricks. London: Longmans, Green, 1969.

Tindall, William York. *Wallace Stevens.* Minneapolis: Univ. of Minnesota Press, 1961.

Todorov, Tzvetan. *Introduction to Poetics.* Trans. Richard Howard. Minneapolis: Univ. of Minnesota Press, 1981.

Vendler, Helen Hennessy. *On Extended Wings: Wallace Stevens' Longer Poems.* Cambridge, Mass.: Harvard Univ. Press, 1969.

———. "Wallace Stevens." *Voices & Visions: The Poet in America.* Ed. and intro. Helen Vendler, 123–55. New York: Random House, 1987.

———. *Words Chosen Out of Desire.* Knoxville: Univ. of Tennessee Press, 1984; rpt. Cambridge, Mass.: Harvard Univ. Press, 1986.

Walsh, Thomas F. *Concordance to the Poetry of Wallace Stevens.* University Park: Pennsylvania State Univ. Press, 1963.

Weston, Susan B. *Wallace Stevens: An Introduction to the Poetry*. New York: Columbia Univ. Press, 1977.

Willard, Abbie F. *Wallace Stevens: The Poet and His Critics*. Chicago: American Library Association, 1978.

Williams, William Carlos. *The Collected Poems of William Carlos Williams, Volume 1, 1909–1939*. Ed. A. Walton Litz and Christopher MacGowan. New York: New Directions, 1986; *Volume 2, 1939–1962*. Ed. Christopher MacGowan. New York: New Directions, 1988.

———. "Comment: Wallace Stevens." *Poetry* 87 (January 1956): 234–39.

———. *Imaginations*. Ed. with intro. Webster Schott. New York: New Directions, 1970.

———. *Selected Essays*. New York: New Directions, 1954.

Wittgenstein, Ludwig. Cited in *Ludwig Wittgenstein: The Duty of Genius*, by Ray Monk. London: Vantage, 1991.

Woodland, Malcolm. "Wallace Stevens: 'It Must Be Abstract' in *Notes Toward a Supreme Fiction*." Unpublished Honours thesis. Univ. of Victoria, B.C., Canada, 1986.

Wordsworth, William. Letter of 24 September 1827. *Letters of William and Dorothy Wordsworth*. 2d ed. Vol. 4, 1821–28. Ed. Alan G. Hill, 546. Oxford: Clarendon Press, 1978.

———. *The Poetical Works of William Wordsworth*. Ed. Ernest de Selincourt and Helen Darbishire. 5 vols. Oxford: Clarendon Press, 1940–49.

Wright, James. Cited in J. D. McClatchy, *White Paper on Contemporary American Poetry 16*. New York: Columbia Univ. Press, 1989.

Yeats, William Butler. *The Collected Poems of William Butler Yeats*. New York: Macmillan, 1976.

———. "A General Introduction to My Work." *Essays and Introductions*, 509–26. London: Macmillan, 1961.

Zinn, Christopher. "Freedoms of Speech: Wallace Stevens's Civic Imagination, 1923–1936." Ph.D. diss., New York Univ., 1990.

Recordings, Videotapes, and Computer Software

Discourse. Computer software. The Daedalus Group (1105 Clayton Lane, #248W, Austin, TX 78723), 1990.

Talking Heads. "Heaven." *Fear of Music*. Sire Records, 1979.

Wallace Stevens: Man Made Out of Words. *Voices & Visions*. A Thirteen Part Videotape Series on Modern American Poetry. The Annenberg-CPB Project. New York: New York Center for Visual History, 1988. (Available from Annenberg-CPB Collection, P.O. Box 2345, South Burlington, VT 05407-2345; or phone 800-LEARNER.)

Wallace Stevens, Reading His Poems. New York: Caedmon Records, 1957.

Contributors

MILTON J. BATES is professor of English at Marquette University. His publications include *Wallace Stevens: A Mythology of Self, Sur Plusieurs Beaux Sujets: Wallace Stevens' Commonplace Book,* and the revised edition of Stevens's *Opus Posthumous.*

MICHAEL BEEHLER, associate professor of English at Montana State University, is the author of *T. S. Eliot, Wallace Stevens, and the Discourses of Difference,* and has published widely on modern American poetry and literature theory. He is currently working on postmodernism and the ethical writings of Emmanuel Levinas.

DEAN WENTWORTH BETHEA is assistant professor of English at Albertson College of Idaho. He has written widely on British, American, and German romantic literature, focusing particularly on William Blake, Hawthorne, and Novalis.

MARIE BORROFF is Sterling Professor of English at Yale University. She is the author of *Language and the Poet: Verbal Artistry in Frost, Stevens, and Moore,* and is currently writing a book on the uses of sound symbolism in twentieth-century poetry.

JACQUELINE VAUGHT BROGAN is professor of English at the University of Notre Dame and a member of the Editorial Board of the *Wallace Stevens Journal* (for which she served as guest editor in the Fall of 1991). Among her numerous publications are *Stevens and Simile: A Theory of Language* and *Part of the Climate: American Cubist Poetry.*

P. MICHAEL CAMPBELL is a lecturer at the University of California at Berkeley and editor of *Occident: U.C. Berkeley's Literary Magazine Since 1868.* He has edited a collection of criticism and is currently completing *The Comedian as Wallace Stevens: The Development of a Comic Tradition in American Poetry.*

JOSEPH CARROLL, professor of English at the University of Missouri, St. Louis, is the author of *The Cultural Theory of Matthew Arnold* and *Wallace Stevens' Supreme Fiction: A New Romanticism*. He is currently working on a Darwinian conception of literary theory.

ELEANOR COOK, professor of English, University of Toronto, is the author of a number of books and articles, chiefly on poetry and poetics, including *Poetry, Word-Play, and Word-War in Wallace Stevens*. She is currently completing a book on the poetics of biblical allusion.

MARGARET DICKIE, Helen S. Lanier Distinguished Professor of English at the University of Georgia, is the author of *Hart Crane: The Patterns of His Poetry, Sylvia Plath & Ted Hughes, On the Modernist Long Poem, Lyric Contingencies: Emily Dickinson and Wallace Stevens,* as well as numerous articles on American literature.

JOHN DOLAN is senior lecturer at the University of Otago in New Zealand. He has published a book of poems, *Slave,* from Occident Press, and is currently completing *Habeas Corpus: A History of Occasionality and Reader Belief in the English Lyric*.

DAVID C. DOUGHERTY is professor of English at Loyola College in Maryland and author of *James Wright* and *Stanley Elkin*. In addition to several studies of James Wright and Robinson Jeffers, his essays include studies of John Updike, Saul Bellow, Walker Percy, John Dos Passos, John Gardner, Robert Coover, Galway Kinnell, Raymond Chandler, Rex Stout, and Warren G. Harding. He is working currently on Dos Passos's political ideology and its impact on his fiction.

CHARLES DOYLE is professor of English at the University of Victoria, Canada. His books include *William Carlos Williams and the American Poem* and *Richard Aldington: A Biography*. He is the editor of *Wallace Stevens: The Critical Heritage*.

JANET M. ELLERBY is an assistant professor of English at the University of North Carolina at Wilmington. Her scholarly interests focus on postmodern theories in twentieth-century literature. Her current projects include locating transgressions of conventional "family values" in contemporary fiction and a reconsideration of trauma theory and Freud.

J. MARKEL FURNISS is a high-school English teacher in Simsbury, Connecticut. He has written about C. G. Jung and Stevens.

ELTON GLASER, professor of English at the University of Akron, has published three volumes of poetry: *Relics, Tropical Depressions,* and *Color Photographs of the Ruins.* He has twice received fellowships from the National Endowment of the Arts and the Ohio Arts Council; other awards include the Iowa Poetry Prize and the first Randall Jarrell Poetry Prize.

B. J. LEGGETT, Distinguished Professor of Humanities at the University of Tennessee, is the author of *Housman's Land of Lost Content, The Poetic Art of A. E. Housman, Wallace Stevens and Poetic Theory,* and, most recently, *Early Stevens: The Nietzschean Intertext.*

GEORGE S. LENSING is professor of English at the University of North Carolina at Chapel Hill. He has published widely on Wallace Stevens, including *Wallace Stevens: A Poet's Growth.*

A. WALTON LITZ is Holmes Professor of Literature at Princeton University. He has held ACLS, NEH, and Guggenheim fellowships, and in 1989–90 was Eastman Professor at Oxford University. He is the author of numerous books and articles on modern literature, including *Introspective Voyager: The Poetic Development of Wallace Stevens.*

JANET McCANN is associate professor of English at Texas A&M University. She has written articles on Wallace Stevens and is coauthor of a text, *Creative and Critical Thinking.* She is also a poet who has won a National Endowment for the Arts Creative Writing Award.

JAMES C. RANSOM is associate professor of English at Haverford College. He is the author of articles on the poetry of Wallace Stevens, on American folklore, and on the pedagogy of the humanities in contemporary higher education.

JOAN RICHARDSON, professor of English at the Graduate School of the City University of New York, is the author of *Wallace Stevens: The Early Years, 1879–1923,* and *Wallace Stevens: The Later Years, 1923–1955.* She is currently completing a book on modernism in New York City, 1905–1915, and a series of essays on Stevens.

ALISON RIEKE is associate professor of English at the University of Cincinnati, where she writes about and teaches courses on twentieth-century literature. Among her publications is *The Senses of Nonsense,* which explores modernist experimental writing by Stevens, Joyce, Stein, and Zukofsky.

LAUREN RUSK is a doctoral candidate in English at Stanford University, at work on a dissertation titled "Reflections in a Three-Way Mirror: Reading Socioliterary Autobiography." She is the author of articles on Wallace Stevens and Adrienne Rich.

ROBIN GAIL SCHULZE is assistant professor at the University of Kansas. She has written on Eliot and Woolf and is currently completing a book-length study of Wallace Stevens and Marianne Moore for the University of Michigan Press.

JOHN N. SERIO, professor of humanities at Clarkson University, is the editor of the *Wallace Stevens Journal.* He has written numerous articles on literature and on desktop publishing and has just completed *Wallace Stevens: An Annotated Secondary Bibliography,* for the Pittsburgh Series in Bibliography.

LISA M. STEINMAN is Kenan Professor of English and Humanities at Reed College. She has published numerous articles on nineteenth- and twentieth-century poetry, as well as being the author of several volumes of poetry. Her books include *Made in America: Science, Technology and American Modernist Poets, All That Comes To Light,* and *A Book of Other Days.*

HELEN VENDLER, A. Kingsley Porter University Professor at Harvard, is the author of books on Yeats, Herbert, Keats, and Stevens, and is the poetry critic for the *New Yorker.* She is at work on a commentary on Shakespeare's *Sonnets.*

Index